Power and Inequality

Power is a broad and complex concept that cuts across all fields in the humanities and social sciences. Written by a leading historian of economic thought, *Power and Inequality* presents a wide-ranging and multi-disciplinary analysis of power as an economic and social issue. Its aim is not to formulate a new abstract theory of power but rather to illustrate the different ways in which power is used to exacerbate social and economic inequality. Issues such as division of labour and its evolution, different forms of capitalism up to the money-manager economy, the role of networks (from the family to masonic lodges and the mafia), the state and the international arena, culture and the role of the masses are considered. The analysis of these elements, causing inequalities of various kinds, is a prerequisite for devising progressive policy strategies aiming at a reduction of inequalities through a strategy of reforms.

ALESSANDRO RONCAGLIA is Emeritus Professor of Economics, Sapienza University of Rome, and member of the Accademia Nazionale dei Lincei (since 2018 in its Presidency Council). He has also been President of the Italian Economists Society. His book *The Wealth of Ideas* (2005) received the Blanqui Prize. He also won the Guggenheim Prize in the History of Economic Thought for 2019.

Studies in New Economic Thinking

The 2008 financial crisis pointed to problems in economic theory that require more than just big data to solve. INET's series in New Economic Thinking exists to ensure that innovative work that advances economics and better integrates it with other social sciences and the study of history and institutions can reach a broad audience in a timely way.

Power and Inequality

A Reformist Perspective

ALESSANDRO RONCAGLIA
Sapienza University of Rome

Shaftesbury Road, Cambridge CB2 8EA, United Kingdom

One Liberty Plaza, 20th Floor, New York, NY 10006, USA

477 Williamstown Road, Port Melbourne, VIC 3207, Australia

314–321, 3rd Floor, Plot 3, Splendor Forum, Jasola District Centre, New Delhi – 110025, India

103 Penang Road, #05–06/07, Visioncrest Commercial, Singapore 238467

Cambridge University Press is part of Cambridge University Press & Assessment, a department of the University of Cambridge.

We share the University's mission to contribute to society through the pursuit of education, learning and research at the highest international levels of excellence.

www.cambridge.org
Information on this title: www.cambridge.org/9781009370523

DOI: 10.1017/9781009370493

First published 2024

A catalogue record for this publication is available from the British Library.

Library of Congress Cataloging-in-Publication Data
Names: Roncaglia, Alessandro, 1947– author.
Title: Power and inequality : a reformist perspective / Alessandro Roncaglia, Sapienza Università di Roma.
Description: Cambridge, United Kingdom ; New York, NY, USA : Cambridge University Press, 2023. | Series: Studies in new economic thinking | Includes bibliographical references and index.
Identifiers: LCCN 2023001410 | ISBN 9781009370523 (hardback) | ISBN 9781009370493 (ebook)
Subjects: LCSH: Power (Social sciences) | Equality. | Social policy.
Classification: LCC HN49.P6 R66 2023 | DDC 303.3–dc23/eng/20230502
LC record available at https://lccn.loc.gov/2023001410

ISBN 978-1-009-37052-3 Hardback
ISBN 978-1-009-37047-9 Paperback

To

ROBERTO VILLETTI

(1944–2019)

Contents

Acknowledgements

The project for this book was defined between 2008 and 2009, after a fair amount of preparatory work and lengthy discussions, together with Roberto Villetti; then Roberto fell ill and work came to a standstill. Even today, however, the ingredients have remained more or less unchanged, despite the mass of notes that I have gradually accumulated and the works that I have published on contiguous themes (Roncaglia 1977, 1983, 2001, 2005, 2009, 2015, 2019).

For years I had hoped to complete the project in collaboration with Roberto, as I considered his experience as an active politician and his remarkable interdisciplinary culture essential; but Roberto passed away, after a long illness, in September 2019. His advice, criticism and suggestions were essential in the setting-up phase of the work; I miss our long discussions very much today. I cannot involve him in the final result, of which I am sure he would as always have had much to say. But I do not think he would have minded having this book dedicated to him, with affection, in memory of our long collaboration.

My brother Gino, an expert in the new media that have taken on such importance in the most recent phase of the struggle for power, gave me a great deal of help, with reading suggestions, food for thought, critical observations.

Together with Roberto and Gino, I would like to thank, without involving them in the final result, two anonymous referees, Michele Alacevic, Marco D'Eramo, Anna Gialluca, Maria Chiara Malaguti, Roberto Petrini, Michele Salvati, Roberto Schiattarella, and above all Arnaldo Bagnasco, Carlo D'Ippoliti and Mario Tonveronachi, who read previous drafts of this work or some of its chapters and provided very useful critical and constructive comments. Finally, thanks are due to Thomas Ferguson for his very useful comments and reading suggestions and for his decisive support for the realization of this English edition, to Inet for a grant covering translation expenses, and to Graham Sells and Thomas Marshall for a most able stylistic revision.

1 Introduction

1.1 WHY THIS BOOK

Sex is much more talked about than practised; by contrast, power is talked about relatively little, while so many spend an enormous amount of time pursuing it, in their own immediate sphere if not in society at large. Yet, at least in principle, reserve should be natural in the case of sex, while it should be equally natural for every citizen to be interested in forming an idea of the distribution of power in society: of the factors that determine it and the changes it undergoes over time.

What we are interested in here is power as a social issue. The topic is of great interest in itself, but also because it cuts across a wide range of research. Power is a 'rainbow' concept: you can never tell where it begins and where it ends, and it has many different aspects that intersect, with boundaries that gradually blur as they pass from one to the other. There is power linked to physical strength and individual charisma or to a role in public administration or justice, or in an organization (e.g. a company), economic power and political power, the power of the state or linked to the social position of the individual, and so on. Precisely for this reason, the subject is difficult to deal with: it is practically impossible to provide a clear and coherent picture of the situation at a given moment in time; the elements that intervene to modify the situation over time are too many and too varied for unequivocal identification of a precise trend, except in extremely vague terms.

It is impossible to master such a broad and complex field. I write as an economist; researchers with expertise in other disciplines, from sociology to law, philosophy or history, political science or anthropology, will inevitably find my laboured forays into these fields simplistic and flawed, though necessary to develop the argument. Indeed, as Bertrand Russell observed (1938, p. 108), 'Economics as a separate science is unrealistic, and misleading if taken as a guide in practice. It is one element – a very important element, it is true – in a wider study, the science of power.'

On the other hand, anyone wishing to change the society we live in for the better, whatever that means – and we have all, or almost all, felt the ethical call of this objective – must confront the problem of power: what kind of power is needed and how to acquire it, in order to be able to play a truly active role; how to assess the situation facing us, in order to understand what direction we should be working in and what constraints will limit our action. For a reformer – a term we will try to clarify later – an analysis of power is, in principle, a prerequisite for action. In practice, it is often the good politician's 'nose', or flair, that guides action, rather than a reflective analysis of power that proves too difficult to make; but a little reflection and reasoning never hurts.

For these reasons, the aim of this work is not to formulate a (more or less new) abstract theory of power, but to illustrate its different aspects for a political use, with the aim of achieving reforms: a transformative use and not a conservative one, for the purpose of change and not defence of the status quo. Hence an alternation between different analytical levels: even the most abstract reasoning is influenced by political objectives.

By structural reforms we do not mean – contrary to current usage – reforms to improve the efficiency of the economic system. We mean reforms to make the distribution of power in society less unequal, without neglecting efficiency. It is precisely the complex nature of power that calls for reflection searching enough to identify political strategies that are useful and not counterproductive for civil progress. Demagogy – demand everything, and then some more – is a practice in which the most reactionary politicians excel, and is in any case the best way to consolidate the pre-existing power structure, if not to worsen it.

With his theory of probability, Keynes (1921) taught that, while surrounded by uncertainty, it is worthwhile to gather information and to reason about it: trust in reason, accompanied by constant caution, has the same cultural roots – the Enlightenment – as trust in the possibilities of progress in human societies. As a rule, research has a normative motivation: to know, to the best of our ability, in order to be able to act usefully.

For these reasons, it seems to me that it is worth making yet another attempt, desperate though it may be, to reason about power – that is, to try to understand its nature and its distribution in society. After all, this is equivalent to studying the elements that at the same time hold together and differentiate society internally: a fundamental problem, which must be addressed, complex and challenging as it is. Illustration of the various aspects of the problem cannot be in great depth, let alone exhaustive, but should be sufficient to show how each aspect fits into the context of the overall problem.

The results of my research must be considered partial and provisional. I hope, however, that this work will suffice to reject two opposing but equally unrealistic ideologies, both of which operate in a conservative sense, as they tend to block any attempt to address the problem concretely. On the one hand, there is the idea that our societies are characterized by a well-levelled playing field where no single competitor is advantaged or disadvantaged compared to the others, and where it is therefore the merit of individuals, together with the randomness of luck, that determines the results of each one of us. On the other hand, there is the conspiracy mythology of an invisible world power centre on which everything depends and to which everyone is enslaved. The reality is much more varied: there are considerable power differentials that generate deep and radical inequalities, but also margins of freedom of action that we can use to counter these inequalities and their causes.

1.2 AN OUTLINE OF THE BOOK

As we shall see in Chapter 2, we have a grid of possible interpretative elements (power as a barrier, as belonging to networks, as weight in society) and fields of application (political, economic, cultural): a complex grid, but perhaps still too simple. This complicates identification of an adequate line of argumentation. It is generally recognized that in the end everything depends on everything else; however, we must not be overawed by the difficulty of finding a logical thread that will not run into criticism. A note of caution is therefore sufficient: the line of argument adopted, even if it has its own good reasons, should not be hypostatized; other lines of reasoning, other links between categories and fields of application of power are also valid, but some choice – obviously open to criticism – is in any case unavoidable.

A possible alternative, which had been suggested to me and which deserves mention, would have involved an analysis of power from the perspective of theories of justice. But rather than starting from 'what should be', and then considering how to get there, I prefer to start from 'what is the case', and then see if and how it can be improved. We should not aim to reach an ultimate, optimal goal, or even to define it: we should rather aim to drive towards a less unequal distribution of power.

Following Adam Smith, we begin with the division of labour (Chapter 3). The division of labour underlies the unequal distribution of labour and social roles, income and wealth; its evolution underlies economic development and changes in the social structure. We will thus consider first the aspects of power that have most directly to do with economics: the differentiation of production roles and incomes.

We will go on to consider, in Chapter 4, the problem of the power of control over the different production units and the relative importance of some of them compared to others. The form in which this control takes place is linked to the mechanisms of finance, which influence the pace and sectoral structure of economic development.

Finance shows the importance of networks as a means of strengthening and centralizing widespread power. While the power of Henry Ford was concentrated in the direct control of a large car company, the power of the Rockefellers, which also started from the control of a single oil company, was already in the second generation spreading through banks, insurance companies, oil companies and conglomerates of various kinds. Is there more power when you control 40 per cent of the shares in a large company, or when, with 3 per cent of the shares in a bank and a network of cross-checks, you exert a dominant influence over large sectors of the economy?

Interlocking shareholders (and the related networks of interlocking directors) are but one type of a more general species, namely networks as a structure for generating and enhancing power, active in the most diverse fields of social life. As we will try to show in Chapter 5, the different types of networks, sometimes but not always endowed with an institutional framework regulating their functioning and favouring their stability, condition political, economic and cultural life. The 'white' (fully legal) networks, based on family solidarity, religious beliefs, political convictions and economic relations, are flanked by what we might consider 'grey' networks, not illegal but with dubious moral foundations, based on the exchange of favours (such as Masonic-type associations) and by 'black', illegal networks, such as Mafia-type associations. Their importance is often underestimated in theoretical analyses of power, whereas they seem to have a decisive influence on the political and economic life, certainly in Italy and probably in other countries as well.

Chapter 6 moves on from the analysis of networks of relations to analysis of state-centred political power. In this regard, it is perhaps worth pointing out here another significant limitation of this work. The central aim is to draw attention to the multidimensional nature of power and its political implications: however, this means that a systematic treatment of political power would go far beyond my scope here.

The nation-state has its own historical path: it was born out of the decline of feudalism and gradually developed its role, which then came to be eroded in the phase of globalization. There are various conceptions of the nature of the state: the Weberian one of a monopoly of legal force, the Marxian one of an instrument of class power, the ordoliberal one of the legal construction of the market and, preceding these, the conception of a social contract (Rousseau, 1762) or of an association based on Hume's (1752) 'tacit consent'. In the internal organization of the state, administration of justice and military defence are important; intervention in the economy is important too, to the point of configuring the role of the state as a countervailing power to private economic power, or as expanding the role of private power. The welfare state has become increasingly important for social cohesion, not only for the redistribution of income but also – above all, perhaps – in containing the economic uncertainty that affects the lives of individuals and families.

This brings us to Chapter 7 and the problem of the relationship between culture and power. Cultural factors play an important role in the evolution of societies over time, involving the Gramscian theme of the quest for hegemony and its relationship with domination. The theme is complex: it is necessary to consider the typical behaviour of the masses (whose role has found its way into debate on the origins and characteristics of totalitarian regimes), the role of civil society and of religions, the various types of elites, and the new social media.

Chapter 8 is devoted to a brief discussion of the spatial dimension of power, from families to international relations. The dynamics of family relations have undergone profound changes, with transition from the patriarchal family to the varied forms present in today's scenario. The distribution of power between the various institutional levels – municipalities, provinces and regions, states and supranational bodies (from the European Union to the United Nations) – is also changing. The Covid-19 crisis has highlighted complex coordination problems at the international level, within the European Union, and in the relations between the central and local authorities within individual countries; a debate has thus been launched that could lead to significant but as yet unassessable changes in institutional arrangements. And now the war in Ukraine raises complex issues in international political and economic relations, but also concerning the relationship between ethics and power. These are undoubtedly critical points for overcoming these multiple crises and reconstructing a better world – which requires a strategy of structural reforms.

1.3 THE POLITICAL OBJECTIVE AND THE STRATEGY OF STRUCTURAL REFORMS

Brief as it is, this analysis of the dimensions of power nevertheless enables us to tackle the next step: possible intervention strategies.

Both the use and the pursuit of power pose major ethical problems, which are outlined in Chapter 9. In itself, power is neither beautiful nor ugly, neither good nor bad: it is a fact which we must come to terms with, neither demonizing nor exalting it. On an ethical level, the problems do not concern its existence, but the judgement to be made regarding its configuration in a given historical moment and in a given society, and the attitude to adopt towards the situation we are faced with, taking into account the objectives of freedom, justice and the common good (which includes prominently the issues of peace and the defence of the natural environment).

If what matters is not the point of arrival – because the final destination cannot be defined unequivocally, nor fully achieved – it is better to focus on the road to follow: the progressive extension of rights and a progressively fairer distribution of powers in their multiple ramifications. These issues are discussed in Chapter 10.

Thus we come, in Chapter 11, to the problem of defining concrete strategies for today's scenario: this, after all, is the objective that lies behind this book. The chapter is focused on the case of Italy: a case that I know by direct experience; however, I believe that – *mutatis mutandis* – its illustration provides useful pointers to what feasible reforms might look like in other countries as well.

Human history as a whole is characterized by undeniable progress, but temporary and/or local setbacks are also possible. Thus, while the first decades after the Second World War saw major steps ahead, since the 1970s significant progress in the field of civil rights (in particular gender inequality) has been accompanied by elements of regression. In the economic field, following the rise of neo-liberalism and the associated financial globalization, the concentration of power and imbalances in the distribution of income and wealth have increased. (The role of neo-liberalism and its theoretical shortcomings will be discussed in Sections 11.3 and 11.4.) In the political sphere, the burgeoning of demagogy and populism is worryingly reminiscent of the manoeuvrability of the masses that favoured the establishment of authoritarian/totalitarian regimes such as fascism and Nazism. The war in Ukraine now adds further dramatic elements to an already worrying situation.

It is difficult, but not impossible, to reverse these trends, and to make progress on the road to individual freedoms and social justice. The 2008 financial crisis and the Covid-19 pandemic with their heavy consequences make it clear that we need to abandon the path advocated by neo-liberalism and followed in recent decades, given the resounding failures of the myth of the invisible hand of the market. The formation of a new consensus around progressive policies requires complementary actions in the cultural, political and economic fields, with a progressive alliance along the never easy path of gender equality, environmental protection, reduction of economic and power inequalities, dissemination of culture and education and defence of civil rights.

For better or for worse, all this justifies yet another attempt to define a more just society – a society in which the distribution of power is less unequal and less conditioned by violence – and to identify the paths along which to move in that direction. The strategy of structural reforms was an important element of my youthful political education; at the time (the 1960s) it was translated into reasoned political choices that were discussed as rigorously as possible in open and in-depth debates between politicians, economists and lawyers. Reflecting on the multifaceted nature of power may be useful to revive this strategy after decades of oblivion, in a radically changed scenario.

PART I The Colours of Power

2 Interpretations and Fields of Application

The Multiple Faces of Power

2.1 A BACKWARD GLANCE

Over time, different definitions of power have been proposed, referring to different areas of social life. They all have something in common, in that they are specifications of the same phenomenon, but they may differ in bringing out particular aspects. The following brief overview, inevitably superficial (especially with regard to the best-known authors), serves essentially to recall the variety of positions on the subject, as the background to our own interpretation.

In the classical age of the Greek polis, between the fifth and fourth centuries BC, following Vegetti (2017, p. 17) we can identify five main 'types of legitimation of power': '1. *plethos*, the majority principle; 2. *nomos*, the principle of legality; 3. *kratos*, the principle of force; 4. *arethè*, the principle of excellence; 5. *episteme*, the principle of competence.' Authors like Plato or Aristotle consider the problem of power as part of their analysis of forms of government. In the same vein, Cicero distinguishes between *auctoritas*, the source of legitimacy to govern, and *potestas*, the power to intervene directly in the subjective sphere of others. Thucydides is the first of a long stream of authors who utilizes the standpoint of a realist balance of power in their analyses of international relations.

In the Christian world, the supreme power is divine authority. In the first centuries, political power was recognized as a reality to submit to ('Give to Caesar what is Caesar's'); later, with the Church's conquest of temporal power, the thesis of the religious origin and legitimation of political power, and therefore of the supremacy of religion over civil life, was upheld for centuries. In partly different forms, the idea of the supremacy of religion over civil life still reigns in many Muslim countries.[1]

Machiavelli, with *The Prince* (1513), provided what is probably the first in-depth treatment of political power analysed in its concrete manifestation, making a clear distinction (rejected by many later authors) between this theme and the ethical problems connected with good governance.[2]

For Hobbes (1651), every human being is endowed by nature with absolute power over his or her own choices, but this leads to a war of all against all; the strife is settled by the constitution of an artificial authority, the absolute state (in which, however, the citizen retains freedom in everything that is not regulated by the sovereign). On the other hand, for the natural-law theorists (such as Pufendorf) and Locke, human beings retain certain natural rights – to life and liberty above all – which constitute a limit to the powers of the state. Montesquieu (1748) moves in a similar direction, favouring moderate forms of government, in which legislative, judicial and political powers are distinct and separate; the distinction of the three countervailing powers determines the degree of freedom of different countries, regardless of their constitutional form, whether republican or monarchical.

Between the sixteenth and seventeenth centuries, consultant administrators (*cameralisti*) and mercantilists considered economic relations from the point of view of the nation state, which is all the stronger the greater is the total national wealth (with gold often utilized as a proxy). Starting with Adam Smith (1776), the point of view of the welfare of citizens, identifiable with per capita income, took on increasing importance.

Karl Marx (1867–94) links power to the class structure of society: the capitalists, who control the means of production, can exploit

[1] Muslim countries, however, have a wide variety of forms of government, especially in relation to the dialectic between nationalism and religiosity; for a discussion of the subject see Mozaffari (1987).

[2] Gramsci (1975) sees a modern version of Machiavelli's Prince in the political party that leads the proletariat to realize the new society.

the workers, extracting surplus value from them. The 'superstructure' (culture, institutions) is influenced by the economic structure more than it influences it. Substantial changes in the social distribution of power occur, after a long preparatory phase, with the transition between successive socio-economic systems: from feudalism to capitalism and from capitalism to socialism (characterized by public ownership of the means of production).[3]

For the history of modern thought on power, Weber's analyses constitute a fundamental point of reference. As Pietro Rossi (2007, p. 248) points out, Weber distinguishes between power understood as capacity – generic or indefinite – to assert one's will, even in the face of opposition, and power seen as a relationship of command and obedience, with a specific content. Weber (1922b) uses different terms to designate different aspects of what we refer to more generically in these pages as power: *Herrschaft* (translated as 'dominion' in the Italian version of the most recent critical edition); and *Macht* (now translated as 'power'). Pizzorno (1963) distinguishes instead between 'power' and 'authority'.

Of his many publications, Bertrand Russell also devoted a book to the issue of power (Russell, 1938). His considerations are wide-ranging, dealing with psychological issues (the impulse to acquire power, relations between leaders and followers), religious and anthropological issues (the power of priests: Russell was staunchly anticlerical), political issues (the power of the sovereign, forms of government), cultural issues (the formation of opinions, conventions as sources of power) and economic issues, up to the distinction between 'power over human beings and power over dead matter or non-human forms of life' (p. 23). Russell (1938, p. 5) places great emphasis on the multidimensional nature of the concept of power: 'power, like energy, must be regarded as continually passing from any one of its forms into any other .... The attempt to isolate any

[3] For none of the authors mentioned in this section can these brief outlines account for their wealth of thought; on Marx, in particular, there is much lively interpretative debate and a boundless literature, not least because of the political importance of his thought.

one form of power, more especially, in our day, the economic form, has been, and still is, a source of errors of great practical importance.'

After the end of the Second World War, in the context of the confrontation between the Western bloc and the Communist bloc, the main analyses of power focused attention on the relationship between the state and individuals. Thus Friedrich von Hayek (1944) indicates as a 'road to serfdom' not only the situation in which the state has total control of the economy through public ownership of the means of production, but also any step in this direction when the state assumes some influence in the economic sphere. In a similar vein, Bertrand de Jouvenel (1945) focuses his extensive historical and philosophical examination on Power with a capital P, referring to 'the controls, both spiritual and material, which modern governments have at their disposal' (p. 3) and illustrating its growth over time. Consistent with this approach, de Jouvenel (1945, p. 18 n.) proposes as a measure of the 'extent of Power' the ratio between 'the resources at Power's disposal' and 'the resources inherent in society', which we can interpret as the share of the public sector in national income. The Power of the state is directly opposed to individual freedom: 'Every increase in the state authority must involve an immediate diminution of the liberty of each citizen' (1945, p. 157).[4]

Perroux (1950, p. 56) points out that economic life 'is different from a network of exchange. It is, rather, a network of forces. The economy is guided by the pursuit not only of gain, but also of power.' Perroux then considers a 'domination effect' for the analysis of economic relations, in particular between companies and states.

A similar conception of economic life as characterized by power relations is developed by Galbraith in his work. In particular, Galbraith (1952) underlines the high concentration of power in large

[4] If this opposition were true, the reconquest by the state of control over a territory previously dominated by the mafia would be considered a defeat of individual freedoms. The opposition thesis actually serves de Jouvenel to support another thesis, common to all neo-liberals, namely the opposition to the welfare state: 'those who seek social security find an authoritarian state' (1945, p. 351).

corporations, which favours a continuous expansion of production and living standards, but requires – and stimulates – countervailing powers: trade unions, large commercial intermediaries, various forms of regulation and public intervention.

Innis (1950) shows that the media system has a direct influence on social structures and the ways of organizing power in time and space, initiating a line of research to which we will return in Section 7.8.

A potentially quantifiable definition of the concept of power was attempted by Dahl (1957). Power is understood as a relationship between individuals: 'A has power over B to the extent that he can get B to do something that B would not otherwise do' (1957, pp. 202–3). A number of elements have to be added: the source or basis of power, the means, the extent (i.e. the set of actions that A can force/induce B to perform), the amount of power (defined as the increased probability that B will perform a certain action if A exercises his power over him), and the number of individuals over whom the power can be exercised. Dahl (1957, p. 214) acknowledges that it is difficult to use this concept operationally, but nevertheless considers it useful, as a point of reference and touchstone for empirical analysis.

This line of reasoning was then developed by Harsanyi (1962), who added a further element, the cost of exercising power. By comparing this cost with the utility of the actions whose performance becomes more probable thanks to the exercise of power, Harsanyi succeeded in bringing the issue of power choices back into a classical utilitarian scheme: agents' choices are guided by the felicific calculation of pleasures and pains, considering for each choice the utility derived from it and adopting those choices that maximize utility. We thus have a treatment of power linked to methodological individualism, that is, to the idea that in the social sciences theoretical constructions must necessarily start from the behaviour of individuals.[5] In principle, this approach opens the way (assuming we

[5] Constructing a theory concerning the behaviour of individuals, as the methodological individualism of traditional marginalist theory claims to do, is different from recognizing an autonomous decision-making capacity ('intentionality') of

have all the necessary information) to giving precise answers to the problem of accounting for agents' decisions. However, these answers concern a totally unrealistic world: non-probabilistic uncertainty is absent; individuals have a well-specified map of preferences assessed in terms of a single quantity (a one-dimensional utility), thus ruling out the possibility that individuals' actions are guided by a diversified complex of motivations (a-rational passions, such as pride or love, and interests, rationally evaluated but not confined to personal enrichment) and that there are qualitative differences that cannot be reduced to quantitative differences between the various types of pleasure. Moreover, the social relations that influence the various elements considered in this model are assumed to be given, whereas in fact they constitute the most complex and interesting aspect of the problem of power.

In an extensive history of social power from antiquity to the present day, Mann (1986–2012) illustrates how the four different forms into which he distinguishes the sources of social power combine over time: ideological, economic, military and political.

Bachrach and Baratz (1962, p. 8) stress that power also consists in creating 'barriers to the public airing of policy conflicts'. Developing this point, Lukes (1974) proposes a three-dimensional view of power: power as the ability to actuate a predetermined agenda, in shaping the agenda, and lastly in influencing people's minds so as to ensure consent ('in such a way that they accept their role in the existing order of things', p. 11). Nye (1990) then identifies power with the ability to make others do what one wants; on the basis of this definition, he distinguishes between *hard power* (coercion) and *soft power* (persuasion). One form of soft power is *nudge*, theorized by Thaler and Sunstein (2008) as a tool available to public authorities as an alternative to the imposition of direct constraints, to induce rational individual behaviour: a kind of compromise between paternalism and

individuals, which leads to rejecting deterministic theories (as Max Weber, 1922a, does, for example).

liberalism. Nye's soft power is an important element for a critique and reappraisal of the realist doctrine then prevailing in the analysis of international relations, stressing the importance of cultural elements in addition to the military and economic ones.

All these definitions, summarized here in basic terms, should not necessarily be considered as mutually exclusive alternatives; each of them, even if one-sided, can be useful to illustrate some aspect of a multidimensional issue like power.

2.2 POWER AS A DIFFERENTIAL OF POTENTIAL, AS A BARRIER TO ENTRY, AS A WEIGHT

How should power be defined in the context of our analysis? A preliminary point to be underlined is that the concept of power, in the sense considered here, is related to society – to a community of individuals – and not to the relationship between individuals, as is the case, for instance, in definitions like: 'Power as coercion consists in enforcing one's own decision *against* the will of the other' (Han, 2005, p. 2). In the relationship between individuals, the multidimensional nature of power also blurs the notion of 'coercion', to be understood rather as the power to influence the other's actions. Han himself (2005, p. 38) reminds us that 'power that works through habits is more efficient and more stable than power that gives orders or uses coercion'. More general than Han's, but still centred on the two-way relationship between those who influence and those who are influenced, is Bobbio's definition (2010, p. 6) which, again following the line of Weber, interprets 'power as the capacity of a subject to influence, condition and determine the behaviour of another subject'.

Of course, the two approaches – analysing power relations between individuals and social power relations – are not mutually exclusive; the intentionality of human action must also be kept in mind, perhaps in the background, in analyses of social power relations.

In the societal sense, power is a multi-dimensional notion; its generic sense is intuitive. However, if we try to pin it down, some important aspect will escape us. No matter how hard we try to define them precisely, by their very nature the concepts remain somewhat indistinct; we can hope they will come into clearer focus – but it may be just the opposite – as we proceed with the analysis. An initial provisional definition can nevertheless be of help.

Let us consider three possible definitions: power as difference of potential; power as barrier to entry; power as weight. On the other hand, we will not be concerned with what we can consider power in the absolute sense: the power of humans over nature, as manifested for example in a lengthening or shortening of the average life expectancy at birth, or in the amount of goods and services available to us.

In the first case – power as a difference in potential – the concept of power indicates a relationship, not a quality intrinsic to the individual. What counts, within society, is the internal ordering of power, whereby some are 'more powerful' than others, on the strength of some dimension of social relations: a difference of potential in social action.

The second definition – power as a barrier to entry – is typical of the economic field, but can also be used for politics and culture. In each of these fields of action, society can be seen as divided into non-homogeneous domains; an ideal, perfectly egalitarian society, in which there are no differences in power, is characterized by total freedom for individuals to move between the different domains. Controlling the barriers to entry into each sphere thus constitutes an element of power for those already placed within – the insiders as opposed to the outsiders (as in the case of network power, discussed in Chapter 5). In the field of economics, as we shall see later, the dominant importance of oligopolistic market forms depends precisely on the existence of barriers to entry in the different markets. In the field of culture, the influence of each protagonist depends on the possibility they have of direct or indirect access to the main media: radio and television, newspapers, publishing houses. In the case of politics, people who have an important role (member of parliament, minister, regional or municipal councillor) have acquired over time a greater reputation and network power than those who are at the threshold of the arena and are therefore at a disadvantage when they try to enter it. In this sense, the concept of barriers to entry is also useful to illustrate the comparative advantages of those who have some power in more than one sphere: take, for instance, the case of the economic group that can exercise indirect political power through the control of newspapers or television networks.

The third definition characterizes power as weight (or importance), in relation to the specific field under consideration: the share of votes received by a political party in the total electorate, the market share of a company, and so on.

Do we have any tools to measure power? Since, let us repeat once again, it is a multidimensional concept, we certainly cannot expect to find a single measuring rod. We can, however, suggest, not four measures, but four types of measure: indices of inequality, heights of barriers to entry, size and strength of networks, and relative weight. It will be a matter of choosing the most appropriate unit of measurement for each particular case, and then establishing an appropriate metric for the specific area under consideration.

In economics, but also in other fields, the height of the entry barrier indicates the power of the incumbent over the potential entrant. For instance, the incumbent in an oligopolistic market enjoys advantages over the potential entrant; the theory of oligopoly, which we will discuss in Section 4.3, defines the determinants of these advantages and measures them in terms of the extra profit that the incumbent is able to obtain without risking new market entry. In a number of areas, the barrier to entry is purely legal: this, for example, is the case for professional bodies, from notaries to lawyers, or for licences, as in the case of taxis, radio or TV frequency bands, and maritime oil exploration areas. Also in these cases, the presence of a barrier to entry allows the insider to gain more than the competitive level; in several cases we can have a direct measurement of the economic value of the barrier through the market value of the licence.

In a way, the network is the opposite of the barrier. In fact, it is not a matter of exclusion, but of inclusion, of linking up with others in order to combine forces: it is the main element of political power, but it is certainly not limited to this area. In this case, there are three possible measures: the size of the network (in relative rather than absolute terms, i.e. as a relative weight with respect to the sector of activity considered as a whole); the strength of the ties of connection (e.g. share of votes in the case of interlocking shareholding); and the degree of centrality within the network, which depends on the structure of the network and the position of each individual within it. In a number of cases, these elements will be difficult to define; take, for example, the case of associations like freemasonry, where the bond of membership often entails a willingness, but not an obligation, to exchange favours.

Weight is a matter of the strength of the individual's presence within the sphere of activity: the market share in the case of a company; wealth and income, intelligence and training, birth status, or even physical appearance in the case of an individual. With respect to these characteristics, we may consider the specific situation of the individual in relation to that of other individuals in his or her field of activity or turn to comparative parameters such as the mean or median value.

Analysis of power in any given situation entails consideration of a variety of elements, and thus the simultaneous use of different types of measurement. Often exact measurement, even if a suitable metric has been specified, will be difficult, and it may only be approximate. In any case, the combination of different elements and measures, which cannot be summarized in a single measure, will bring qualitative assessments to the fore. Nevertheless, even with all the limitations, cautious application of power metrics can be useful.

Democracy, which is also a very complex and multidimensional concept, can be linked to the notion of power, considering it to be more fully realized the more egalitarian the distribution of power proves to be. In this sense, the problem of defining and analysing the concept of power is equivalent to that of defining and analysing the concept of democracy; policies designed to achieve a fairer distribution of power, in its various dimensions, are *ipso facto* designed to achieve a higher level of democracy. The quest for an 'alliance of democracies' called for in response to the war in Ukraine now involves international relations and adds urgency to the issue. Similarly, the problem of power is linked to that of justice, in particular distributive justice, which is achieved not only through an egalitarian, or less unequal, distribution of wealth and income, but must be extended to the different dimensions of power: the problem thus becomes enormously complex. But we will be returning to these issues as our argument unfolds.

2.3 TYPES, AREAS, INSTRUMENTS, MOTIVATIONS OF POWER

We will have to approach the subject step by step, taking the main aspects of power one by one: first the bolder colours, and only subsequently the nuances of the intersections, which constitute the dominant feature of the real world.

As for the areas of power, the economic, political and cultural spheres seem to predominate. The military and technological areas can either be treated separately or included, as instruments of power acquisition and defence, in the political and economic areas respectively. (Technology plays a decisive direct role with respect to 'absolute' power in the sense indicated above, i.e. the relationship of human beings to nature). As for the instruments, we may list some examples: newspapers, television networks, content distribution platforms, universities and publishing houses for culture; shareholding and networks of business and financial alliances, entry barriers and antitrust rules for the economy; political parties, associations and networks of financial support for politics.

As for motivations, we should reject the utilitarian tradition centred on the maximization of utility (in Bentham's felicific calculus, the algebraic sum of the pleasures and pains resulting from each action) by each subject. This tradition has the apparent advantage of giving precise answers, but it requires such drastic simplifications as to distort the problems it is meant to address. Instead, we can resort to the distinction between passions and interests: the former are a-rational, not necessarily irrational (e.g. love, pride, lust); the latter are susceptible to rational analysis (e.g. the quest for wealth and income, but also for knowledge or justice, fame or prestige). Motivations concern individuals, but in a climate of sufficient cultural affinity they can also be applied to groups of individuals.

Power types are a very useful analytical tool, as Weber shows with his notion of 'ideal types' – indeed, the only one available to the researcher to avoid getting lost in a myriad of case observations – but a delicate one. They are creations of our minds and not factual realities, even though we have to refer to actual facts to construct them. Weber considers them in the context of macro-social analyses; however, there is no reason why they should not be used, with the necessary caution, for more specific analyses as well. To give just a couple of examples that we will be coming back to later, the power of money managers in the contemporary finance-dominated economy is different from that of corporate executives in the age of managerial capitalism; the cultural hegemony of traditional societies centred on religious practices and traditional rites is different from that of the age of mass media (radio and TV), just as the latter is different from that of the digital age based on social media (WhatsApp, Twitter, Facebook, Instagram and the like).

To put it simply, we can focus on three ideal types of power: charismatic, traditional and legal. In other words: the dominant personality of a leader, the force of tradition to which the behaviour of the members of a society conforms and the set of legal norms that organize social coexistence.[6]

If we try to put together the classifications by area and type of power, we get a 3 × 3 table. Each box can help us isolate an aspect of a multiform reality. Thus, we can try to describe the state of a society from the point of view of the theme of power at a given moment in its history by attributing a low or high value (from 1 to 3, for example) to each box.

[6] See Weber (1922b) for an in-depth discussion of the three concepts and their interrelationships.

For instance, in a society like that of Italy today we may perhaps attribute a low – but not zero – value to charisma in the economy, medium in politics and high in the cultural field; the role of the forces of tradition can be considered medium in the economy (due to the hereditary transmission of assets and control of companies, tempered especially in periods of rapid technological change by the emergence of new agents), medium in politics and medium in the cultural field; the legal rules of the game will be of high value in the economy, medium in politics (which can change them, albeit – revolutionary leaps aside – following well-specified formal procedures), and low value in culture.

	Power type		
Area of power	Charismatic	Traditional	Legal
Economy	1	2	3
Politics	2	2	2
Culture	3	2	1

A similar table can be constructed to represent, in stylized form, the transition between different historical stages. For example, in the transition from feudalism to capitalism, charismatic and traditional power decrease, while legal power increases; in the transition from the age of the press to that of the Internet, charismatic power increases and traditional power decreases; and so on.

Weber proposed a historical sequence in the relevance of the three types of power, with the predominance of charismatic power in primitive societies, traditional power for a long subsequent phase, and finally legal power for the modern age, but always recognizing the possible coexistence of the three (also due to the importance, in each social order, of the legacy of the past). The double classification proposed here, by types and areas of power, complicates the picture, though never enough given the unclearly defined nature of the triads of categories used; but it can be useful in highlighting the profoundly differentiated nature (the rainbow) of power. To the two-dimensional classification (by types and by areas) we can then add other dimensions: such as that of motivations (passions and interests) or that of the instruments of power mentioned above.

Clearly, the classifications are complex and at least in part arbitrary; it is better not to justify them a priori, but to see how they work in practice. We can only add, as a general rule, that extreme choices should be avoided: on the one hand, simple dichotomies would make us lose sight of important phenomena while, on the other hand, too many categories would get in the way of reaching useful conclusions for interpretation and action. For example, in the analysis of social classes Sylos Labini (1974) taught us that, compared to the simple dichotomy between capitalists and proletarians or to considering *n* social groups with practically no limit to *n*, an intermediate level of abstraction/simplification suitable for the purpose at hand – in his case critique of the Italian Communist Party strategy of messianic expectation of the growth of the proletariat – is preferable, adding to the binary bourgeois-proletarian classification a single category defined as the middle classes (within which further distinctions can then be introduced if and when they prove useful to deepen the analysis). Similarly, when considering market forms, faced with the simple competition-monopoly dichotomy or, at the other extreme, the idea that each market constitutes a case in itself, it may be useful to introduce the category of oligopoly, which in turn may be subject to further subdivisions (concentrated, differentiated, mixed oligopoly). The classifications must have concrete foundations, but they are still creations of the researcher, made (and justified) insofar as they are useful for interpretation of the phenomenon under analysis.

2.4 CUMULATIVE PROCESSES AND BALANCING PROCESSES

In the analysis of power, static vision and dynamic vision (considering the structure at a given moment or its evolution over time) are complementary. The static vision, as understood here, does not imply the idea of a situation in equilibrium but more simply a 'snapshot' of the situation at a given moment, useful for grasping its structure, regardless of postulating its stability or persistence over time. The issues analysed so far essentially concern the static vision; but in the case of power the evolutionary potentialities inherent in the different situations are important.

For this aspect, we can distinguish two main cases (together with a reference case, namely static processes in which the situation tends to remain unchanged or to follow a constant trend over time): cumulative processes and balancing processes.

In the first case, a process characterized by a progressive acceleration of change is set in motion. For example, a position of political power can be used to boost economic power, which in turn feeds back into strengthening the political position, in a self-fulfilling spiral. Again, a strong economic position can be exploited to gain cultural hegemony (e.g. through ownership of newspapers or television networks or subsidizing them through advertising, or through the use of paid trolls on social media), which opens the way to gaining political strength, which in turn can be used to strengthen the economic position yet further.

A special case of cumulative processes is lock-in. This is the case of the QWERTY typewriter keyboard, still utilized though not the most ergonomic one, discussed by David (1985), or the case of the petrol versus the electric car recalled by Nelson (1995): at the beginning of the twentieth century, the petrol car and the electric car had equivalent costs (and advantages and disadvantages of use); however, when one of the two technologies – in our case, the petrol car – gained a slight advantage, albeit for contingent reasons, there was a tendency to invest more in that technology, which favoured its improvement (cost reduction, qualitative advances); thus a cumulative process took place which became stronger as the cumulative advantage grew, until switching to the other technology was practically impossible. Today we can see that the problem was not one of insurmountable technological difficulties: under the impetus of environmental concerns, incentives for the electric car were adopted, which were strong enough to allow the initial disadvantages to be progressively offset. Breaking lock-in positions is not impossible, but it is so difficult that exogenous interventions (such as strong public incentives) are needed to get round the lock-in situation.

In the case of balancing processes, reaction to a dominant position sets in motion mechanisms that tend to limit it. For example, the rise of a firm within a market may stimulate alliances between competitors, or the adoption of anti-trust measures. At least from Montesquieu (1748) on, if not before, institutional rules ensuring the presence of countervailing powers have been considered the main element that can act as a brake on absolutist tendencies.

In actual games of power, cumulative processes and balancing processes overlap. In general, the former are stronger than the latter. Appropriate institutional rules are therefore needed to facilitate balancing processes so as to achieve a distribution of power that does not tend to become increasingly unequal.

At any given time, we may speak of an equilibrium, determined by balancing processes, with respect to certain aspects considered in isolation. However, these equilibria will always be local and unstable, due to the simultaneous action, in areas related to the one under consideration, of cumulative processes that come into play systematically as elements that break the equilibria. The result is a complex dynamic of social systems that is generally non-linear, periods of relative stability alternating with phases of rapid and drastic change. The constant evolution of technology may well be the main systemic source of change, with cumulative effects that make reversal impossible. Currently, for example, new information technologies have entailed revolutionary changes in the political field and in the competition to emerge and gain a footing in the field of culture.

Both the difficulty and, often, the impossibility of predicting technological change and the overlapping of cumulative and balancing processes are constitutive elements of the uncertainty inherent in social evolution.

3 The Origin of Inequalities

The Division of Labour

3.1 DIVISION OF LABOUR AND THE WEALTH OF NATIONS

The division of labour is a source of both economic wealth and social stratification, of prosperity and alienation: in short, it is the root of all the issues we are going to discuss.[1]

Adam Smith, who in *Wealth of Nations* (1776) based his analysis on the division of labour, overall took an extremely positive view of it (although, as we shall see, far from purely rosy). In his view, in fact, the wealth of nations – that is, roughly, the per capita income of a country's citizens – depends to a large extent on the stage reached by the division of labour, which determines productivity.

As he reminds us in the famous example of pins (Smith, 1776, pp. 14–15), a worker doing everything alone can produce at most a dozen pins a day, whereas a small factory with ten workers can produce about 50,000 pins a day. As the division of labour progresses, then productivity grows – and grows a lot.

The link between productivity and the wealth of nations is obvious. National income is given by the number of workers employed in production multiplied by the amount of output that each on average manages to produce, that is, by productivity. Per capita income is equal to the national income divided by the population. It is, therefore, equal to the share of employed workers in the total population multiplied by productivity.[2] In the long run, it is mainly the

[1] In parts of this chapter I use, and rework, material from my book *The Wealth of Ideas* (Roncaglia, 2001).

[2] In symbols: given Y = national income, L = number of workers; π = output per worker (i.e. labour productivity) and Pop = population, from $Y = L\,\pi$ we derive per capita income, $Y/Pop = \pi\, L/Pop$.

second element, productivity growth – linked to a greater division of labour – that drives increase in per capita income.[3]

Smith's thesis is also obvious, but it is not trivial. Implicitly, Smith assumes that the wealth of nations is a good indicator of the well-being of citizens and perhaps also of the power of a state; moreover, he considers it possible to overlook, at least in an initial approximation, the role that the composition of production may play.

This last aspect must be kept in mind. A well-known example is the proverbial alternative between producing guns or butter, with its impact on the availability of food or the military power of a country. There is a similar alternative, as far as the well-being of citizens is concerned, in the case of drugs and medicines. However, without diminishing its importance, this aspect can be deferred to a separate discussion.

The second aspect, the link between per capita income and the economic power of a state, has no unequivocal answer. Identifying the wealth of nations with the welfare of citizens rather than the overall economic size of the country is generally seen by economists as an undoubted step forward by Smith compared to his predecessors (the mercantilists, often advisors – or would-be advisors – of a ruler). The latter focused on a country's total output as a source of power (both economic and, consequently, military and political), whereas Smith takes as his object of analysis the standard of living of its citizens. In this sense Sweden is richer than China or Russia insofar as its citizens enjoy a higher standard of living. However, when looking at political weight in the international arena the ranking changes. At the same time, when assessing the strength of a state we have to distinguish between its economic power and its political and military power: the two are related, but only partially. The Soviet Union, before its collapse, was considered a great economic power as well as a political and military power; when all is said and done, it turns out

[3] Indeed, the presence of a significant share of inactive people in the total population is compatible with the survival of society only if productivity is high enough to compensate for the associated reduction in per capita income.

that per capita income is also an important indicator of a country's economic strength.

It is also to be borne in mind that per capita income is not the same as a citizen's well-being: it is an important component and a very useful indicator, but it is certainly not everything. Smith is well aware of this, and in the scale of his personal values he gives the economic dimension a far more limited place than many of our contemporaries do.[4] Moreover, there are jobs that are more or less unpleasant, more or less satisfying. The satisfaction or dissatisfaction one can derive from work is important: work is not only a necessary sacrifice to earn a living, but can in itself be a source of satisfaction. But freedom from economic need is a prerequisite – though not the only one – for a pleasant life and attainment of a certain degree of civilization, including, Smith himself recalls (1983, p. 137), the development of letters and the arts. In fact, there is a high, though far from perfect, correlation between per capita income and indicators of human development such as literacy, life expectancy at birth or, on the negative side, infant mortality.[5]

Productivity – and, behind it, the division of labour – is not the only factor determining per capita income. The share of employed workers in the total population also counts, and thus the trend of employment (leaving aside the problem, important as it is, of whom to include among the active workers, which is linked to that of what

[4] 'What can be added to the happiness of a man who is in health, who is out of debt, and has a clear conscience? To one in this situation, all accessions of fortune may properly be said to be superfluous; and if he is much elevated upon account of them, it must be the effect of the most frivolous levity' (Smith, 1759, p. 45).

[5] High correlation, of course, does not mean perfect coincidence. Fuà (1993), well ahead of today's trends, showed that the correlation weakens when sufficiently high levels of per capita income are reached, and argued that when environmental problems are taken into account, an increase in per capita production of material goods does not necessarily lead to a better quality of life. It may be agreed, then, that productivity gains should better fuel a general reduction in annual working time rather than an increase in per capita and overall output. On the issue of output measurement and the environment, see Fitoussi, Sen and Stiglitz (2009). Another crucial flaw of GNP statistics is that they do not take into account the many hours of labour lent especially by women within the family. We will return to these issues later on.

to include in the product).[6] Let us take Smith's example: 10,000 workers, each working alone, produce a daily total of 100,000 pins, while with the division of labour two factories of ten workers each are sufficient to produce the same quantity of pins; if total pin production remains unchanged, employment falls by 9,980, to only 20 workers. The average per capita income would be unchanged, but the social outcome would be disastrous.

Smith draws on the historical experience of previous centuries to argue that, as a rule, when productivity increases, per capita product also increases; generally speaking (unless the number of employees or the number of hours worked per employee falls in proportion to the increase in productivity), overall income also increases. However, this historical rule is not a logical necessity, and it leaves open a major problem: is the market able to ensure that productivity increases translate into increases in welfare (identified with per capita income) and not in unemployment?[7] Or are public interventions needed to support employment, and of what kind?[8] The issue is also relevant from the point of view of the distribution of power between social classes: if technical progress generates an increase in unemployment, this reduces the bargaining power of workers vis-à-vis employers (an aspect we will return to later on).

In part, the increase in productivity has not translated solely into an increase in per capita income, but also into a reduction in working time, which in the long run has been very significant. The conquest of free time by workers has led to significant changes in lifestyles. The 'right to idleness' mentioned by Lafargue (1880) has also been considered an advance in civilization and a goal of the

[6] The issue of the distinction between productive and unproductive workers (and, within the latter category, between useful and useless unproductive work) has been the subject of a large body of literature, and can be key to constructing alternative models of economic and social development and the different roles of classes and strata within them – issues that we will touch on later.

[7] Technological unemployment tends to affect those sectors where there is a strong increase in productivity.

[8] This issue has seen lively debate among economists. For an illustration, see Roncaglia (2019).

working class, allowing for the gradual reduction of constrictive work. The disappearance of the unproductive classes (the rentiers) and a restructuring of consumption could also work in the same direction, as Lafargue points out, including through the abolition of rentiers and luxury consumption (what Veblen, 1899, calls 'conspicuous consumption', arising from the wealthier classes' desire to show off their status). We will return to these aspects later on.

It is worth distinguishing between two different aspects of productivity growth: the increased availability of goods and services that is made possible and the reduction in their production costs. Ricardo distinguishes in this respect between *riches* and *value*: the division of labour increases the former and reduces the latter.[9] The two elements are linked by the fact that technical progress proceeds at different speeds for different products, so that value, as an index of the difficulty of production, varies differently from product to product. The very structure of the economic system is thus modified; in the absence of perfect competition, which would guarantee a full and continuous adaptation of the prices of products to their difficulty of production, an unequal distribution of increases in sectoral production and income rewards some sectors more than others. We will come back to these aspects in the next chapter, dealing with the theme of market forms: a central theme for economic power relations.

Last but not least, the division of labour generates not only productivity gains; it also generates social stratification, and not only that. For example, industrial development undermines the institution of the traditional patriarchal family, associated with agricultural activities; in a context of rapid technical progress, the body of knowledge – not only technological – of the elderly loses weight, and gradually their prestige is also affected. Above all, as will

[9] 'Value ... essentially differs from riches, for value depends not on abundance, but on the difficulty or facility of production' (Ricardo, 1817, p. 273). Before Ricardo, Smith distinguished between labour commanded (the quantity of goods and services that the remuneration of an hour's work allows to purchase) and labour contained (the quantity of labour required, directly or indirectly, to obtain a given product): with technical progress, the former increases and the latter decreases.

be discussed later, the division of labour contributes substantially to determining those negative aspects of work commonly referred to (by Marx, among others) as 'alienation'. A big problem opens up here with the relationship between the positive and negative effects of the division of labour: how are we to interpret them? What is to be done in the face of them?

First of all, is there any contradiction between the positive and negative effects of the division of labour (as some economic historians argued at the beginning of the twentieth century)? In fact, it seems very difficult to think that when he speaks of the negative effects, at the end of the fifth book of the *Wealth of Nations*, the great (and meticulous) Scot forgot what he had argued in the first part of the book. The thesis of a contradiction is therefore clearly absurd: more simply, like so many other things in human life, the division of labour has both positive and negative effects. Without assuming that the two kinds of effects are directly comparable, we can – indeed we must – make an assessment: Smith's is that the positive effects of the division of labour are too important to be given up.[10] In fact, every human civilization that we know of is, and has been, characterized by a certain degree of division of labour. Industrialization has accelerated this process, which has constituted a formidable boost to growth and, in general, to the improvement of our living conditions, in spite of its heavy negative collateral effects on the quality of life and the environment, which deserve today, and would have deserved in the past, far greater attention to counteract them, especially through public intervention.

Comparison with primitive populations ('the stone age', although ethnologists and anthropologists study groups on the fringes

[10] In addition to the increase in the quantity produced, there was also an improvement in the quality of the product: compared to the barber-doctor-dentist recalled in western films, we are very happy today to have specialist dentists, equipped with improved instruments and properly trained in their use. In the initial phase of the debate on the division of labour, authors such as Xenophon or Diodorus Siculus considered precisely the improvement in the quality of the product as the main advantage of the specialization of craftsmen.

of modern society, while archaeologists can say little about primitive societies) may help illustrate this point. Sahlins (1972, p. 133) notes that among these peoples 'Production is not forced to pursue its maximum physical or remunerative capacity, but rather tends to stop when subsistence is momentarily assured'. There is thus a limitation of compulsive work to a minimum, and a share of free time that appears to be greater than we have today. Provocatively, the primitive society could thus be considered a society of plenty.[11] However, if we consider the standard of living of these peoples (average life expectancy, morbidity, education, etc.), it is clear that none of us would prefer to live in their conditions. Rather, their example can be considered in defining the characteristics of a utopian society, with the same level of scientific and medical knowledge and productivity as ours, but in which other aspects of the primitive society are taken as a paradigm: reciprocity, the relative preference for leisure over opulent consumption, less inequality (guaranteed among other things by the institution of gift-giving by those in positions of power).

Both positive and negative assessments are also possible concerning the functioning of the market, the most widespread form of organization in societies based on the division of labour, generally accompanied by private ownership of the means of production.[12] When each productive unit needs the means of production produced by others, which it obtains by giving up at least part of its own product to others, there is a network of repetitive exchanges that ensure the continuous functioning of the economy; naturally, this network becomes increasingly complex as the division of labour progresses. The alternative to the market, namely top-down centralized planning, has proved less efficient. The myth of the invisible hand of the market (wrongly attributed to Adam Smith – a grave error for

[11] See Marchionatti (2020, p. 440). On similar lines, Graeber and Wengrow (2021) stress the variety of forms of social organization found in primitive societies, contradicting both Rousseau's positive and Hobbes's negative idealizations.

[12] On the link between the market, private property and coercive labour, see Villetti (1978).

historians of economic thought) has failed in theory as well as in practice:[13] unemployment and job security, pollution and global warming, poverty and distributional inequalities need to be addressed with public intervention precisely to ensure the social sustainability of the market.

What can we do, then, about the negative effects? Do we have to accept them, as an ineliminable corollary of the positive ones? Smith's answer (and that of many other progressives of his time, such as Condorcet in France) is, along with other interventions, recourse to public and free elementary education: in the context of the time, a strikingly innovative strategic indication.[14] We will be coming back to this; what needs underlining now is that the division of labour is accepted as an ineliminable characteristic of the economic systems in which we live, given its positive effects, but whose (very considerable) negative effects must also be recognized, so as to intervene to contain them.

3.2 THE ORIGINS OF THE DIVISION OF LABOUR AND SOCIAL STRATIFICATION

The extreme ideas of a primitive society in which the division of labour had yet to come into existence, or of a society at the end of the development of human history in which the division of labour has ceased to exist, can at best be considered ideal references. The history of human societies – those of the distant past as well as those of the foreseeable future – is based on the division of labour, albeit in constantly evolving forms. The debate on the origins of the division of labour therefore concerns not so much its emergence at a particular stage of history (or prehistory), but its nature and effects.

[13] See Rothschild (1994) and Roncaglia (2005) for a critique of the myth of the invisible hand of the market and its attribution to Adam Smith; Roncaglia (2019) for a review of the most recent economic theories.

[14] Little attention was paid at the time to the environmental issue – which is not limited to global warming – on which the spotlight was finally turned relatively recently. The first well-known economist to address environmental issues was John Stuart Mill (1848) in the mid-nineteenth century.

In a society based on the division of labour, differences in income and social status (and the very satisfaction one can derive from work) are to a significant extent related to the role one plays in the production process. Thus we may ask what determines our position in the division of labour: fate, inheritance from the past, or our innate abilities.

An important tradition, starting with Plato and Aristotle if not before, attributes a decisive role to innate abilities. One is by nature an Athenian citizen or, going down the ladder, a woman or a slave. This thesis is of course schematic, but it captures the substance of a position that was predominant in antiquity and was still widespread at the time of the nineteenth-century debate on the abolition of slavery (and we must remember that the position of John Stuart Mill, the abolitionist, was not the majority position in his day, dominated rather by the naturalness of slavery theses of a Ruskin or a Carlyle).[15] Even nowadays, in marginalist economic theory, wage (and, in general, income) differentials are attributed primarily to differences in the endowments of the innate capacities of each individual, which also affect the second element considered relevant, known as the accumulation of human capital, that is, the acquisition of greater labour capacities through the use of time and money.

An interesting episode in this debate occurred immediately after the publication of the *Wealth of Nations*. Pownall, former governor of Massachusetts, reacted with a short pamphlet to many of the theses put forward by Smith in his book, criticizing, among other things, his ideas about the origin of the division of labour (Pownall, 1776).

In the *Wealth of Nations,* Smith argues that the origins of the division of labour can be traced back to the human propensity to barter and exchange, in other words to the propensity of human beings as social animals – according to Aristotle's influential definition – to relate to one another. Differences in individual capacities are not the origin of exchanges: on the contrary, they derive mainly, if not

[15] See Levy (2001) and Canfora (2004).

exclusively, from different work experiences. The latter – the fact of doing a certain job – are implicitly attributed to a large extent to one's initial position in the social structure and to occasional factors.[16]

Pownall, on the other hand, argues that the origins of the division of labour and the consequent distribution of roles among individuals are rooted in innate differences in ability: for example, strength or manual dexterity or eyesight or stature and so on. This thesis, as mentioned above, has a long tradition, and provides a justification for the social stratification associated with the division of labour, as if everyone is 'naturally' predestined by their innate capacities to a certain role. Indeed, it is in this way that Plato presents his distinction between peasants, warriors and philosophers, or Aristotle argues that slaves and women have naturally subordinate roles in society.

Coming to more recent times, in the field of anthropology, the seminal research by Margaret Mead (1935) showed 'the determining force of social conditioning' (p. 296) – culture, not biology – in the assignment of social roles to men and women. The work is based on field studies and comparisons between populations in New Guinea: the Arapesh, the Mundugumor and the Ciambuli. In the first and second cases, men and women have similar characters, although of opposite types in the two populations: among the Arapesh a gentle character prevails and among the Mundugumor an aggressive character, with a strong spirit of competition. Ciambuli men and women,

[16] 'The difference of natural talents in different men is, in reality, much less than we are aware of; and the very different genius which appears to distinguish men of different professions, when grown up to maturity, is not upon many occasions so much the cause, as the effect of the division of labour. The difference between the most dissimilar characters, between a philosopher and a common street porter, for example, seems to arise not so much from nature, as from habit, custom, and education. ... Without the disposition to truck, barter, and exchange, every man must have procured to himself every necessary and conveniency of life which he wanted. All must have had the same duties to perform, and the same work to do, and there could have been no such difference of employment as could alone give occasion to any great difference of talents.' (Smith, 1776, pp. 28–9). The availability of natural resources is obviously relevant for the geographical distribution of labour, especially in the most backward societies, as in the exchange of fish and game between coastal and inland populations; even in this case, however, we can assume that the ability to hunt or fish is a consequence and not a premise of the work performed.

on the other hand, have different characters, more in line with the traditional conception; it is the Ciambuli women, however, who manage the family resources. Mead's work sparked off wide-ranging debate, both in the anthropological field in the strict sense and in the field of gender studies, where it has played a formative role in the thesis that the biological reality of sex is open to different cultural constructions, which exert an important influence on social cohesion.

On the other hand, in the economic field, the traditional marginalist approach, which is widespread today, is characterized by the thesis that the economic problem consists in the comparison between the original scarce endowments of resources of each individual and his/her needs. The so-called accumulation of human capital, whereby individuals improve their skills by investing in education and training, adds to this basic framework but does not eliminate it. In this way, the marginalist approach follows both its own internal logic and the traditional hierarchical view of society defended by Pownall against Smith.

In this respect, we can cite as an example an article by Samuelson (1971, p. 405): 'A woman is not a man, and men are not at any age homozygous twins. Thus, let women be three times as efficient in beaver production and two times as efficient in deer production. ... To understand the statics and dynamics of men-women distributive shares requires use ... of simple general equilibrium pricing'. In essence, according to Samuelson, the original capacity endowment determines the optimal allocation of workers between different work tasks and their relative wages.

Note that, in Samuelson's example, women are – with ironic chivalry – considered superior to men in both trapping and big game hunting; however, since their advantage is considered superior in the former, they should limit themselves to this and leave the latter to the males. The reasoning is similar to that of Ricardo (1817) when, in his theory of international trade, he traces the comparative advantages of different countries to their original endowment of resources. Thus, the main criticism of the latter theory also applies to the issue of the allocation of workers between different jobs: the static character, implicitly considered unchangeable, of the original allocation of resources, in reality clashes with important phenomena of increasing returns, both static and dynamic, which have different signs and different strengths in the various activities. If England specializes in industry, leaving agriculture to India, the productivity gap in favour of England (not only in industry, but also in overall terms) will grow over time; the same happens, in terms of social location gap, when the division of labour leads to distinguishing plumber from lawyer, or typist from manager.

The conclusion of Aristotle, Pownall and Samuelson is that, except for accidental events (and except for the influence of the family endowment of wealth and power, often decisive in reality, which we will consider later), it is our original capacities that determine our work placement and thus our social placement.[17]

The distribution of innate capacities among individuals has also been referred to in connection with the 'Pareto law' (Pareto, 1896) concerning the personal distribution of income: a 'law' apparently applicable to different populations and epochs, thus called upon to support allegedly natural differences in income and wealth. In reality, as more recent research has shown, not only are the empirical foundations of the 'law' far from solid, but above all its explanation can be found not in an original distribution of innate resources that follows the Gaussian law of the random distribution of an event around the mean, but as the result of stochastic processes (Markovian chains), in

[17] A problem arises here: if abilities are innate, and not generated in response to social and market self-regulating mechanisms, who can ensure that the availability of different types of talents corresponds to the needs of the economy? Abbot Galiani gives his answer: only divine providence – 'Men are born by providence to various trades disposed, but with unequal proportion of rarity, and corresponding with admirable wisdom to human needs' (Galiani, 1751, p. 49). Before dismissing this thesis with a weary smile, it is worth remembering that the argument based on divine providence is theoretically indemonstrable, either positively or negatively – it is, in fact, a matter of faith – while the myth of the invisible hand of the market is, theoretically, a demonstrated error: the confidence placed in the self-regulating capacity of markets is less scientifically justified than that placed in divine providence.

which each individual's income depends on income in the previous year plus a random variation with the probability of a given percentage change remaining constant from one year to the next.[18]

On the other hand, if we adopt Smith's thesis on the origin of the division of labour, we may consider individual work skills as substantially acquired in the course of work experience. According to this view there is a cumulative-circular process in which the original social position contributes to determining our job position and the latter tends to self-perpetuate through the acquisition of experience and skills. Whoever starts to specialize in medicine will become a doctor, whoever starts to be a lion tamer will continue to be a lion tamer; not because one has genetically inherited the skills of Hippocrates and the other those of Mr Togni, but – even if one is the son of a doctor and the other of a lion tamer – because the original social position contributes to directing cultural and work training towards one field of work rather than another. Even when the work of the children is not exactly the same as that of the parents, the family influence is felt; in this way it contributes to crystallizing the social structure, in so far as it is determined by the division of work roles.

It is precisely for this reason that progressive liberalism – of which Adam Smith can be considered one of the founding fathers – attaches so much importance to the conditions for achieving the greatest possible equality of opportunity in access to different types of work. This requires equal access to training, especially schooling (three cheers for state schools!) and entry into different careers (three cheers for open competitions!). However, in order to give these aspects the truly decisive importance due to them, we have to reject the position of Aristotle, Pownall and Samuelson and share that of Smith.

Of course, this is not to deny that there are differences between individuals. Short-sightedness or acute eyesight, for example, are at least partly hereditary; absolute pitch, that is, the ability to identify the frequency of a sound, seems to be linked to a specific genetic

[18] For a collection of essays and a review, see Corsi (1995).

mutation; and so on. But Smith's thesis, shared by a broad tradition of thought, is that these differences are secondary to the influence of other factors, primarily the social position of the individual at birth.

Here we come across an aspect in which the 'Smith-like' and 'Samuelson-like' positions can find points of contact, even if in the end they appear distinct: the theme of meritocratic selection, the subject of so many heated discussions. Good exam marks should be given to those who have studied, not to those who are recommended, so – for example – exams should be public. Students often call for an end to meritocratic selection, but this would be counterproductive. If all the CVs submitted showed practically the same grade, selection being inevitable, candidates for posts would end up being selected on the basis of recommendations.[19]

We will return to meritocracy later (Section 5.1). Suffice it here to recall that recently the notion of meritocracy has been repeatedly used to defend inequalities; merit is attributed with the results achieved in social competition, which are seen as evaluating each individual's effort and ability. The premise of this thesis is the decidedly unrealistic assumption of a society characterized by perfect social flexibility, that is, among other things a 100 per cent inheritance tax rate and absolute irrelevance of the social position of individuals at birth. The notion considered above, on the other hand, relates to a limited aspect: the procedural mechanisms of selection for access to educational qualifications or certain jobs. Such mechanisms are certainly insufficient in themselves to ensure intergenerational social mobility, and are therefore to be complemented with other measures, but they are nevertheless useful, if not necessary.[20]

[19] For an interesting analysis of the various forms that recommendations can take and the broad spectrum of ethical evaluations they receive, see Zinn (2001).

[20] In an interesting paper, Heckman and Landers (2021) compare Denmark and the USA, pointing out that Denmark's quite significant redistributive policies have proved insufficient to ensure an intergenerational mobility systematically higher than in the USA, due to the role of within-the-family skills transmission across generations, as soon as policies targeted to the least advantaged groups (such as universal day-care, free college tuition, support to state education) had been rolled out in favour of universality

If skills are innate, the problem (no minor one, in any case) concerns the possibility of preventing the hereditary transmission of power – economic, political and social – from playing a dominant role in the selection of job roles and in crystallizing social stratification. If, on the other hand, skills are largely acquired, then the problem becomes more complicated and additional interventions, which would appear illogical in the case of purely innate skills, become decidedly necessary. For example, if ethnical origin is not accompanied by innate differences but by differences of opportunity in the acquisition of those skills on which meritocratic selection itself is based, then the implementation of active equal opportunities policies is correct. It is precisely for this reason that in many American universities, in the case of roughly equivalent capacities, there is a preference for employing lecturers of Hispanic or African origin, with the aim that the quotas of lecturers from the various groups should correspond to those in the population as a whole. This is why, again, in politics, quotas for female candidates are proposed (which is partly ineffective if few women are elected). With interventions of this kind it is hoped to counteract those cumulative mechanisms that contribute to determining the acquisition of work skills.

In reality, social stratification tends to perpetuate itself through instruments that vary according to the institutional set-up and that, although less strong in market economies than in feudal or planned ones, are nevertheless present in them too.

In the slave economies of antiquity or in the feudal economies of the Middle Ages, the position of the individual in society depended, almost exclusively, with very few exceptions, on birth. If you are born into a family of slaves or serfs, you are *ipso facto* a slave or a serf. In a dictatorial regime, be it fascist or communist, if you are born the son of a party official, a general or a top bureaucrat, you are much more likely to go to the right schools and have the right

in education policies. In particular, the authors stress the role of purposive choice of neighbourhoods by parents in hindering intergenerational social mobility.

support in the decisive early stages of your work experience than if you are born into a family of unskilled workers.

In market economies the factors behind family transmission of social position, and hence the rigidity of the social structure, are less important than in a caste system, but far from absent. It is precisely the centrality of the economic element that means that family wealth (or, perhaps better, family economic and social power) plays an important, if not decisive, role in determining the quality and quantity of children's education and then their occupational and social position; in this way social stratification is independent of ability, and in part determines it through the cumulative mechanisms mentioned above.[21] Other mechanisms of hereditary transmission of job roles are even more subtle: if we leave aside the widespread nepotism afflicting our universities, have I made a career as a professor because I was born intelligent, inheriting my parents' genes, or because, coming from a family of professors, I acquired from childhood – more from the concrete example of my parents than from a targeted education – a system of values that attaches importance to study and research and an ordered method of intellectual work? What is important is not to claim that the first element is completely irrelevant, which would be absurd, but to recognize that the second element is decisive. (As every teacher knows, cases of wasted intelligence, whenever students give priority in their value systems to activities other than study, are all too frequent; moreover, truly brilliant personalities – the like of Einstein and Keynes – are very rare, and the case of people of normal ability who obtain excellent results through application and a good working method is much more frequent.)[22]

[21] Lamberto Maffei, a well-known neurobiologist, points out that the development of brain circuits reaches its peak at around three years of age and therefore recommends, in order to guarantee greater equality of opportunity, to make pre-school 'no longer optional', but universal and compulsory, and to 'start structured learning as early as nursery school, at around 3–4 years of age when the child's ease of learning is at its greatest' (Maffei, 2021). This proposal is fully in line with the structural reforms discussed in Section 11.6.

[22] Milos Forman's film *Amadeus* (1984), which presents Mozart as an intemperate genius, forgets to mention the long hours spent studying the piano that his father forced on him from his early childhood.

The liberal tradition (e.g. Luigi Einaudi, 1949, pp. 213 ff.) maintains that it is necessary to guarantee the equality of starting points while, depending on individual merit, the arrival points can be characterized by even considerable differences in income, wealth and social power. However, this implies radical policies of active intervention, in particular with an almost total taxation of inheritances (Einaudi proposes a rate of 33 per cent, confiscatory over three generations) and public education able to compensate for cultural differences between families of origin. Above all, it would imply an egalitarian distribution of social power. In the absence of these requirements, which are far from being met in reality, policies aiming at levelling out the starting points must be accompanied by policies aiming at reducing the imbalances at the finishing points, which would otherwise end up generating cumulative spirals of differentiation. We shall be returning to these aspects in various contexts.

3.3 DIVISION OF LABOUR AND ALIENATION

As mentioned above, Adam Smith graphically points out the negative implications of the division of labour:

> In the progress of the division of labour, the employment of the far greater part of those who live by labour, that is, of the great body of the people, comes to be confined to a few very simple operations; frequently to one or two. But the understandings of the greater part of men are necessarily formed by their ordinary employments. The man whose whole life is spent in performing a few simple operations, of which the effects too are, perhaps, always the same, or very nearly the same, has no occasion to exert his understanding, or to exercise his invention in finding out expedients for removing difficulties which never occur. He naturally loses, therefore, the habit of such exertion, and generally becomes as stupid and ignorant as it is possible for a human creature to become. The torpor of his mind renders him, not only incapable of relishing or bearing a part in any rational conversation, but of conceiving any generous, noble, or tender

> sentiment, and consequently of forming any just judgement concerning many even of the ordinary duties of private life. Of the great and extensive interests of his country, he is altogether incapable of judging. (Smith, 1776, pp. 781–2)

This is, in essence, the problem of alienation, which for Smith derives directly from the division of labour.[23] In Marx's characterization of it in the *Economic-Philosophical Manuscripts* of 1844, alienation derives more specifically from three circumstances: the worker only performs part of the labour process (so rather than dominating the technology he/she is dominated by it: the production process is alien, it is 'other than himself'); the worker obtains a product that must be sold on the market because it has no direct use to him/her, and indeed in a capitalist society it is not the property of the worker but of the employer; the means of production are not the worker's property but the capitalist's, who consequently has the choice of production techniques. These characteristics are partly inherent to the division of labour per se, partly to the form it takes in a capitalist society.

The theme of alienation, however, disappears in Marx's later writings, to be replaced in *Capital* by the theme of commodity fetishism. The interpretation we can give to this fact is that alienation, as characterized by Marx, would remain even in the socialist society he prefigured by attributing ownership of the means of production to the state, while commodity fetishism would be inherent to capitalist society alone. What is of interest here, however, is at least in part a different problem: the impact of divided labour on the broader

[23] The term 'alienation' commonly brings to mind Marx's *Economic and Philosophical Manuscripts* ([1844] 1932); in fact, the problem had already been addressed by other authors; in addition to Smith we must remember at least Ferguson (1767, pp. 207 ff.). Outside of economics and philosophy, other fields of research, such as psychoanalysis, deal with it; we can also mention two films, Fritz Lang's *Metropolis* (1926) and Charlie Chaplin's *Modern Times* (1936). Before Smith, the notion of alienation can be traced in the writings of Jean-Jacques Rousseau, whom Smith had met through Hume. Unlike Smith, Rousseau is a radical critic of the market economy: see Colletti (1969, pp. 195–292).

culture and psychology of the workers, reverberating on their self-awareness and political choices.

Divided (and compulsory, in the sense of an activity necessary to ensure survival) work leads to a partial or total loss of awareness on the part of the worker of the meaning of his/her activity within the social production system, and therefore of his/her role in society. Work thus has a negative connotation, as a sacrifice necessary to earn a living; simultaneously, it has a positive connotation, as an activity with which the individual contributes to the progress of the community of which he/she is a part and which guarantees him/her a positive role within society, in essence as a means of self-realization, without taking into account the (rather rare) possibility that work activity be in itself gratifying. This positive outcome is favoured by three conditions: a specific professional content, however moderate; the recognizability of the work of an individual, or of a small group; and, above all, a strong work ethic.[24]

The coexistence of positive and negative effects to varying degrees from person to person is an element that often goes hand in hand with differences in income in generating inequalities. For this reason, it is important to stimulate a widespread culture of accepting and valuing even low-skilled jobs as necessary and useful to society; reducing pay differentials would greatly help in this.

3.4 SOCIAL CLASSES

So far we have considered the social stratification deriving from each person's occupation within a society characterized by the division of labour. In market capitalist economies, however, a fundamental form of social stratification is the traditional class distinction (adopted

[24] As Primo Levi observes in *La chiave a stella* (1978, p. 61), through a skilled fitter in conversation with a chemist: 'If we exclude prodigious and individual moments that fate may bestow upon us, loving one's work (which unfortunately is the privilege of the few) is the best concrete approximation to happiness on earth: but this is a truth that not many know.' (This may apply, for example, to university lecturers who manage to remain uninvolved in academic quarrels.)

since Adam Smith's *Wealth of Nations,* 1776) between capitalists, landlords and workers.

Between classes, and within each class, conflicts arise. The classical economists stressed their centrality for the evolution of the economy and society, albeit with different approaches: Smith emphasized the structural difference in bargaining power between capitalists and workers; Ricardo linked investment, and thus economic growth, to profits (which he contrasted with rents: duties on grain favour the latter to the detriment of the former, and thus hinder overall growth); finally Marx, by focusing on the conflict between capitalists and workers, elevated the class struggle to the ultimate motor force of history.

Traditional marginalist theory, on the other hand, traces the distribution of income between social classes to the scarcity and relative productivity of the production factors labour, capital and land. The corresponding distributional variables wage, profit rate and rent are determined as equilibrium values which under competitive conditions lead to equality – for each factor of production – both demand and supply, and marginal productivity and price. The distribution of income thus determined has optimality characteristics, guaranteeing the full employment of available resources; distributional conflicts can only lead to deviations from this optimal situation, in cases where one of the conflicting parties enjoys greater bargaining power than the others, that is, in cases where perfect competition does not obtain.[25]

In much the same way, sociologists like Drucker and Mayo see conflict as 'a "deviation" from a normal situation of integration and cooperation', as Dahrendorf (1959, pp. 185–6) reminds us; according to him, society constitutes instead 'an evolving structure composed of factors of integration and factors of disintegration'.

As we shall see in various contexts, the traditional tripartition of social classes (capitalists, workers and landlords) gradually became

[25] For a broader illustration of the theories of classical and marginalist economists, see Roncaglia (2001).

less useful as an instrument of analysis as a result of developments in the division of labour (in technology) and in society's lifestyles. There is thus an increasing tendency to redefine social classes – for example, with the entry of the middle classes into the arena, the loss of importance of landlords, the growth in number and weight of financial operators – while at the same time sociologists increasingly have tended to develop classifications based on a variety of characteristics.[26] Each of these classifications makes a choice of the aspects considered most significant for analysis of the societies in which we live and must be judged from this point of view. Debate on this subject ranges far and wide. For example, Goldthorpe's (1992) scheme envisages seven categories: big entrepreneurs and professionals, lower-level professionals and managers, lower- and higher-level clerks, the urban and agricultural petty bourgeoisie, low-level technicians and supervisors, skilled workers and unskilled workers. An important role is played by the categories adopted for statistical surveys; thus in its 2017 Annual Report, ISTAT (Italy's National Institute of Statistics) adopted a scheme based on nine categories: young blue collar, retired blue collar households, low-income households with foreigners, low-income households of Italians only, traditional provincial households, lonely elderly and unemployed young people, white collar households, silver pensioners and the ruling class. After examining various classifications, Bagnasco (2016, pp. 111–12) proposed seven classes: elite, established middle class, new affluent workers, traditional working class, emerging service workers and precariat.

Piketty (2019) classifies modern societies as 'proprietarist', that is, based on private property, with social stratification depending on the distribution of wealth and income, emphasizing the role of 'proprietary' ideology (laissez-faire, neoliberalism) and changes in institutions. The decline of property-owning societies after the Second

[26] The problem is not limited to market economies. For example, for communist countries, new classes of bureaucrats, oligarchs, and so on have been considered. On the distribution of income and wealth in communist, and then former communist, societies, see Piketty (2019).

World War was characterized by the rise of social democracy, the welfare state, and the conception of property as temporary: with progressive income taxes, together with wealth and inheritance taxes, some wealth was put back into circulation every year.[27] However, with the rise of neo-liberalism there has been a drastic reduction in the tax burden on the richest, and the drive for wealth circulation has turned into a tendency towards increasing concentration, with the share of the top 1 per cent increasing both in income and (especially) in wealth.

Beyond the examples, the central problem remains the existence of a complex social stratification in each society and at each moment in time, and its dynamics, that is, the change in importance of the various categories and the mobility between them over time.

To a greater or lesser extent, class pertaining and class distinctions are transferred from one generation to the next, with a crystallization of the social structure that affects not only the distribution of income and wealth but also, and above all, that of power (and culture as its instrument). In periods of economic growth, upward mobility – in the sense of improvement in the standard of living – is widespread; it can thus obscure the much lower mobility in the sense of changes in relative positions, the only one relevant to the analysis of power in our sense. Things become more complex when economic growth is accompanied by an incisive technological change, with the creation of new professional figures that imply growth in workers' skills and fragmentation of their qualifications. We will see later, when illustrating Babbage's second law, that even in this case there is a general advancement but not necessarily a change in relative positions, although given the increasing differentiation of jobs the hierarchy may be more difficult to identify.

To what extent is the class distinction that characterizes a capitalist society linked to the division of labour? While it is clear that

[27] Piketty (2019, p. 655) recalls in this regard that according to 'the German Basic Law of 1949 ... the right to property is legitimate only to the extent that it contributes to the general welfare of the community'.

the division of labour is an indispensable precondition for a capitalist society, should we also consider the reverse connection to apply, that is, that capitalist society is the inevitable outcome of a productive organization based on the division of labour?

In market economies, economic power is linked to the control of enterprises, that is, the ownership/control of the means of production and the control of financial capital. Here arise the problems of the connection between market economy and private property, between private property and ownership of the means of production (of 'capital' and land), between private accumulation (savings) and the right to inherit wealth, between financial capital and politics. These are complex issues: often opposing positions in the debate contain useful elements while appearing one-sided at the same time. For example, one might argue (with Oskar Lange) that the market economy does not necessarily imply private ownership of the means of production, with the inequalities that follow, but is compatible with state ownership of enterprises; and it might be replied (with Luigi Einaudi and Friedrich Hayek) that public ownership of the means of production generates inefficiency and entails a centralization of power that inevitably ends up by constricting political freedoms. In this second thesis, taxation of inheritances may be considered a measure of fairness, rather than a revolutionary attack on capitalist power. We will have to return to these issues – in general, to the issue of social classes – as we proceed with our reflections on power.

3.5 OTHER ASPECTS OF SOCIAL STRATIFICATION

The division of labour within a capitalist society is thus mirrored in social stratification between the classes of workers, capitalists and landowners, as well as between the workers themselves according to the type of occupation.

Economists often overlook two aspects. First, the power differentials associated with social stratification concern not only market power, but also the world of politics and culture in the broadest sense. Second, the concept of social classes that we use here, following a long tradition in the history of economic thought, is an abstraction. As such, it must be useful for analysis and have a real foundation. However, in order to assess the social position (and thus the position of power) of each individual or group of individuals, we need to consider various other elements besides the source of income (wages, rents, profits). For example, we need to consider culture as a possible source of some form of hegemony, or personal or family networks as a possible source of political power. The use of one classification does not preclude the use of other categories; moreover, there may be no contradiction between the various classifications, but rather complementarity; indeed, it will be necessary to take into account as far as possible the interrelationships between the different types of classification.[28]

If we focus on the differences between workers, the division of labour can be considered from three points of view: distinction of roles within the same production unit, distinction by professional qualifications and distinction between sectors of activity. As regards the first aspect, the distinction of roles implies not only a stratification of salaries (linked both to the greater or lesser qualification required, and to the implicit responsibility – for example, having to work with very expensive materials and machinery – as well as the riskiness and the hierarchical role held within the enterprise), but also a stratification of power and greater or lesser rewards associated with the type of work carried out. The distinction by sector of activity has similar implications; in this case, wage differentials depend at least in part on the degree of competition in the sector (in general, the extra profits that are allowed in an oligopoly by the presence of entry

[28] The various types of classification must be kept distinct, however attractive it may be to link them into a single scheme. In fact, analysis progresses when different aspects of the same classification are separated into several distinct classifications. Thus, for instance, Richard Cantillon (1755) linked the division by social classes (peasants, artisans, merchants and nobility) to the division by sectors (agriculture, handicrafts, trade) and the organization of society on the territory (countryside, village, city), while later – at least since Adam Smith – the three aspects have been kept distinct, increasing the flexibility of analytical schemes, without necessarily losing sight of the links between them.

barriers translate at least in part into higher or lower extra wages depending on the height of the entry barriers). As regards the distinction by occupational qualifications, contrary to common belief, the relative wage differentials often depend more on social factors than on training costs (the 'human capital investment') or the probability of success; in particular, wage differentials in favour of high management grades have grown considerably in recent years without any substantial change in qualification requirements, while the availability of suitably qualified people has increased. Finally, the risk of unemployment is different for different areas of the country, job qualification and sector of activity.

As we shall see, the complexity of the division of labour has increased over time, and the average level of complexity of work activities has grown in parallel; consequently, the grid of wage differentials between sectors, by qualifications and by hierarchical position within firms has also become more complex. The notion of the 'wage jungle' points to the difficulty of identifying logical criteria for explaining wage differentials, beyond the obvious reference to the conditions determining relative bargaining power.

Specific analyses of pay and power differentials (relative difficulties in gaining access to higher hierarchical levels in different careers) have focused on gender and race. These are mainly empirical analyses, which point to a process tending in the direction of less inequality, albeit with considerable slowness and some temporary setbacks. In this respect, it is interesting to observe the importance of change from one generation to the next. When I enrolled in Statistics, there were 6 female freshmen out of more than 600 (and there were similar situations in Engineering, while the opposite situation prevailed in Literature); today, women and men are more or less numerically equal among the enrolled students. Analyses of university careers in the field of economics show that the proportion of women is increasing, mainly at the first level (researchers) to start with, the effects gradually spreading to the second level (associate professors) and, with some delay, to the third level (full professors).

In the Accademia dei Lincei the delay is still considerable, but the proportion of women has risen from slightly above zero to around 10 per cent in just over five years.[29] In spite of its slowness, the depth of change helps to show that the thesis of innate differences must be abandoned in favour of one based on social, cultural and political conditioning.

3.6 EVOLUTION OF THE DIVISION OF LABOUR AND SOCIAL STRATIFICATION

The debate on the lines of evolution of the market economy (the so-called 'laws of motion of capitalism') is vast, and here we can only focus on the theses most directly relevant to the issues discussed. We will discuss the issue of industrial concentration later on; for now we will consider the link between the division of labour and social stratification. For this aspect, what we can call the two 'Babbage's laws' are of fundamental importance – and, compared to their importance, they are decidedly little known.[30]

The first of these laws states that the division of labour is driven by the quest to reduce labour costs. The division of labour consists in separating the different phases within each work process; it therefore allows the use of less skilled workers for each phase, who can be paid a lower wage. If you build a house yourself, you have to be a bricklayer and painter, an electrician and plumber, an architect and a carpenter, so you have to have a truly extraordinary skill set, and your pay per hour worked will have to be high; with division of labour, on the other hand, the skills required of everyone can be more limited and the cost of labour reduced.[31] In this way, the task assigned to

[29] See, for example, Carabelli, Parisi and Rosselli (1999) and the documents of the Commissions on Gender Issues of the Italian Society of Economics at www.siecon.org, and of the Accademia Nazionale dei Lincei, at www.lincei.it.

[30] Cf. Babbage (1832). Corsi (1984) rediscovered Babbage's 'second law'. Both 'laws' were already outlined in Smith's *Wealth of Nations* (1776).

[31] This argument is independent of manual workers earning more or less than white-collar workers. The fact that skilled manual workers in various cases (e.g. plumbers) are in fact paid more than the large strata of university graduates, together with the

each worker becomes increasingly specific, and thus simpler and deskilled. The work process is continually reorganized: skilled workers, responsible for a set of stages, are replaced by ordinary workers, each engaged in a single stage of the work process.

This thesis was taken up by Marx with his 'law of increasing proletarianization' (albeit in a subsidiary form, as Marx relied mainly on the gradual growth in the number of wage-earners at the expense of independent peasants, artisans and small entrepreneurs). The increasing division of labour would lead to a continuous growth of the share of unskilled labour, and thus to a continuous expansion of the proletariat formed by ordinary, unskilled workers. This aspect is central to Marx's thinking, as it underpins his thesis of the inevitability of the revolutionary transition, whereby the vast majority of society, which has nothing to lose but its chains, would expropriate the capitalists (reduced in number by the process of industrial concentration) of their economic and political power, with the nationalization of the means of production and establishment of the dictatorship of the proletariat.[32]

In the first half of the twentieth century, the 'scientific division of labour' supported by engineer Frederick Taylor seemed to confirm the Marxian thesis of proletarianization. Taylorism, as is well known, requires that each production process be broken down into

increasing availability of leisure time allowed by the reduction of working hours, may favour a modest regression of the 'off-market' division of labour, with the development of domestic DIY. However, the tendency to outsource at least part of previously domestic activities to the market remains stronger.

32 The fact that the proletariat would be the great majority of the population allowed the dictatorship of the proletariat to be characterized *ex ante* as democratic. Of course, this conception of democracy is closer to that of Rousseau, linked to the existence of a 'general will', than to that of John Stuart Mill, who interprets the majority principle essentially as a decision rule – the decision rule par excellence in the political field – and is careful to defend the rights of minorities from the risks of a dictatorship of the majority. See Colletti (1969) on the relationship between Marx's (and Lenin's) thought and that of Rousseau, and Urbinati (2002) on Mill's political thought. Let us also recall the debate (which involved Marx himself) on the possibility of a communist revolution in Russia, a backward country in which the majority of workers were peasants, not the industrial proletariat: strictly speaking, the revolution should have broken out first in England and then in Germany.

its elementary components, measuring their execution times, and then reassembled in the most efficient way, assigning each worker one or more well-defined operations, with pre-determined execution times, thus promoting the standardization of each step in the work process. Taylorism accompanied and supported the spread of the assembly line, which originated before the end of the nineteenth century (perhaps in the manufacture of Colt pistols, or possibly in Chicago's slaughterhouses, where a predefined part of the animal carcass, hanging from a hook that moved along a predefined path, was cut off at each 'station'). Fordism, established with the famous Ford Model T assembly line, inaugurated in 1912, perfected Taylorism through strategies of product standardization (as Henry Ford said, you can choose your cars any colour you want, as long as you want them black).

We may consider as a variant of Taylorism (aimed not to strictly technical but to wage cost and organizational advantages) the tendency, in recent decades, to 'fissuring', namely to shed to subsidiary organizations through subcontracting or franchising segments of work done internally. Strict guidelines allow the head firm to retain full control over the working process, while subsidiary organizations operate under tight margins, with lower wages and benefits and less stringent work safety conditions.[33]

According to Marxist theory,[34] the continuous subdivision of every production process into elementary stages that allow the use of unskilled workers also applies to new production processes introduced through innovations: only in the first stage do major innovations improve the situation, but proletarianization invariably follows. When computers were introduced, the technician who

[33] For an analysis of the 'fissured workplace', cf. Weil (2014).

[34] See, for example, Braverman (1974) who illustrates the early stages of the development of information technology. As will become clear later, the computer revolution and the development of the so-called new economy, based on the diffusion of information and communication technologies, constitute rather a demonstration of the limits of the traditional Marxist position and the importance of Babbage's second law.

wrote the programs was also in charge of translating the programs into machine language and then inputting the data, which at first meant using special machines to punch the cards or the tape with which to feed the computer. Later, there was a subdivision of tasks and the technician, who was better paid, was limited to writing the programs, while the work of punching the cards had disappeared and that of inputting the data into the computer, when it was not done automatically, was entrusted to less qualified personnel.

However, the division of labour, precisely because it allows attention to be focused on each individual phase, makes it easier to devise process innovations that allow for the mechanization of the simplest operations, such as the translation of the programme into machine language, or the input into the computer of data that are already available, for example from digital archives. This is, in fact, 'Babbage's second law'. In short, the division of labour, through the simplification of work operations, favours technical progress and in particular the replacement of less skilled labour by machines. Indeed, it is much easier to design new machines when the work task is simple than when it is complex. When we are faced with an assembly line, in which each worker performs a few simple and repetitive operations, the problem of mechanizing a production process as a whole is also broken down into a series of specific problems, and is easier to solve. This same principle had been used by Babbage in his attempts to build calculators capable of performing arithmetical operations: each of these operations, for example multiplication, is broken down into a series of sums, with a subdivision of the mental work into simple operations that allows for its mechanization.

Hence the gradual emergence of what is known as Industry 4.0, with the use of numerically controlled machines.[35] The pioneers of Industry 4.0 operate in highly dynamic contexts, such as those of

[35] For a social history of industrial automation, with particular reference to numerically controlled machines, cf. Noble (2011).

robotics; they are therefore subject to dynamic competitive pressure, on the side of technological innovation, which hinders, if not prevents, the formation of concentrations of power, strongly favoured by economies of scale and network. (To a certain extent this is true even of software giants, such as Microsoft or Google; it is certainly true of computer hardware, as the decline of IBM or Nokia and many others testify. In the field of traditional business services, highly successful companies such as Amazon are introducing revolutionary organizational innovations based on the use of information technology.)

Babbage's second law is very important, because it links the division of labour to technical progress and simultaneously also to changes in the qualification structure of the labour force. Thus, if we take Babbage's first and second laws together, we have a kind of dialectical movement within the process of economic development: on the one hand, the division of labour reduces work to increasingly specific, ever less skilled tasks; on the other hand, the simpler tasks are eliminated from the scene because they are replaced by machines.

What is the overall effect of these two tendencies to divide each production process into simple operations and invent machines to carry them out? First, the amount of general education required of ordinary workers tends to increase over time, due to their employment in increasingly complex work processes using increasingly sophisticated machinery. Secondly, the share of skilled workers in the labour force grows, due to increasing mechanization that implies more work for the design and maintenance of machinery, and due to the increased complexity of the economy based on a progressively more advanced division of labour, which requires an increasing share of indirect labour for the functioning of the system (services for production and public administration).

This last aspect is also highlighted by Weber's (1922b) thesis of a progressive bureaucratization of the economy and society, in connection with the increasing rationalization of every aspect of life, in the transition from feudalism to capitalism and then within capitalist development. Schumpeter (1942), taking up this thesis, points out how it applies to the growth of large companies and even to their research and development activities. Accompanying the process of division of labour and mechanization, the growth of per capita income gives rise to a progressive growth of consumer services, some of which are specialized services requiring highly skilled labour. The education sector also expands; so does research and development, as the drive to innovate becomes a crucial element of competition in a rapidly changing technological environment.

If we distinguish between the microeconomic division of labour (within the individual production unit) and the macroeconomic division of labour (between economic sectors), we can see that Babbage's second law has given rise, over time, to the development of an increasingly important 'qualificative sector'. This sector includes research workers (both theoretical research, mostly in the public sector, and applied research, mostly in the private sector), teaching and vocational training workers, and the technicians needed to control and optimize technological change. The processes of accumulation themselves change in nature, directed towards acquiring the cognitive capital needed to bring about technological change rather than towards isomorphic expansion of the productive base. The 'qualifying class' grows in size and importance, assuming distinctive characteristics (including lifestyles) and its own specific power within the economy and society.[36]

The acceleration of technological change brings with it an increasing speed and extent of social change, which also affects culture: we find ourselves in what Bauman (2000) calls 'liquid modernity'. The traditional division into the three social classes of workers, capitalists and landowners gradually loses its meaning; in addition to the growing importance of the middle classes, there is a veritable

[36] See Villetti (1978, pp. xliv–xlvii). Study of the growth of the 'qualificative sector' deserves to be developed, in the context of research on the evolution of the social structure, also for its influence on the dynamics of cultural and political life.

deconstruction of class conflicts. As Bauman (2003, p. 40) notes, there is 'a progressive disintegration of social conflict into a multitude of conflicts between groups and the proliferation of battlefields'. The growth of the skills sector, and the parallel development of what has been called Industry 4.0, is nonetheless progress: while it does not eliminate coercive work, it does make it, at least in part, considerably less monotonous, more interesting.[37]

Overall, as a result of all these elements, instead of a process of proletarianization we have growth of the middle classes of technicians and professions, research and teaching, bureaucracy and politics. With a diversified spectrum of activities, interests, lifestyles and cultures also diversify, and these become increasingly important elements of aggregation, even independently of job location.

This has radical implications for political perspectives. As it is based on the 'law of proletarianization', which has proved erroneous, Marx's thesis of the inevitability of proletarian revolution falls apart. The dictatorship of the proletariat is no longer even remotely democratic (in the sense of Rousseau and Lenin, whereby the rulers, though a small group – the vanguard of the working class, according to the Leninist theory of the state – would represent the 'general will' of the vast majority of the population). In concrete terms, in the countries of Western Europe after the Second World War the problem was posed somewhat differently, but always as a crisis in the political strategy of the communist parties. These parties, having abandoned the revolutionary option (also as a consequence of realistic acceptance of the division of the world into blocs sanctioned at Yalta), set themselves the objective of the democratic conquest of power: if the proletariat had grown to become the overwhelming majority of

[37] As Sylos Labini (2006, p. 148) observes, 'in order to increase the number of agreeable jobs and to increase job satisfaction, there are two main ways. The first is to develop research, which normally multiplies highly skilled and therefore non-monotonous and non-repetitive jobs. The second way is participation, a formula with different meanings.' This second way, which is very important, corresponds to themes that we will deal with later: democracy within the company and the world of work in general (cooperatives, co-determination, workers' statute *et de hoc genus omnia*).

workers, the party representing the proletariat should have been able to win the majority of votes in the elections.[38]

All of this collapses as soon as it is recognized that the majority of workers are instead accounted for by a diversified group of professionals, technicians, researchers, teachers and administrators, with widely differing qualifications, cultures, lifestyles and interests. Representing the interests of less qualified workers, even if one manages to win all their votes, is not enough to win over the majority of voters: we need to pose the problem of alliances, between different social groups if not between different social classes, finding a positive composition for the coexistence of interests and cultural positions that may differ considerably. Abandonment of an over-simplistic perspective opens up a situation in which the task of the progressive politician becomes more difficult but also more interesting.[39]

[38] Obviously – and here is the difference with the dictatorship of the proletariat, exercised by a self-proclaimed vanguard – conquest of the electoral majority implies that the workers recognize their authentic interests, behind the smokescreen of religions, nationalisms and localisms, and all the other 'opiums of the people'. Hence the importance attributed to the pursuit of cultural hegemony: in the wake of Gramsci's indications, but above all with Togliatti's reduction of culture – as well as the trade union – to a transmission belt of the political line elaborated by the party. Cultural hegemony took on an even more decisive role when, faced with the acknowledged impossibility for the 'party of the working class' to win an electoral majority on its own, a strategy of alliances between the working class and the middle classes was proposed, but always under the banner of the former.

[39] This was the central thesis of Sylos Labini (1974). He argued, against the prevailing thesis in the Partito Comunista Italiano (PCI) – and much of the left – that the development of Italian society was characterized by the growth of the middle classes, whose role in political life had become dominant, and by internal differentiation of the working class. The book had a wide circulation, accompanied by criticism and negative reactions; however, it won the day, favouring the abandonment of Marxist orthodoxy and the gradual transition of the PCI towards a modern reformist and progressive political force. The year 1989, then, with the collapse of the communist regimes, marked an epoch-making break that drove the majority of the PCI towards the shores of social democracy. The transition accelerated when the Socialist Party disappeared under the blows of Tangentopoli (bribery scandal), leaving a void in the political field that the now renamed Democratic Party, which had miraculously escaped the same fate, has every interest in occupying. Sylos Labini's thesis, supported by a rich empirical apparatus, holds up perfectly to criticism; if anything, what the book did not deal with (but which Sylos Labini considers in other writings) was the link between the evolution of the division of labour (Babbage's laws illustrated above) and the evolution of the social structure.

Tendencies in income and wealth distribution over the past decades, with the growing share conquered by the top 1 per cent, do not contradict the thesis of a growth of the middle classes, as defined here on the basis of their role in the production structure. The impoverishment of important strata of the middle classes and the growing gap between rich and poor opens the door to an alliance between the traditional working class and the majority of the middle classes, provided that the specific roles, interests and cultures of the variety of social groups called to form the alliance are recognized and taken into account as part of a well-balanced political project.[40]

3.7 THE INTERNATIONAL DIVISION OF LABOUR

After the end of the Second World War, the system of international economic relations built up at the Bretton Woods Conference (1944) allowed for a remarkably vigorous expansion of international trade, thanks also to the gradual elimination of customs duties and other constraints,[41] a sharp fall in transport costs and a more stable and efficient currency system. Economic globalization has also entailed the development of foreign direct investment and, within it, of investment tending to relocate production phases to countries with lower labour costs or less stringent regulations. This has led to the creation of 'international value chains', or supply chains in which the final product is obtained through the cooperation of production facilities

[40] The sociological literature on middle classes is boundless; various definitions have been given of this category. In fact, as Bagnasco (2016, p. 83) notes, 'the middle class is a social construction'. Thus the motto of the 'dual economy', focusing attention solely on income distribution, appears simplistic – though this possibly is not true for the detailed analyses on the tendencies of income distribution in the recent stage synthesized by that motto.

[41] The GATT (General Agreement on Tariffs and Trade) agreements initiated in 1947, and then the World Trade Organization (WTO) founded in 1995, have given a strong impetus to globalization. The neo-liberal approach of the WTO results from the fact that (as Crouch, 2003, p. 95, notes and as was evident in the Covid-19 pandemic) 'The only right that the WTO protects against competition is the patent right'.

located in different countries, each of which relates to a single stage of the production process.[42]

The division of labour thus saw a new phase of development. From the subdivision of a work process into several successive stages within the same plant (e.g. the assembly line), we initially moved on to the subcontracting of semi-finished products (such as magnets for cars). While this trend continued, there was also a progressive relocation outside the company of some collateral activities entrusted to specialized companies (for example, call centres for marketing, cleaning or guarding the factory, or processing payrolls), taking on increasing importance thanks to the growing role of services within manufacturing companies, following the mechanization of work processes. Finally, there is a delocalization of fragments of the work process, mainly aimed at exploiting localization advantages lying in the availability of raw materials or cheap labour, or even tax and regulatory incentives of various kinds granted by developing areas or countries. The information technology revolution favours this trend, making it possible to maintain close logistical coordination between plants located in different parts of the world without losing control over product technology and all business functions, from research to marketing.

The worldwide delocalization of supply chains contributes to globalization processes with closer production integration between different countries, which in principle should bind them to more cooperative behaviour: Khanna (2016, p. 17) contrasts 'connections' with 'divisions'.

The development of international value chains modifies the international division of labour between developed manufacturing

[42] Khanna (2016) richly illustrates the importance of this phenomenon, pointing out that 'Supply chains are the first true *world wide web*' (p. 36) and observing that in international power confrontations 'the strongest power will not necessarily win, the most connected will win' (p. 43); 'the conflicts of the future will no longer be about creating more borders, but about controlling connections' (p. 48).

countries and backward countries concentrated on the export of raw materials (and therefore hampered in their development, as the 'dependency theorists' point out).[43] While control of the supply chains is exercised by managers in the oldest and richest industrialized countries, preserving an important element of dependency, the new situation favours industrial development and rapid economic growth in some of the less wealthy countries. This leads to a reduction in income inequality on average on a global scale, while inequality within the major countries grows, with the income share of the richest growing in all countries, accompanied by stagnating incomes for the middle and lower classes in the richest countries (Milanovic, 2016, 2019).[44]

The tendency to strengthen the central positions in social stratification thus gives way to a renewed trend towards polarization, characterized, however, by the emergence of a phenomenon of 'multiple inequalities' with a diversification between social segments, compared to the traditional one between proletarians and capitalists.[45] This complicates the interpretation of social evolution and creates fragmentation in the political debate.

The absence of global political integration, however, can lead to the temporary fragmentation of international value chains, as seen in the Covid-19 pandemic. The interruption of a fragment of the production chain (e.g. lockdown in China) or political interventions that distort the system of supply flows (e.g. by prioritizing domestic supplies over foreign supplies under existing contracts, as happened in the case of medical supplies or intermediate materials for the pharmaceutical industry) can lead to a significant, albeit temporary, drop in production and income, especially when no precaution was taken against the possibility of interruptions in international trade.

[43] See Prebish (1950); Furtado (1964).

[44] According to Patel (2021), these trends re-propose similar tendencies in previous episodes of globalization over the past 500 years (but, of course, there are also interesting differences).

[45] See Bagnasco (2020). For example, the phenomenon of insecure employment has different effects by gender, by territorial area, by age, by nationality and ethnicity (among migrants), and by level and type of education.

An important reversal in international value chains is taking place after the Russian Federation invaded Ukraine on 24 February 2022, mainly – but not only – due to economic sanctions on the Russian Federation. Changes of expectations and strategies on the side of many important transnational corporations are also taking place; their importance is likely to be significant and protracted beyond the end of the war. Restructuring of value chains is likely to take time and to give rise to temporary upheavals in production and to inflationary pressures.

3.8 UTOPIAS ON THE DIVISION OF LABOUR

The division of labour within each production process implies an increase in the size of the enterprise. Within the firm, the production process designed to obtain a product (or a set of products, in the very common case of joint production) is organized from above (at least in its fundamental structure)[46] through hierarchical chains of command and an appropriate system of rules (e.g. on working hours: if the workers do not all start working at the same time, the assembly line cannot start).

Control over an enterprise gives enormous power, precisely because, as they say, the market stops at the enterprise's doorstep.[47] This means that, even if we were to consider the market as an institution characterized by equal relations between the participants in

[46] We may recall here the possibility of setting up 'islands' along the path of the production process, within which to entrust workers with the self-organization of work: a system suggested, in the wake of Elton Mayo and the theory of 'job enrichment', to motivate workers by involving them to some extent in organizational choices, albeit in a very limited sphere. The improvement in productivity observed in these cases confirms the importance of worker motivation for the smooth running of the production process.

[47] Coase's theory (1937) justifies the existence of the enterprise, and thus of areas of command within the market economy, by the fact that in certain areas – for example, to coordinate the operation of an assembly line – transaction costs would be much higher than those of top-down coordination. In its absence, each worker in the chain would have to negotiate with their upstream colleague for the purchase of semi-finished products and with the downstream colleague for the sale of the product, with the owner of the plant for the rent of the workstation and with others for the purchase of energy and raw materials – more time would be spent negotiating than working.

the exchange, we certainly cannot consider the entire market economy in the same way, since a large part of economic life takes place within companies, and therefore under the banner of command and hierarchy.

Hence the importance of issues commonly gathered under the label of enterprise democracy: co-determination, in which workers in some respects participate in the management of the enterprise; co-participation, in which workers share a part of the profits; consumer and production cooperatives. Management efficiency and egalitarianism in the distribution of power and income often appear to be in opposition. However, the institutional imagination has run wild; among the many proposals it is not impossible to find some reasonable ideas which, by involving the workers in the interests of the enterprise, can move simultaneously in the direction of greater equity and greater efficiency. (In particular, workers can play an important active role in technological change, especially in process innovations; above all, when work acquires a significant technical content, worker involvement can increase productivity and improve product quality.)[48]

There are, however, several limits to what can be done in this direction. In the case of co-management in companies with more than a small number of workers, delegation of corporate responsibilities is necessary, since trivial reasons of efficiency make management by workers' assembly impossible.[49] Employee profit-sharing

[48] Giddens (1998) identifies a 'third way', between the planned economy and the market economy, in a stakeholder's society in which enterprises are managed in the interest not only of shareholders (or in general of the owners of capital) but also of workers, consumers and interested third parties (e.g. citizens in general, as interested in environmental protection). This view was conceived in the context of a managerial economy; its foundations become shaky with the transition to a money managers economy.

[49] Self-management, in which control of the enterprise is taken over by the workers, has had a strong appeal as a model of 'power from below' as opposed to the 'top-down' hierarchy that characterizes capitalist enterprise. However, it has essentially remained in the realm of utopia. The need to designate and delegate management has meant that, where this model has had some form of application (Tito's Yugoslavia), power has actually been concentrated in an authoritarian-hierarchical form in the

(which is used by an increasing number of listed companies through the distribution of shares to employees) can be useful in terms of efficiency, by involving workers – especially those with management responsibilities – in the smooth running of the company. However, to have some influence over the distribution of power it is necessary for a significant proportion of shares to be in the hands of the workers; the practical need then arises for delegation – generally entrusted to trade unions – to plan management strategies, often restricted to the selection of candidates for the board of directors: the element of 'democracy from below', although not nullified, is severely curtailed. In most cases, the workers' participation in company ownership is a minority one, so co-participation is limited to a modest redistributive effect. Currently, the idea that the interests of the shareholders should be taken into account alongside those of the stakeholders (workers, customers, citizens interested in the environmental impact of production activity), while gaining ground in public debate, has in fact been pushed into the background by the thesis that managers' main task is to create value for the shareholders, that is, to maximize the value of the shares, in a short- or very short-term perspective, given that this is the perspective that governs stock prices in markets dominated by financial speculation.[50]

One of the lines of enterprise organization that have been most explored, both in theory and in practice, is that of cooperatives. Born

hands of the party bureaucracy, just as (or perhaps only slightly less than) in centrally planned countries.

An example of a proposal for co-management is the one put forward in 1977 by the Bullock Commission in England (recalled recently by Piketty, 2019, p. 666): 'that in all companies with more than 2000 employees, shareholders and workers would each elect x members of the board of directors, while the state would complete the representation by appointing y independent directors'. Piketty (2019, p. 1281) speaks of 'participatory socialism', which he contrasts with 'state-centred socialism', to designate the case of co-determination accompanied by progressive taxation in order to guarantee the 'circulation of capital'.

German co-determination (*Mitbestimmung*), approved in 1976, provides for equal representation of shareholders and employees, but with the chairperson chosen by the shareholders having the deciding vote in the event of a tie.

[50] On this, cf. Lazonick and Shin (2020).

spontaneously and progenitors of the trade unions, consumer cooperatives were initially simple forms of collaboration between workers to procure consumer goods at a low cost, when factories were far from shopping centres.[51] From collaboration in one field came collaboration in others: in trade unions, negotiating working conditions; in production cooperatives, collectively controlling the enterprise worked for. Production cooperatives are obviously compatible with a market economy; so much so, indeed, that they may have the same defects as private enterprises, such as exploiting monopoly conditions, disregarding environmental effects, or the risk of leaving their employees on the breadline in the event of bankruptcy. Moreover, the growth in size, with the associated financialization and the need for management delegation to managers, greatly reduces the value of this form of economic organization as an alternative to capitalist enterprise. However, their original democratic force is undeniable, and has led in some cases to their being given regulatory advantages over private enterprises, for example through forms of preferential taxation. Even irrespective of the fact that they may constitute a general form of organization of the economy, as has been suggested[52] but remains hard to believe,[53] there is no doubt that in a market economy their presence may constitute an important contribution to the formation and development of a civic practice of cooperation. For this reason the increasing assimilation of cooperatives to capitalist

[51] In the early phase of British industrialization, textile factories located close to waterways that provided motive power for the looms often had dormitories for the workers and an employer-owned shop, which, not being subject to competition, could charge relatively high prices. It would have been absurd for the individual worker to make the necessary journeys to shops in the nearest village, but it was easier and cheaper to organize a shop run by the workers themselves. It was precisely these forms of self-organization that later led to the emergence of trade union organizations.

[52] See, for example, Vanek (1970) and, more recently, Jossa (2010).

[53] Indeed, we have to take into account the economies of scale that can only be exploited by large firms in various sectors, as well as the difficulty of organizing large firms into cooperatives. Moreover, given that coordination through hierarchy and command prevails within enterprises, it is difficult to imagine large enterprises, even if formally constituted as cooperatives, really responding fully to the cooperative spirit.

enterprises achieved in recent years through a series of legislative interventions is not to be viewed favourably.

In fact, industrial democracy, with the exception of important but relatively limited cases of co-determination and co-participation, is generally sustained above all through the attribution of rights to workers and their trade union organizations, and through trade union confrontation. This is a complex issue, since any strengthening of workers' rights can only hold out over time if these rights are exercised in a way that does not undermine the productive efficiency of the companies.[54]

Here we may briefly recall some other social reform projects based on reorganization of divided labour: the utopia of fully surpassing coercive labour thanks to technological progress; a way of organizing society by virtue of which it is possible to leave behind not coercive labour itself but the inequalities in income and power that it entails.

The first utopia was traced out by Marx in the *Critique of the Gotha Programme* (1878). Two steps are envisaged. The first is transition from capitalist to socialist society, characterized by the public ownership of the means of production and the political domination of the proletariat. At a later stage, thanks also to the acceleration of technological progress favoured by the state management of the economy, there is transition to a communist society: in it, the productive forces will be so developed as to allow people to obtain everything they need without the need for compulsory labour, but simply on the basis of voluntary activity.[55] As a matter of fact, state ownership of

[54] We will be returning to this theme later in Section 11.1, when we consider the Italian Workers' Statute (Law No. 300 of 20 May 1970). Here we can point out, in this respect, that the microcosm of the workplace has its own structure of social relations that reproduces, in partial and simplified form, that of society as a whole. However, because of their immediacy the relations within this microcosm are of considerable importance, not least because of the prominence they place on certain power relations. This applies both to the hierarchical structure in which all work is organized and to that particular form of power relationship that is the employment contract.

[55] 'In a higher phase of communist society, after the enslaving subordination of the individual to the division of labour, and therewith also the antithesis between mental and

the means of production, apart from giving enormous power to the government (Hayek, 1944, speaks of the 'road to serfdom'), has also proved ineffective – beyond the stage of primitive accumulation – in fostering productive growth and technical progress, and in particular in qualitative improvement of products. It also led to the formation of an elephantine, inefficient and greedy government bureaucracy (the so-called *nomenklatura*). The exploitation of the workers thus remained, albeit to the benefit of a different class from the capitalists. The ultimate goal of completely surpassing coercive labour was just as utopian as in market economies, serving in reality to justify the harshness of the dictatorship of the proletariat as a means to achieve (in the fullness of time) the ultimate goal.

The second utopia, which is more realistic,[56] is the one formulated by Ernesto Rossi in *Abolire la miseria* (1946): the labour army as a means of distributing coercive labour among all, for a limited period of time in each person's life. In short, each citizen would have the right to a 'citizenship wage' adequate to guarantee lifelong survival (at a level linked to the state of development achieved by society, thus potentially increasing over time), in exchange for the provision for a limited period of time, equivalent to a period of military service, of the less pleasant forms of divided labour. In this way, coercive work would cease to be a life sentence for the less fortunate classes, while specific work of a higher technical level (of a surgeon, for example, or a concert pianist) could be chosen voluntarily by some as a means to secure a higher standard of living, as well as a form of personal fulfilment. The organizational details are left open to discussion: for example, whether or not public ownership of companies – at least of the larger ones – is necessary, and what space

physical labour, has vanished; after labour has become not only a means of life but life's prime want; after the productive forces have also increased with the all-round development of the individual, and all the springs of cooperative wealth flow more abundantly – only then can the narrow horizon of bourgeois right be crossed in its entirety and society inscribe on its banners: 'From each according to his ability, to each according to his needs!' (Marx, 1878, p. 160).

[56] On the distinction between reasonable and fanciful utopias, see Section 9.6.

should be left to the market. What is important in this proposal is the idea of a social distribution of the lowest forms of coercive labour through the labour army, accompanied by the elimination of poverty: an institutional arrangement that certainly has a profound effect on the functioning of the market economy, but which can be made compatible with it through an appropriate regulatory system: no light undertaking, but not impossible to outline.[57]

The division of labour and coercive work are probably inescapable. However, radical but not impossible interventions – such as the labour army proposed by Ernesto Rossi – can limit its negative aspects, including the most odious forms of social stratification. Moreover, as we will try to show in the following chapters, there are various reform policies, even less radical, that can facilitate social mobility, so as to prevent such stratification from crystallizing over time.

[57] A similar proposal was made by Carmen Sirianni (1981), who aimed at eliminating the '*detailed* division of labour' (p. 70 of part 1, my italics) and ensuring 'a structure of work choices that can lead to a relatively flexible and fluid life course for each individual' (p. 72). The aim is not totally to surpass coercive work, but rather to reduce it to the point where a classless society can be achieved. This requires expansion of leisure time, increase in production according to artisanal criteria, development of education (p. 5 of part 2), and above all (although the author does not say so) superseding structural differences in economic power, and therefore private ownership of the means of production, so as to enable 'the equivalent exchange of socially necessary labour' according to appropriate pre-established 'standard criteria' (p. 80 of part 1), allowing a more egalitarian distribution of coercive labour and a greater sphere of choice for each worker. Although highly suggestive, the proposal appears rather vague and decidedly challenging to implement.

4 Modern Capitalist Property and Finance

4.1 FROM PRIMITIVE ACCUMULATION TO MERCHANT CAPITALISM AND MANUFACTURING CAPITALISM

In order to understand modern capitalist property, we must see how it has evolved over time and clear the field of two opposite myths: either it is a miraculous institution, the only one capable of guaranteeing personal freedom and economic development; or it is the root of all evils, the harbinger of an inevitable collapse of social coexistence. Like various social institutions, private property has both positive and negative aspects.

A widespread myth concerns its origins, with small private property being born of hard work and savings, and then accumulating (or decumulating), generation after generation, thanks to the tenacity and skill of some and the indolence and inability of others.

In fact, the transition from the feudal regime of 'domination' (the lord's power over his subjects, a combination of legal, political, economic and civil power) to the capitalist regime of private property is marked by a 'primitive accumulation'. Its main element is the passage of land from traditional forms of use, which in some ways constituted a guaranteed source of subsistence for the serfs themselves, to the regime of private property. The lords are freed from the constraints of tradition, free to fence off the land (starting in England, with the enclosures) expelling the serfs and assigning the land to cattle breeding, which offers a higher net income than cereal cultivation precisely because of the need for less labour: thus, the production of means of subsistence is reduced, but the lords have fewer mouths to feed. Poverty spreads, but the landowners get richer.

Other forms of primitive accumulation are based on force and violence, such as the wealth accumulated through piracy, military expeditions and colonization in the sixteenth–seventeenth centuries. Finally, we have financial activities, from the ubiquitous usurious loans to the financing of large-scale and equally high-risk operations, such as the construction of waterways or colonial expeditions, long-distance maritime trade or public expenditure, particularly on war. Victory or defeat in wars led to either sensational enrichment (as in the case of the Merchant Adventurers who shared out the lands of Ireland after Cromwell's expedition, or the Rothschilds after the Battle of Waterloo) or equally sensational bankruptcies, like that of the Florentine bankers.[1]

Primitive accumulation, as Marx calls it, is followed by capitalist accumulation; wealth grows on itself, in a self-feeding process. In the mercantile capitalist phase, the main source of wealth accumulation is profits from international trade. The large private mercantile enterprises that dominated this sector did not disappear until after the middle of the nineteenth century (when, for instance, the East India Company was dissolved and its power over the Indian colony was transferred to the British state). Accumulation on a smaller scale occurred with the development of handicrafts, then of small manufacturing industry; apart from exceptional cases, characterized by state intervention (such as the manufacture of tapestries in France), companies were relatively small. The development of small manufacturing industry marks the transition from the phase of merchant capitalism to the phase of manufacturing capitalism, often considered – at least in part erroneously – as dominated by competition.

This interpretation is not universally accepted. Among authors who emphasize other aspects of the transition to capitalism we may recall Karl Polanyi, who held that analysis of modern societies themselves should be carried out by comparing different economic

[1] For various interpretations of primitive accumulation, which highlight its different aspects, see the essays collected in Dobb et al. (1954).

and social systems. In primitive societies, the mechanisms of social integration are based on the reciprocity of gifts (within families, groups of blood relatives, tribes) and, at the same time, on forms of redistribution ensured by the central power, achieved through compulsory tributes to political and religious authorities (especially in the form of transfers of goods or provision of services). Conversely, in market societies, where income depends on the sale of one's labour or, for capitalists, on making profits,[2] social relations are embedded in economic relations. The degradation of workers does not come from exploitation, as Marx argued, but from the disintegration of the culture based on the social relations of reciprocity.[3] In this way, the economic structure influences the cultural superstructure, introducing elements of disintegration into modern societies, which, without reaching a systemic breakdown, generate social malaise and even violent tensions.

Polanyi criticizes the thesis, characteristic of the Austrian school, that the *homo oeconomicus* who compares resources with desires in order to make rational choices represents the archetype of the human being. In reality, economic man only comes into being later, together with the system that integrates/subordinates society into the economy; the market economy is not the natural epilogue to the history of human civilizations.[4]

[2] 'The motive of gain was specific to merchants, as was valor to the knight, piety to the priest, and pride to the craftsman' (Polanyi, 1968, p. 67). Trade – exchange – was different from the market. In the trade of traditional societies, prices were generally set by custom or political power (as was the case, for example, in medieval guilds): the exchange was a mutually beneficial exchange of benefits (Polanyi, 1968, pp. 109–10), a 'giving and receiving of thanks', as Albert the Great used to say (Roncaglia, 2001, p. 38).

[3] 'Not economic exploitation, as often assumed, but the disintegration of the cultural environment of the victim is then the cause of the degradation' (Polanyi, 1968, p. 46). One of Polanyi's main contributions to the comparative study of economic and social systems is to show how money and foreign trade, present in all kinds of societies, operate differently and play a different social role in market economies or in societies based on reciprocity and centralized redistribution.

[4] After recalling that, as Aristotle states, man is a social animal, Polanyi (1968, p. 65) states: 'Man's economy is, as a rule, submerged in his social relations. The change from this to a society which was, on the contrary, submerged in the economic system was an entirely novel development.'

By limiting their analysis to the functioning of the price mechanism in a market economy, theoretical economists lose sight of the problems relating to the very structure of societies embedded in the market.[5] Institutions such as the gold system and the balance of power in the international arena, or the market and the liberal state at home, generate contradictions; in particular, the market has a destructive effect on the system of reciprocity, hence on the social nature of humans, and generates distributive conflicts that lead inevitably, for better or worse, to an extension of social control (dictatorships, but also the New Deal and the welfare state).

Social integration achieved through market exchanges and the associated dominance of the economy over other aspects of social life (i.e. the system in which it is the economy that integrates/subordinates, embeds, social life) is contrasted with two other ways of organizing economic life: systems in which not exchange, but redistribution from the centre, or reciprocity, regulate economic life, allowing the economy to be integrated into society.

Developing Polanyi's theses, Immanuel Wallerstein (1974, 1980, 1989) distinguishes two types of world-systems: world-empires, characterized by centralized management of economic resources and in which the economy is, to use Polanyi's term, embedded in society; and the world-economy, that of the capitalist market, in which it is society that is embedded in the economy.

4.2 FROM COMPETITIVE CAPITALISM TO MANAGERIAL CAPITALISM

The contrast between economies based on reciprocity and/or centralized redistribution and market economies, alluded to in the previous section, concerns two 'ideal types' of basic structure of society. Economic history and theory have since developed a number of categories to illustrate different types of market economies, often

[5] 'The "economistic fallacy" consisted in an artificial identification of the economy with its market form' (Polanyi, 1968, p. 142 n.).

considered in sequence: merchant capitalism, early-stage manufacturing capitalism (considered competitive), trust capitalism (or managerial capitalism, although the two categories have at least partially distinct features), and financial or money manager capitalism.

Obviously, the distribution of economic power (or, more precisely, of the power to direct economic life) is substantially different in the various types of capitalism. In merchant capitalism, the big companies that control international trade, such as the East India Company, and the bankers who finance them (while also financing, as mentioned above, sovereigns and their wars) dominate. In the phase of manufacturing capitalism, the smaller size of firms limits, through competition, the power of the capitalists (without cancelling it – far from it, especially in relation to the workers and the communities where the manufacturing plants are located).

Large-scale production economies and mechanization favoured the processes of entrepreneurial concentration in what can be called the second industrial revolution, characterized by an increasing scale of investment. In this phase, a differentiation emerged between Anglo-Saxon capitalism, in which limited liability companies resort to the market (by issuing shares and bonds) to raise funds, and the German model, in which companies resort mainly to banks.

The growth in size of companies, in particular the rise of large joint stock companies, raises two issues: who controls the companies? Is the dominant market form still (assuming it ever was) competition, albeit far from perfect?

The second problem will be dealt with in the next section. The first problem arises from the fact that in joint stock companies the managers are usually persons other than the owners, who may be very numerous, and each of whom often owns a small proportion of the share capital.

Adolf Berle and Gardiner Means (1932) point to joint-stock companies and the separation of owners and managers as the basis of a new institutional arrangement, managerial capitalism. In the first phase of the industrialization process, competitive capitalism, small enterprises managed directly by the owner prevailed. Later, with the rise of large enterprises organized as joint-stock companies, ownership was divided among many small shareholders (the system of public companies, no longer controlled by an individual or a family group). The managers of the companies succeeded in acquiring sufficient autonomy to guarantee their re-election in shareholder meetings dominated by voting agreements inspired by the managers themselves, who thus became the real protagonists of the economy, taking all the decisions concerning not only the day-to-day management of the companies but also long-term strategic choices.

Several economists (including, among the first, William Baumol, 1959), sharing the thesis of Berle and Means, deduce a change in the objectives of the firm. More precisely, the objective of profit maximization should prevail in the phase of competitive capitalism, when firms are managed directly by their owners. In the stage of managerial capitalism, other objectives prevail – in particular, maximizing sales, which better serves the power interests of the managers.

Of course, managers have to take into account the risk of being replaced at the company's shareholders' meetings. This can happen when many shareholders, dissatisfied with the performance of the company and in particular with the dividends paid to them and the growth in share prices, sell their shares on the stock exchange, encouraging the takeover of the company by a new controlling group. The so-called theory of managerial capitalism developed by Robin Marris (1964) is based on this constraint on managers' freedom of action.

At the same time, as part of their business development strategy, managers can influence the choices of public authorities in their favour, either through lobbying (often entrusted to specialist operators, and often with considerable investment of money), or through trade associations endowed with strong bargaining power vis-à-vis the political class.

Managerial capitalism can then be seen in its actual working, considering the changes that are continually occurring in the market forms of the various sectors and in the decision-making processes of firms, as Chandler (1990) does when he reconstructs the history of the major manufacturing firms in the United States, Germany and Great Britain from the last decades of the nineteenth century to the middle of the twentieth. These aspects concern the distribution of power among firms and their owners, and are actually major elements when considering the links between economic and political power. Unfortunately, short- to medium-term historical reconstructions often overlook these links, which are very important indeed.[6]

Interactions between economic and political power can influence the selection of managers, on whom depend not only the strategic choices of companies, but also their technical and productive efficiency. This aspect is underestimated by those who focus attention on the links between economic and political power: in the long run, managerial choices, at least in part politically motivated, can be decisive for the success or crisis of companies. As Leibenstein (1966) points out with the concept of *X-inefficiency*, firms using similar techniques and similar amounts of capital and labour can have very different efficiency (productivity). Inefficiencies are attributable to management inefficiency, lack of worker motivation (e.g. absenteeism), and lower quality of production inputs. The actual importance of the problem, confirmed by numerous studies, indicates the limits of the assumption of given techniques commonly adopted in the theories of the firm, and the relevance of studies on organization (such as those by Cyert, Simon and many others), the sociology of work and

[6] The importance of these connections is illustrated, for example, in some classic works such as Ernesto Rossi's *I padroni del vapore* (1955), on the relationship between the capitalist bourgeoisie and fascism, or Scalfari and Turani's *Razza padrona* (1974), on the power structure in the Italian economy in the 1960s. Good journalistic investigations into these topics cast more light on the political events of a country than inquiries into the pure political power games, or even more than the vast historiography on political parties. We have many reconstructions of the history of individual companies, often stimulated and financed by the owners or top managers of the companies themselves; they are useful, but should be taken gingerly because they are biased, especially as regards the power games within the company itself, in relations with other companies and, above all, in relations with politics.

actual market structures, and above all the importance of the greater or lesser managerial capacity of those appointed to lead firms through selection mechanisms that do not necessarily favour competence.[7]

Theoretically, the power structure of the company is dominated by the shareholders' meeting, which chooses the management, approves the financial statements, and can guide major strategic decisions. In reality, the shareholders' meeting is dominated by the management, unless there is a takeover. Even when there is a majority voting bloc, if there are several autonomous parties in the bloc, the management assumes the role of interpreter of the compromise that made it possible to reach agreement on the voting bloc. Between management and majority shareholders there is a relationship of relative autonomy, characterized by partial exchanges of information (on the part of management, on the real internal situation of the company; on the part of the shareholders, on the prospects of change in the shareholding structure). Especially within large companies, information flows, which are obviously of great importance for decision-making processes, are part of the internal power game.

The internal organizational structure of the company shows significant degrees of autonomy at various levels, even within the framework of a sufficiently well-defined hierarchical order. In a large company, top management control over all activities is practically impossible. In a transnational firm, the various national branches may enjoy a more or less significant degree of autonomy (generally, little autonomy with regard to transfer prices between the various firms of the group and to financing flows; practically complete autonomy with regard to the purchase of means of production necessary for the activity of the national subsidiary, including the selection of personnel with the sole exclusion of top

[7] Especially in family-controlled firms, such choices are often influenced by varying degrees of favouritism towards relatives (in Italy even more frequently than in countries with a Protestant ethical tradition). In the case of public companies, managers' choices are often influenced by the political authorities and, in the case of larger firms, by company trade unions.

management; intermediate autonomy with regard to relations with the government authorities of the host country). The same holds in a conglomerate (a group of companies controlled by a parent company, operating in different lines of business). In the case of a company with several plants, the management of each plant also has autonomy in organizing the production process, but often with controls based on inspections and detailed comparison of results with those of the other plants.

Financial managers generally have considerable margins of autonomy, in particular for the management of current liquidity, which often leaves room for manoeuvre for speculative activities. With the financialization of the economy and the development of derivatives, speculative activities may acquire greater importance in the company's profit and loss accounts than productive activity itself; in this way, by generating very considerable profits (or losses), financial managers acquire greater power in the company structure than the engineers who manage productive activity. Precisely as a consequence of the margins of autonomy of each sector of the company, the system of internal controls is of great importance, covering all activities, including the control of financial risks as well as the actual production activities: management control officers report directly to the highest levels, and are autonomous vis-à-vis branch managers, though not having direct management powers.

The market power of a large company is reflected in the personal power of its managers. The head of the financial management of a large multinational company deals on an equal footing with the top executives of the financial institutions; the head of the foreign network or local subsidiary of a multinational company may have more importance in some countries than the ambassador of the country where the parent company is based. In the power networks we will be discussing later, including freemasonry, managers of large companies are often present, contributing to the overall power of the network and using it in power struggles even within the company itself.

4.3 OLIGOPOLY AS THE DOMINANT MARKET FORM

The second issue mentioned at the beginning of Section 4.2 concerns the dominant market form in the phase of managerial capitalism and the elements that account for the market power of large firms. This prompts some considerations on the transition from a (at least partly hypothetical) competitive phase to an oligopolistic phase of capitalism.

In contemporary economies all sectors are, to a greater or lesser extent, moving away from the perfect competition studied in economics textbooks. Monopoly is present, by definition, in all cases where there is only one supplier; very often, however, there are product substitutes occupying relatively close market spaces. Thus, oligopoly – the case where producers are relatively few in number and enjoy appreciable market power – is the most common case, along with imperfect competition, which occurs when, as in retail trade, sellers differ somewhat from each other.

Paolo Sylos Labini and Joe Bain, in two books both published in 1956, develop a theory of oligopoly (focusing respectively on the cases of concentrated and differentiated oligopoly) in which pure competition and monopoly constitute the two extreme borderline cases. In the case of oligopoly, firms in the market are partially protected from competition from potential entrants by a 'barrier to entry'. This barrier is not insuperable (which would mean falling back into monopoly, whereas the case of non-existent barriers corresponds to pure competition); its height, and hence the difficulty of overcoming it, depends on a number of factors.

In the case of concentrated oligopoly, the height of the entry barrier – that is, the barriers to entry for new firms in the industry – depends mainly on economies of scale, which force a hypothetical new firm to enter the market with a minimum output of significant size, which cannot be absorbed at current prices. The entry of the new firm then leads to a price reduction and the disappearance of extra profits, thus making entry unprofitable. The price reduction depends on the growth rate of demand for the firm's product and its price elasticity, which determines the cumulative loss that the entrant faces after entry before the price returns to a level sufficient to guarantee pre-entry profits. In the case of differentiated oligopoly, it depends on the expenditures for advertising and the like necessary to establish the new brand on the market. It also depends on the assumption – known in the literature as 'Sylos Labini's postulate', although in reality it is a widespread pattern of behaviour – that incumbent firms are unwilling to make room for new entrants by reducing their output to avoid a fall in the price of the product.

In both cases, in concentrated oligopoly as in differentiated oligopoly, the ratio of fixed costs (including overhead costs, thus also marketing costs) to variable costs is high. As a result, the traditional adjustment mechanism of competitive markets based on the interrelationships between prices, demand and supply is lost. Firms keep prices relatively stable when faced with changes in demand that are considered short term, responding with changes in the degree of capacity utilization; they respond uniformly (manifesting a kind of implicit collusion) to changes in labour or raw material costs through proportional price changes (the so-called full cost principle). In the event of a substantial and non-transitory fall in demand affecting all firms in the sector, firms may raise prices – instead of reducing them, as traditional theory would have it – to compensate for the increase in fixed costs per unit of output. In conditions of low capacity utilization, larger firms can wage price wars (even driving prices below variable unit cost) to eliminate smaller firms and capture their market share.[8]

Under the shelter of entry barriers, incumbent firms can enjoy above-competitive profits and a certain freedom of action, albeit

[8] When the ratio between fixed and variable costs is very high, as in the case of network services (e.g. telephone companies), economies of scale tend to lead to monopoly conditions. If an attempt is made to ensure the presence of several companies in the sector, as happened in Italy after the privatization of telephony, the result is a fierce battle over market shares, with an enormous increase in marketing costs (which then fall on the users, who are moreover subjected to intrusive and unrelenting forms of advertising).

within limits determined by the risk of new entry. These extra profits often translate into wages, salaries and bonuses for workers higher than those prevailing in sectors where competitive pressure is stronger.

According to the Keynesian view, firms' investment decisions are the *primum mobile* in the evolution of the economy. Once they have decided on the level of investment to be made, firms have to decide how to finance it; for various reasons they prefer to use internal sources (profits not distributed as dividends to shareholders) rather than borrowing and issuing new shares. Therefore, according to a post-Keynesian theory of the firm, entrepreneurs price their products so as to obtain a sufficient profit margin to finance the desired investments.[9]

Of course, this theory can only be applied to firms with market power, which are able to set the prices of their products independently and in doing so are not rigidly constrained by competition from other firms. However, even in the case of oligopolistic firms, prices cannot be set freely, so as to generate enough profit to finance any amount of investment projects the firms wish to carry out. We can therefore interpret this theory as relating to the use of the margins of choice available to managers in the presence of strong elements of uncertainty as well as oligopolistic conditions.

One development of the theories of market forms based on barriers to entry is the theory of contestable markets (Baumol et al., 1982). The perfectly accessible markets are those for which there is no entry or exit cost. In such markets no firm can earn extra profits. Indeed, any opportunity for extra profits, even if temporary, immediately attracts new firms to the market. The absence of exit costs allows new firms to avoid any risk, for example, of reaction from

[9] See Steindl (1952), Eichner (1976) and Wood (1975). The Modigliani–Miller theorem, according to which under conditions of perfect competition and perfect knowledge the different sources of financing are equivalent (cf. Modigliani and Miller, 1958) is considered inapplicable, as non-competitive market conditions and imperfect knowledge prevail.

incumbent firms. Indeed, if market conditions change and extra profits become negative, the new firm can immediately exit an accessible market at no cost (hit-and-run tactics). Exit costs arise mainly from having fixed capital assets that cannot be reused once the activity for which they were purchased has been abandoned: the sunk costs. This element constitutes the main novelty of the theory of accessible markets compared to the theory of market forms based on barriers to entry.

Oligopolistic market forms, when a few large companies dominate a sector, can encourage collusive behaviour, whether formal (cartels) or informal.[10] Cartels have played very important roles in the past, sometimes even used as instruments of industrial policy (the fascist corporations were essentially no more than compulsory cartels). Cartel agreements between large companies dominated the international oil industry for decades, starting in the 1930s (see Roncaglia, 1983, ch. 4). In the most recent phase, antitrust rules have discouraged formal collusion and cartel formation; however, informal collusion remains widespread, difficult to prove and therefore largely overlooked by antitrust authorities.

Oligopoly theories based on barriers to entry emphasize a logical sequence from structure (technological characteristics and product differentiation perceived by buyers) to conduct (decisions on investments, production levels and prices) and from there to performance (degree of market power, profitability and market shares). This interpretative

[10] This aspect had already been pointed out by Adam Smith, stressing both the greater bargaining power of capitalists compared to workers ('The masters, being fewer in number, can combine much more easily': Smith, 1776, pp. 83–4) and their influence, in Smith's opinion systematically negative, on the choices of the legislator, that is, on policy ('The interest of the dealers, however, in any particular branch of trade or manufactures, is always in some respects different from, and even opposite to, that of the publick. ... The proposal of any new law or regulation of commerce which comes from this order, ought always to be listened to with great precaution, and ought never to be adopted till after having been long and carefully examined, not only with the most scrupulous, but with the most suspicious attention. It comes from an order of men, whose interest is never exactly the same with that of the publick, who have generally an interest to deceive and even to oppress the publick, and who accordingly have, upon many occasions, both deceived and oppressed it' (Smith, 1776, p. 267).

paradigm has been challenged through the systematic use of game theory, which forms the basis of a new paradigm linked to a different logical sequence, starting from conduct (linked to achievable objectives) and ending with the structure of the industry. Although the new paradigm is now dominant (thanks also to the advantages for academic careers offered by the possibility to publish formally sophisticated models linked to the many possible variants of the rules of the game), its heuristic power is doubtful; the developments in game theory, especially with repeated games, hardly seem to be pointing in exciting new directions: 'Too many equilibria and no way to choose', as Kreps (1990, p. 95) comments. Under these conditions, a skilful theorist can deduce any desired result (conforming to the observed reality) through appropriate specification of the rules of the game, while actual power relations disappear from the horizon of the analysis.

Barriers to entry appear to be dominant, given the importance of fixed costs and administrative and marketing overheads over variable costs. It can therefore be argued, as observed above, that oligopoly – that is, the case where barriers to entry exist but are not completely insurmountable – is the general case, compared to which perfect competition (no barriers to entry) and monopoly (insurmountable barriers to entry) appear as the borderline cases. The actual distribution of power between economic sectors then depends on the relative height of the barriers to entry and the factors that determine it.[11]

4.4 DOMINATION POWER AND NETWORK POWER

The economic power of the great capitalist (Rockefeller or Ford, Agnelli or Del Vecchio) comes in two substantially different forms: direct power of possession/control (power of domination), and indirect power of network (power of influence/hegemony).[12] The first

[11] Later on, in Sections 6.7 and 6.8, we will consider the role of state intervention on firms' market power through antitrust and regulatory policies.

[12] The various types of network powers will be considered in the next chapter. Here we focus attention on a specific case of networks, cross-shareholding. Important enquiries on the power structure of the US economy were conducted in the late 1930s to

case occurs when the company, or group of companies, is controlled through the possession of a majority of shares sufficient to avoid having to negotiate strategic decisions with other co-owners. Among other things, this is what happens in the case of conglomerates, enterprises operating in different branches of activity gathered under a single umbrella of ownership: present everywhere, but notably central to the Korean (the *chaebols*) and Japanese (the *zaibatsu*) economies.

Control by domination can be the result of a cascade organization: if I have 51 per cent of a Luxembourg limited partnership, which owns 51 per cent of a Dutch financial holding company, which in turn owns 51 per cent of an Italian industrial company, my control over the industrial company is practically absolute, even with an investment of little more than 13 per cent of its share value (much less, if external financing intervenes at each step).

There is a network control system when, with perhaps 3 per cent of the shares, I am the first shareholder of a financial institution which in turn is the first shareholder, again with only 2 or 3 per cent of the shares, of an industrial company of which I in turn am the second shareholder, with the possibility that this industrial company is in turn the owner of a modest but significant share package of the original financial institution. The example may seem intricate, but it is perfectly simple compared to many real-world cases.

Interlocking directorates, that is, the presence of the same person on several boards of directors of potentially competing companies, often accompany interlocking shareholdings; again, the limits set by law are of great importance in favouring the concentration or diffusion of economic power. In general, this applies to all anti-monopoly legislation. In the early days, at the turn of the twentieth century, the emergence of anti-monopoly legislation in the United States was supported by a popular movement against large concentrations of

early 1940s by the Temporary National Economic Committee of the US Congress; some of the Committee's publications have been digitalized by the University of California and are now available as Google books.

power, both economic and political (such as Rockefeller's Standard Oil Trust). The same orientation, but strictly related to the economic field, was taken in the interwar period by neo-liberalists of various orientations (from German ordoliberals to exponents of the first Chicago school, such as Henry Simons). After the Second World War, first the 'Free market studies' group directed by Aaron Director in Chicago, then the Mont Pélerin Society as a whole, adopted an attitude of hostility towards any state interference in economic activity, hence also towards 'hard' anti-monopolistic regulation (which led to the exit of the ordoliberal group from the Society). These brief outlines of the history of antitrust policies hardly reflect the complexity and scope of the matter, but they are sufficient to show the influence of the prevailing economic culture on the concentration or diffusion of economic power.

Section 8 of the Clayton Act, passed in the USA in 1914, prohibited interlocking directorates. The prohibition was then interpreted as applying only to companies operating in the same sector, allowing the establishment of a network of control of some of the largest oil companies mediated by interlocking with financial institutions.[13] In Italy there are no such prohibitions, but only a limit (often violated) on the number of boards of directors on which the same person may sit, motivated not by anti-collusive aims but by the need to ensure serious commitment on the part of directors, who all too often operate as well-paid front men or paper pushers.

Financial institutions, especially the large investment funds in recent years, have become increasingly important in the system of cross-shareholding; at the same time, the role of individual owners of shares, the 'big capitalists' of the past (who still exist, but with a reduced role), has declined. The importance of shareholder interlocking networks and interlocking directorates is enhanced by the other types of networks discussed in the next chapter, namely 'grey' networks.

[13] See Neale (1970, pp. 201–2).

One case will suffice to show the importance of these networks, with analysis of the oil market in the first decades after the Second World War (Roncaglia, 1983). The situation can be reconstructed thanks to the research work of the US Senate collected in two hefty volumes published in 1978, dealing with the subject of interlocking shareholdings and interlocking directorates. (It is worth noting that, as far as I know, public studies of this type and magnitude have not been carried out since the rise of neo-liberalism.) As can be seen from the graphs in Roncaglia (1983, pp. 72–4), four of the 'Seven Sisters' (the major oil companies of the time) were inside the 'Rockefeller network', resulting in collusive behaviour on major strategies, which among other things may have had some co-responsibility for the outbreak of the first oil crisis in 1973–4.[14]

4.5 MARKET CONSTRUCTION

From what we have so far seen and indeed from what we will be seeing, it is clear that the hypothesis of competitive markets is completely unrealistic. Supporting it actually constitutes a powerful conservative ideological distortion, since it tends to present the market as a neutral ground with respect to the distribution of power and to obscure the role of its institutional set-up – regulations, antitrust policies – in favouring, also dynamically, power differences.

Some (Hayek, 1944; Clark, 1940 and various others) have argued that the market, even if imperfectly competitive, is preferable to a centrally planned economy, which tends to favour dictatorial political power. In many respects, this is a valid argument. However, between a centrally planned economy and an economy totally dominated by the free market there is a vast intermediate area, and it is in this area that we find ourselves today as in the past. Moreover, in positing a clear-cut dichotomy between state and market, sight is lost of an essential aspect: what forces determine the institutional set-up of

[14] See Roncaglia (1983, pp. 67–79); Blair (1976); Federal Trade Commission Staff Report (1952).

markets, which in turn has so much influence over the distribution of power?

There are at least two opposing positions in this regard: that of the neo-Austrian school, in particular Hayek, and that of the German ordoliberal school.[15] Hayek emphasizes the contrast between *taxis* (made order) and *kosmos* (grown order); in line with his liberalist convictions, he expresses a clear preference for the latter, which originates from individual free choices. The ordoliberals share with the Austrians the myth of the invisible hand of the market which, if perfectly competitive, is considered capable of guiding the economy to an optimal equilibrium corresponding to the full use of resources, and in particular full employment of labour. However, they also believe that the competitive market must be constructed with and supported by laws and regulations, as well as customs, which block the spontaneous tendency towards monopolistic situations; they therefore see as utopian the idea that individual choices can spontaneously lead to the creation of a competitive market and preserve it over time. Hayek's position is not supported by any theoretical evidence or historical experience; on the other hand, it is strongly supported by big corporations, since it implies the substantial irrelevance of antitrust policies, to which the ordoliberals, on the contrary, attach great importance.

The situation becomes more complex if we reject the myth of the invisible hand of the market. As Foucault (2004, p. 108) comments, the power to construct the market that ordoliberals entrust to the state does not constitute a deviation from neoliberal ideology, far from it: the institutional construction of a competitive market is the condition for having 'a state under the surveillance of the market, rather than a market under the surveillance of the state'. By contrast, abandonment of the myth of the invisible hand of the market implies attributing an active role of intervention in the economy to the powers of the state: not only with fiscal and monetary policies

[15] See Roncaglia (2019, chs. 4 and 8).

for management of the economic situation, but also with policies designed to deal with the many cases of market failure caused, for example, by the presence of externalities, as in the case of environmental protection, or policies created to tackle power inequalities and their frequent tendency to become self-perpetuating.

For this last aspect, the intertwining of economic, political and military power needs looking into. John Kenneth Galbraith made major contributions in this direction in a series of works that have been widely circulated, centred on analysis of the power structure of American capitalism based on the interrelationship between large corporations and the political and military leadership (Galbraith, 1952, 1958, 1967).

According to Galbraith (1952), the paradigm of perfect competition equilibrium analysis is totally unsuited for interpretation of contemporary economies. The dominance of large corporations in the US economy and society is justified by their efficiency, which allows for continuous expansion of production and living standards, but requires – and encourages the formation of – countervailing powers of buyers of products and sellers of means of production (the workers' unions included). While these do not lead to the same diffusion of power as competition in markets according to traditional theory, they do constitute a means of reducing power differentials in society.

In subsequent publications these themes were taken up again, underlining (Galbraith, 1958) the ability of the large corporations to direct consumer choices and the formation, in the face of private opulence, of a 'public misery', that is, a largely unsatisfied need for culture (schools, but also museums), public infrastructures (road networks, public transport), security services, and action against environmental degradation.[16] The evolution of American society is mainly determined by the interaction between large and powerful players, such as the government, the major corporations, the trade

[16] The contrast between 'private affluence' and 'public misery' echoes the themes of Veblen (1899); Galbraith links it more directly to issues of power.

unions, and the military leadership, which together constitute the 'technostructure' (Galbraith, 1967).[17]

While the role of the market is diminishing, the role of planning is growing: not the centralized planning of Soviet-style communism, but multi-polar planning carried out by the state-military apparatus and by the big corporations, each in its specific field and, in connection with each other and with the government, for the economy as a whole. The importance of education is also growing, both in the sense of technical training and in the broader sense of cultural training; it, too, constitutes a decisive element of social stratification (and of the persistence of social stratification inherited from the past).

In the wake of Schumpeter, but with a contrary conclusion,[18] Galbraith sees a possibility of salvation: 'The industrial system, in contrast to its economic antecedents, is intellectually demanding. It brings into existence, to serve its intellectual and scientific needs, the community that, hopefully, will reject its monopoly of social purpose' (1967, p. 400).[19]

[17] 'So far from being the controlling power in the economy, markets were ever more accommodated to the needs and convenience of business organizations' (Galbraith, 1967, p. 9). 'The accepted sequence', which goes from consumers' choices to the market and from it to the producer, is replaced by the 'revised sequence', running from the choices of big business to the control of consumer orientation and market regulation (1967, p. 216). Consumers and the public sector also adapt (or perhaps better, are driven to adapt) to the demands of the corporations; the power of the trade unions itself saw decline from 1956 onwards (1967, p. 15). The importance of military expenditure, in particular but not only in orienting scientific research (take the case of research on nuclear energy, favoured over research on solar energy), has subsequently been explored by various authors; see e.g. Mirowski (2002, pp. 153–231).

[18] For Schumpeter (1942), with its critical activity the intellectual class would corrode capitalism from within, thus leading to socialism (i.e. in the opposite direction to the one he preferred).

[19] At the same time, as an alternative outcome to the one indicated above in the text, Galbraith seems to foresee the advent of populist movements, such as Berlusconi's and Trump's: 'suspicion or resentment is no longer directed to the capitalist or the merely rich. It is the intellectuals who are eyed with misgivings and alarm .... Nor should it be a matter for surprise when semi-literate millionaires turn up leading or financing the ignorant in struggle against the intellectually privileged and content. This reflects the relevant class distinction in our time' (1967, p. 250). To the financiers may perhaps be added authoritarian powers such as Russia and China, which have been accused to use both direct subsidies and the new social media to undermine Western democracies from within by supporting populist or sovereignist movements.

The paradox of opulent consumption that favours the segmentation of society, already illustrated by Veblen, was taken up by Fred Hirsch (1976), using the notion of 'positional goods' that contribute to determining the social position of the individual and that are desired and demanded for this reason, even at the expense of objectively more useful goods and services, with negative consequences for the civil development of society. In particular, material consumption is favoured, sacrificing education and time dedicated to others while generating social malaise (alienation, deterioration of urban living conditions, inflation and unemployment, loss of humanity in relationships with others).

James Galbraith (Kenneth's son) in his book *The Predator State* (2008) takes up the Veblenian notion of 'predator' to argue that contemporary capitalism, far from being competitive, is centred on the shift from a system built for the middle class to one in which the middle class is systematically plundered in favour of a class of predators, who control the economy and politics: a state run like a corporation, with a system of lobbies (pharmaceutical, oil, financial, military) guiding its actions.[20]

Another aspect to consider, already mentioned and to which we will return in Section 6.8, is the variety of forms of capitalism, competing with each other since the collapse of the communist regimes, which certainly did not mark 'the end of history'. The differences that exist between countries and groups of countries in labour policies, welfare state institutions, corporate governance and their financing models (see Hall and Soskice, 2001) have profound implications for the distribution of power within countries, as well as for economic dynamics and thus for the evolution of power relations

[20] 'Predation' is defined as 'the systematic abuse of public institutions for private profit' (Galbraith, 2008, p. xiii). This has led to 'a process of dispersion of the technostructure's power' (2008, p. 118), mainly to the advantage of financiers and big managers, and thus 'the rise of a new class – very small and unbelievably rich' (2008, p. 98; and if Galbraith is talking about the United States, one cannot help thinking also of the oligarchs of the former communist countries).

at the international level. In particular, as Kalecki (1943) points out with his theory of the political cycle, macroeconomic policies supporting employment contribute to strengthening the bargaining power of workers. As far as financing models are concerned, in economic systems in which firms are mainly financed through banks, the latter also play an important role in directing investment, that is, the growth of production capacity, towards certain sectors rather than others.

The financial sector actually has significant allocative power, directing the sectoral development of the economy, even in market-centric systems where firms are mainly financed through the stock and bond market: a power that is not recognized in the traditional theory that assumes a competitive financial system, therefore passive with respect to the choices of entrepreneurs, whereas in reality it is the centre of a web of power relations, as we shall see more clearly later (Section 4.7).

4.6 THE CAPITALISM OF FINANCIAL MANAGERS

The economic growth of the 1950s and 1960s generated an increase in wealth and, within it, in the share of financial assets. As a result, the role of the professional asset managers, previously dedicated mainly to managing the wealth of the wealthy, grew in proportion. The development of their role was favoured by the privatization of part of public welfare (pension funds, supplementary health insurance, etc.) and by the growing complexity of financial portfolio management (financial innovations such as money market funds and funds of funds, the spectacular proliferation of the use of financial derivatives for hedging and especially for speculative purposes, the development of mathematical-statistical models, and the spread of algorithms for computerized operations on the stock exchange and in organized financial markets). Financial globalization has been moving in the same direction. It has grown dramatically since the collapse of the Bretton Woods system and repeated financial liberalization measures in the United States and elsewhere.

This leads to a phase (which Hyman Minsky, 1990, called money manager capitalism) in which finance dominates the real economy. To a considerable extent, this does not take place through organized financial markets such as stock exchanges, but through over-the-counter operations, directly between the contracting parties, and therefore in a relatively opaque manner. There is a substantial change in the modus operandi: while in previous phases the validation of the choices of economic operators was linked to profitability throughout the life of an investment (e.g. of an industrial plant), in money manager capitalism validation is linked to the increase in the price of positions held by operators, composed of real and financial assets and liabilities, and is verified moment by moment.

Gains (and losses) are amplified by the use of high leverage, which indicates the extent to which a firm uses external sources of finance. In the case of financial institutions, the advantage of using external sources of finance is that they can increase the return on their capital if they make a profit; but if things go wrong, the burden of losses increases.[21] In this way, financial operators boost their ability to make profits but also their risks, together with the financial fragility of the system and the volatility of the markets. In addition, this makes the economy less effective in terms of productivity growth or ecological and social sustainability, as less attention is paid to long-term problems such as the pursuit of technological progress, more unstable in the face of changes in the climate of opinion, and more difficult to control with traditional economic policy instruments. In Minsky's view, the main problem facing economic policy is not the cyclical instability of capitalism, but its systemic instability, that is, its susceptibility to large-scale crises.[22] The risk of crises affects

[21] Leverage is defined as the ratio between the value of assets (or liabilities) and the value of equity. If, with a capital of 100, I borrow 900, and invest the total 1,000 in the purchase of a property or a stock, a 10 per cent increase (or decrease) in the price of that stock leads to a doubling of the capital (or to it being reduced to zero). Hedge funds typically operate with high leverage ratios.

[22] For an illustration of Minsky's theory (Minsky, 1975, 1986), see Roncaglia (2019, pp. 279–86).

economic policy choices at all levels, even to the extent of affecting political events.

The financial sector is diversified, with segments that differ in terms of the type of transaction and the characteristics of the operators, although the various segments are closely linked. We can distinguish two extremes, that of operators with a very short time horizon (known as short-termism) in which the use of computerized transactions is widespread, and that of private equity managers active in the field of the control of share packages with a significant weight in the ownership of companies. The former, often operating in the financial derivatives markets, continuously buy and sell assets to gain from even minor price changes. The latter favour operations of change of ownership or control (or consolidation, with the so-called buy back operations, that is the purchase of packages of own shares, which have had considerable development in recent years), mergers or dismemberment of companies, with the aim of 'value creation', that is, earnings on the value of shares. The previous phase of managerial economics has been superseded as the managers of large corporations can no longer count on substantial power in the face of an audience of small shareholders, but have to face financial operators – such as the managers of hedge funds – who can put together (or sell) share packages of significant size, sufficient to climb the boards of directors or cause a collapse in share prices.[23] In this way, the prevalence of a short-term view is transferred from the financial sector to the directly productive sectors (industry, services, agriculture): entrepreneurial choices concerning new production capacity or the research and adoption of new technologies are affected by contingent motivations that distort the long-term view congruent with such choices.

One aspect of money manager capitalism lies in the high salaries of managers, commonly equated with wages whereas they

[23] On the growth of the financial sector of the economy in its various components and the implications – positive and especially negative – of this trend, see Greenwood and Scharfstein (2013). On the link between financialization, asset inflation and economic fragility, see Toporowski (2000).

should be equated with profits. The form taken by these remunerations (bonus on annual performance, or stock options on the shares of the managed company) constitutes a strong incentive for short-term or very short-term oriented choices. In particular, the remuneration of financial operators is very high, not least because the financial sector is characterized by oligopolistic market forms in which extra profits easily translate into higher managerial remuneration than that prevailing in competitive conditions.[24] This leads to a change in the relative social importance of engineers/technicians and financial managers, to the detriment of the former; this discourages investment in the training of technical-scientific human capital, holding back production efficiency and technical progress, but also has negative effects on culture in the general sense, with an undervaluation of lasting commitment compared to the orientation towards very short-term bets. Moreover, these soaring salaries constitute a non-negligible element in the growth of distributional inequalities that has occurred in recent decades, to such an extent that it also leads to a growing polarization of power relations and the social structure.[25]

Then there is a field that is set to expand and is full of implications of various kinds, namely the development of electronic currencies, such as bitcoins. As long as they are not issued by central banks, they will be fiduciary currencies, destined to vary in price in relation to the official currency, and therefore subject to speculation and, if its mass expands sufficiently, increasing systemic risks. The advantages in terms of facilitating trade are undoubted, but so are the risks that the confidentiality of this type of transaction will encourage development in the illegal and criminal economy: drugs, human organs, money laundering, blackmail, fraud and tax evasion are traded via bitcoins.[26] In addition, monetary policy loses its impact with the

[24] On the transformation of oligopolistic extra-profits into higher wages, see Sylos Labini (1984).

[25] See Milanovic (2016).

[26] For an assessment of the very significant weight of illegal and criminal activities in the bitcoin and other cryptocurrency markets, see Foley, Karlsen and Putniņš (2019).

development of parallel currencies. Among other things, this is an area of ideological controversy: neo-liberals, starting with Hayek (1999), are in favour of private currencies as part of a programme to limit the state to the bare minimum; Keynesians are opposed.

In money manager capitalism, the scope of economic policy interventions cannot be limited to the short-term control of aggregate demand through monetary and fiscal policy instruments. Monetary policy should give central importance to changes in asset prices to prevent the formation of asset bubbles. It is also, and above all, necessary to keep the financial fragility of the economy under control as far as possible in order to limit the scale and frequency of financial crises and their impact on the real economy. This implies paying attention to the regulation of finance, for example with constraints on the leverage of financial firms and on their size, to prevent their possible failure from entailing systemic risks,[27] or with rules aimed at curbing speculative activities (e.g. by taxing trading in derivatives, or with constraints/bans on high frequency trading). Preventive interventions are preferable to *ex-post* interventions, which generate moral hazard by fostering confidence in state intervention to bail out troubled operators and thus a tendency to take excessive risks; moreover, to avoid this tendency, any bailout of financial institutions must be done in a way that makes the costs fall primarily on managers and shareholders, rather than on the public finances.[28]

4.7 POWER IN THE AGE OF FINANCE

Between the eras of managerial capitalism and money manager capitalism there are significant changes in power relations within the

[27] Bailing out banks in difficulty, which is already very costly for the public purse but inevitable when failure would generate a systemic crisis (too big to fail), risks becoming an unsustainable burden for the public purse (too big to be rescued), as Iceland discovered to its cost in the 2008 crisis.

[28] 'We have to establish and enforce a "good financial society" in which the tendency by businessmen and bankers to engage in speculative finance is constrained' (Minsky, 1982, p. 69). See e.g. Montanaro and Tonveronachi (2012) for some proposals in this regard.

economic field, and between this and other areas of power: the world of politics, information and culture.

First of all, in the age of financial globalization, the convenience of and opportunities for behaviour on the fringes of legality, if not beyond, are growing. The development of a complex financial system, which among other things allows for choice of the laxest national taxation and regulation regime, favours tax elusion and evasion by the wealthier classes, money laundering and operations on illegal markets. Moreover, in speculative operations, it is the first to discover a profitable line of operation ('buy on rumours, sell on news') who gain most: exchange of information – up to and including insider trading – between financial operators and the ganglia of other areas, including the world of politics or the judiciary, is a winner; the result is the constitution of transversal information networks in the various areas of activity, with the formation of 'grey networks' centred on the exchange of information and favours. All this, in turn, generates a system of blackmail, which can also involve the political, information and judicial worlds.

The financialization of the economy has also led to a sharp increase in inequalities in the distribution of income and wealth, with an increasing share concentrated in the richest 1 per cent of the population.[29] Correspondingly, the position of the middle classes has worsened in several respects, accompanied by a reduction in intergenerational social mobility.[30]

As we have seen, with money manager capitalism, the managers of large companies lose some of their power, while the managers of large investment funds and large financial institutions gain some, as they are able to organize takeovers of public companies on the basis of the principle of seeking shareholder's value, that is, maximizing the value of the shares, even in the very short term and regardless

[29] See Piketty (2013).

[30] See Bagnasco (2016). The power elite, identified in the mid-1950s by Mills (1956) as the political directorate, the richest industrialists and the highest military ranks, now expands to include in positions of absolute prominence the exponents of finance.

of the long-term prospects of the company being taken over. A conglomerate can be taken over because it is believed that the value of its separately sold parts (especially real estate) is higher than the value resulting from the stock market listing, or that fierce restructuring with a drastic reduction of staff, even if accompanied by a reduction in production levels, leads to a higher shareholder's value: the social costs of such operations are in fact irrelevant for the perpetrators.[31]

The political authorities themselves, especially in countries with large public debts, are forced to recognize the new role of the financial institutions. At a time when there can be sudden changes in the composition of the portfolios of financial institutions, waves of buying or selling public debt securities (or derivatives such as credit default swaps [CDS]; see Roncaglia, 2010) can determine the salvation or fall of a government.

The spiral connecting wealth, income and power is therefore characterized by strong elements of increasing dynamic returns (self-reinforcing spirals). Wealth influences power, power enables income and wealth to increase. This circuit is so obvious that it is worth focusing attention on the elements that limit the strength of its internal connections.

These elements are essentially constituted by the strength of autonomous resistance in each sphere, particularly in politics and culture. Politics, for example, is at least partially autonomous with respect to economic power in Italy, while private funding for the electoral expenses of parties and candidates plays a fundamental role in the United States, to the point of being decisive.[32] If we consider the opposite causal link, the dependence of economic power on political

[31] On the negative effects of the new gospel of shareholder value maximization, cf. Lazonick and Shin (2020).

[32] See Ferguson (1995) and Ferguson et al. (2019); the latter work concludes by highlighting the 'money-driven political system' side of the United States. Bekkouche and Cagé (2018) find a correlation between spending per voter and candidate's vote shares in French municipal and legislative elections between 1993 and 2014. Some political parties in Italy received, and probably still receive, substantive amounts of foreign funding in addition to corruption-driven funds.

power is stronger in countries with substantially dictatorial regimes; it is less strong in the democratic countries of Western Europe.

One aspect to remember is that the influence of economic power on political power also – perhaps above all – passes through the media: television networks and newspapers. In this respect, much depends on anti-trust rules, which should therefore be stricter in the field of information, where it is better not to leave room for concentration tendencies resulting from economies of scale, unlike in the manufacturing industry, where economies of scale should, rather, be favoured for the productivity gains they allow.

Another aspect to consider is the way this web of causal relations – between wealth, income and power – has been modified by the growth of information technology, particularly with the role acquired by the new social media. On the one hand, it is argued that their pervasiveness and low cost of use has a democratizing effect, as it bypasses the barriers arising from the economic costs of traditional media (newspapers or television networks). On the other hand, paid bloggers, the organized dissemination of fake news and the development of automatic message-sending programs is limited to those who have the economic means and, above all, the possibility to operate in a grey area between moral impropriety and outright illegality; recent experience has shown that the dissemination of fake news for political purposes is conducted from extra-territorial bases, in regulatory paradises or in countries – generally with dictatorial regimes – interested in supporting certain political factions. We will come back to these issues later on.

5 The Networks

5.1 THE UTOPIA (OR DYSTOPIA?) OF THE MERITOCRATIC SOCIETY

The myth of the invisible hand of the market guiding the capitalist economy towards an optimal equilibrium, in which the distribution of available resources between the different uses corresponds to the maximum possible satisfaction of consumers' needs and desires, calls for certain conditions. The first, already mentioned, is that the economic system should operate at full capacity, using all available resources; in particular, there should be no unemployment. But in actual fact, unemployment and partial utilization of available productive capacity occur systematically, all too often with alarming peaks, especially in certain geographical areas or among young people. The second condition is that not only should there be perfect competition in the economic system (and perfect information, which is a prerequisite for this), but also perfect social mobility, and that everyone should play the most appropriate role and receive a salary corresponding to their contribution, in other words that society should be a perfect meritocracy. In society, as in the markets, the participants in the competition should be able to count on a level playing field, a playing field without irregularities that might favour some to the detriment of others. Only in this way can the prices of productive services ensure a balance between supply and demand by encouraging the supply of services where demand is strong and discouraging supply where it is relatively weak; insofar as they ensure the optimal allocation of resources, equilibrium prices can be said to be 'fair', even if they correspond to serious inequalities in the distribution of income.

Neither of these conditions can be considered realistic. What is of interest here, however, is the second one. The questions that arise here are twofold: can a perfectly meritocratic society be considered an ideal? If meritocracy has both positive and negative aspects, what obstacles stand in the way of achieving the former and what can we do to counteract the latter?

The first is an ethical question. Marx, for example, saw meritocracy as a criterion of justice valid for pre-communist societies, but which would be superseded in a society where the development of social wealth would make it possible to break the link between what each gives to society and what each receives from it. If what one gives to society depends not only (and not so much) on personal effort, but also on the circumstances in which one happens to find oneself (including innate capacities, or the presence of physical handicaps, but especially the circumstances deriving from the wealth and power of the family one is born into and similar aspects), a meritocratic distribution of the product (as well as of power and social roles) does not have sufficient ethical justification, compared to an egalitarian distribution.

Conversely, meritocracy rises to the level of an ideal for the mainstream economist who subscribes (perhaps with some marginal note of caution) to the ideal of the invisible hand of the market. Any deviation from meritocracy, that is, from the market prices of services of productive factors, appears as a departure from the optimal condition of efficiency in the productive set-up of society.[1]

Actually, the term 'meritocracy' was coined (by the English sociologist Michael Young, 1958) precisely in the context of a critique of this vision, presenting a terrifying image of a futuristic

[1] Uncritically held, this thesis can provoke arrogance among the successful, humiliation among the defeated, and generate fractures in the social fabric. See Young (1958) and Sandel (2020). For a balanced illustration of the different aspects of meritocracy, see Santambrogio (2021), who defines meritocracy as a society in which not only do jobs go to those who deserve them, but in which equality of opportunity is also ensured (primarily through substantial investment in state schools).

society – a dystopia – in which meritocratic criteria are fully established, and the social position of each individual is determined solely by his or her intelligence quotient and work capacity.[2] In a society with blocked intergenerational social mobility, the use of meritocratic ideology by the elites can foster the growth of populist ideologies, which confuse the equal rights of all with the (inevitably different) abilities to fill roles that require specific knowledge and skills. In this way there is a risk of simultaneously blocking social change and provoking the malfunctioning of political institutions.

The answer to the second question implies reformulating the ethical problem: given that – fortunately or unfortunately – we do not live in a perfectly meritocratic society, can a little more meritocracy be considered better than a little less? Put in these terms, the dilemma has no clear-cut answer: much depends on the specific characteristics of the situation at the outset.

On the one hand, given the difference in starting points (particularly in terms of wealth, social position and family culture), uncompromising adoption of meritocratic criteria tends to make the social structure more rigid over time. For the same reason, state education should be favoured over private schools and universities where students are selected on the basis of ability to pay rather than academic merit. Also, in the face of inequalities in remuneration (which among other things often depend on bargaining power rather than merit), a progressive tax system (more accentuated for higher incomes) is an appropriate response, as is high taxation of inheritances. Equally important are policies to alleviate disadvantages for people with disabilities, such as the removal of architectural barriers or a system of subsidies to compensate for the costs of disability.

On the other hand, the reasons most frequently given for calls for greater appreciation of meritocratic criteria have their own

[2] Young was reacting to the educational system then prevailing in Britain (later dismantled in the 1970s), which provided for an examination at around the age of 'eleven plus', which steered children towards differentiated school profiles, helping to crystallize class differences.

validity and importance. In the previous chapter we considered the distorting effects that elements like oligopolistic market forms or the financialization of the economy can have in generating differences in income, wealth and power between workers in different sectors: these distorting effects violate the rules that should in principle guide a perfectly meritocratic society. In the following sections we will consider the obstacles to meritocracy constituted by networks of connections between agents that throw power relations out of kilter, preventing real correspondence between merit and occupational and social position.

As we shall see, the networks in question are of various kinds. We will start with the 'white' ones, in the sense of being not only perfectly legal but also useful for civil development, because of the solidarity and support they provide: the community spirit that is so important for the maintenance of social cohesion. However, in the absence of democracy – a participatory and transparent democracy, sustained by a widespread civic spirit – even white networks can become grey, in the sense of introducing deviations from meritocracy that can be condemned as inefficient and immoral, as contrary to criteria of fairness. White networks are essentially based on family or ideological affiliation (e.g. party or religious affiliation); but they can also be based on affinities of taste and customs (from a philharmonic to a bridge club, from members of a sports club to the old-boy network). They are 'white' as long as they remain within the limits of a secular spirit, that is, devoid of sectarian strictness: as long as helping those who belong to the same network does not penalize those outside the network.

We will then consider the 'grey' networks, which are less acceptable but not illegal (except in extreme cases). This includes, first of all, the deviations of white networks, such as the distorted use of power or influence to the advantage of one of the members of the network, as long as this does not lead to violations of the law. Then there are the formalized organizations, which are not forbidden by law, but which concentrate their activities on the exchange of favours, and which are in any case opaque to public scrutiny. The typical example for this aspect is Freemasonry, which as a degeneration (not inevitable, but not unexpected) has led to the formation of sinisterly secret associations like the P2 in Italy, seeking to influence the political and economic life of the country and, in extreme cases, resorting to violently illegal actions with bombs, the 'strategy of tension' and the coup d'état.

The 'black' networks are the unequivocally illegal networks, from secret associations like the P2 to criminal organizations like the mafia, the ndrangheta and the camorra.

White networks, and to a certain extent also grey networks, have ambivalent characteristics; it is the way in which the individuals in them behave that brings out the positive or negative aspects.

Before going into the details, it is worth recalling that network analysis has developed into a branch of scientific research in its own right, with techniques that can be used in the most diverse fields, from study of the spread of viruses to analysis of the network economy, from the diffusion of new social media to the links of kinship and indirect knowledge between human beings (the famous thesis of a maximum of 'six degrees of separation' between any two individuals in the world population).[3] Regarding more directly the question of power, a general rule is that individuals who are part of several networks may have a role in linking them; this role constitutes in itself a source of power; when two networks are connected by a single individual, his/her power of mediation may indeed be significant. Another important element to consider is the internal structure of the network. In other words, the number (relative to the total) of direct connections with neighbouring nodes (degree centrality), the number of times the node constitutes the shortest link between

[3] See the pioneering work by Barabási (2002) and, more recently and devoted in particular to the field of economics, Glattfelder (2013). As Piselli (1995, p. xl) points out in the introduction to a useful collection of essays on network analysis methodology and application, 'network analysts do not study groups and institutions. They study individuals *within* groups and institutions.'

other nodes (betweenness centrality) and the 'closeness' of the node to all the other nodes in the network (closeness centrality); the latter is an index of global centrality, while the other two are indices of local centrality.

5.2 WHITE NETWORKS: FAMILIES, RELIGIONS, PARTIES

Families can be regarded as white networks par excellence, because of the solidarity cemented in affection and the continuous flow of aid and assistance that may not excite immediate counter-performance but are transmitted backwards and forwards in time, between successive generations. These links are so strong that families can be regarded as economic units, for both regulatory and statistical purposes. Of course, households are not only this: they are also in themselves a power structure (as we shall see more fully in Section 8.2; here we may recall the theme of gender roles); moreover, as we shall see in the next section, solidarity between members of the same family clan can translate into antagonism towards others, with a breakdown of solidarity in society at large.

In this section we focus attention on white networks based essentially on ideological and cultural identity in the broadest sense, in particular religions and political parties. As many authors point out, these networks constitute intermediate bodies between individuals and society that foster habits of cooperation and solidarity essential to the development of a civic spirit, counteracting tendencies towards social disintegration.[4]

In principle (according to the canons of a meritocratic society), affiliations should constitute neither an advantage nor a disadvantage in social competition. In fact, we can only speak of white nets as long as ideological affiliation does not lead to sectarian behaviour, with other ideologies being regarded as inferior, or even denied the

[4] Intermediate bodies of a different kind, but with the same essential function of social glue, are political parties and trade unions, which make citizens' participation in political life more active and aware; for the same reason the progressive tradition, from Cattaneo to Rosselli, tends to enhance the role of local institutions.

right to exist. In this respect, in the multicultural society there is a real need to share a secular moral code ensuring the equal rights of all to pursue their own adherences, all recognised as equally worthy. And this must apply to any kind of adherence, to religious faith as well as football teams, to political convictions as well as musical preferences.

However, it is usually the case (and considered quite natural) that political and religious organisations set up support networks for their members. Parishes, for example, organise support networks for the care of the elderly and the sick, provide activities for the children (e.g. catechism schools), and for the care of the poor. Local organizations of political parties are centres for debate and political education, but also networks of human relations and an outlet for leisure time. Of course, party affiliation is essential for political posts, whereas it should not be – although it often is to some extent – essential for technical positions that are politically appointed.[5]

In these practical aspects we find a vast range within which network whiteness may tend to the opaque. For example, support networks may be closed or open to the outside world; in the latter case, they may have simple humanitarian aims, or aims to assimilate the 'different', using support as a vehicle for proselytizing activities. Of course, among those who share the same religion or ideology, there can be 'rigorists' (traditionalists and conservatives, culturally closed to differences) and 'broad-minded' (with varying degrees of openness); the recent history of the Catholic Church is marked by lively confrontation between the two positions, at times raised to the stormy level of a head-on clash. In other cases, like the world of football, there are multimillion-dollar businesses that may occasionally

[5] Clientelism has harmful effects in this field. Placing an unsuitable person in positions of responsibility, for example as chair of an authority, can be devastating for the authority itself. (In some cases, for example in the case of supervisory authorities, choice of an unqualified person may be prompted by the desire to favour the supervised.) Rules, such as the publicity for job contests documentation, together with the critical function of public opinion, informed by a free and independent press, can stem this drift.

see lapses into illegality (like hooliganism) or exploitation of fans to build political consensus (mixing different types of membership, which should remain separate).

There are therefore two rather blurred boundaries, beyond which the physiology of white networks is prone to pathology. The first boundary lies in the distinction between defending one's roots in a multicultural society and rejecting any form of cultural integration. The second boundary concerns the use, acceptable or distorted, of the networks of social/religious groups.

Two fundamental elements in the first case are confessional schools and 'ghettoization', that is, territorial separation into areas dominated by one or another religious (or football, or other) denomination, limiting opportunities to meet 'others' in a common living environment. Religious and political affiliations are part of the family and community roots of most individuals: rejecting them is possible, but implies a falling-out with the community or family of origin that may have even heavy social costs. At the same time, interactions between individuals with different affiliations in a multicultural society should not be confrontational, for otherwise there is a risk of societal disintegration. For this reason, opportunities for open exchange should be encouraged, and embraced as potential for cultural and human enrichment.

In Italy, the insistence on preferential treatment for Catholic schools, putting them on an equal footing with state schools when it comes to funding, risks leading to a society deprived of the fundamental pillar of common integration that consists in secular school education,[6] guaranteed by the state for all. Currently we have witnessed increasing calls for public support for all types of private schools, backed by a widespread neo-liberal culture; this policy goes

[6] A secular education does not need to be agnostic or atheistic: the teachers in state schools more or less reflect the composition of the population, thus (in Italy, for example) with a majority presence of Catholics but ensuring that students are exposed to a variety of different positions (whereas in denominational schools this is by definition not the case).

in the same direction of social disintegration as that of the denominational schools, with the aggravating circumstance of opening the way to a sharp increase in class differentiation in the quality of school education.

State schools play (or should play) a particularly important role in the integration of different political and religious cultures; incentives for denominational schools – or private schools in general – are a contradiction in terms. Centres of religious education can, on the other hand, play a useful complementary role, flanking state school education with private education that encourages cultural growth and conscious integration into the reference community.

What we have said about the risks of religious affiliations applies, albeit to a lesser extent, to political affiliations. The risk in this case is of political affiliation degenerating into membership of clientele clans; political education, regular exchange of views and open debate can help ward it off. Rules (preferably codified in binding legal provisions) that create forms of control and countervailing power in relation to political appointments (governmental or parliamentary) can also be useful, with requirements for reinforced majorities, hearings and confirmation votes by bodies other than the nominating body, and preliminary assessment of candidates by groups of experts. The media can play a useful role if they enter into the merits of individual cases without sectarian opposition but with external control functions, if public opinion is sufficiently aware of the importance of adequate selection. Here the anti-meritocratic culture ('one is as good as any other') that is so widespread in populist political organizations is a breeding ground for the worst kind of nefariousness, and the costs can indeed be heavy.

White networks, in themselves, play a positive role when they are embedded in an adequate context of rules and widespread culture, in particular when cultural integration is pursued as a political priority and responds to a common sentiment, widespread in the community. They can play a negative role when non-membership becomes a reason for differential treatment, to the point of hostility and exclusion from civil relations (for example, opposing inter-religious marriages). Compared to these extremes, favouritism in occupational choices is so distinctly a lesser evil that it is all too often considered morally acceptable, although it opens the way to deep fault lines within society.[7]

The communities of researchers can be seen as white networks, subdivided by fields of work and orientations, but sharing some characteristics: the dominance of meritocracy (at least in principle) and of a critical mentality (and of self-critical capacity, although often less than would be desirable); passion for one's own work and strong motivation; a perhaps inevitable but often exaggerated concentration in one's own specific field of research; and the sheer curiosity to understand, which as a rule constitutes the dominant motivation. In this field, however, it is worth noting the deviations of family or Masonic networks that influence careers, together with the use of a distorted meritocracy and the growing importance of private funding, which, especially in the economic and social fields, favours conservative orientations.

Among the white networks, in the economic field we have the workers' associations (trade unions), which play a fundamental role of assistance and representation. Much the same can be said of the employers' associations, if we exclude lobbying activities (to which we will return later), which may border on political corruption.

In all these cases, the endowment of 'social capital' can count for a lot: the willingness of each to collaborate with others, to help them if necessary, confident that he or she can in turn receive help when needed, and in general trust in the others.[8] Putnam (2000, p. 14) speaks of 'social capital concerning relations between individuals,

[7] The Italian 1970 Workers' Statute, which prevents employers from gathering information on workers' political or religious orientations (Article 8), only partially interrupted a practice that is unfortunately still widespread.

[8] Putnam (1993) notes, in an analysis of Italian geographical areas, the existence of a long-lasting cultural influence detectable in the differences between the areas that had seen the diffusion of the communes in the late Middle Ages and those that had undergone different experiences. The work is the result of twenty years of research, but the factors to be considered are in fact more numerous, while comparisons

social networks and the norms of reciprocity and reliability that derive from them', and then distinguishes (p. 20) 'between *bridging* and *bonding social capital*'; the former can be considered a civic virtue (albeit ambivalent, in that it can be both a resource and an obstacle to external integration), while the latter can characterize closed communities (such as the family clan or the mafia). Sovereignism is, to all intents and purposes, a 'social capital that closes', preaching closure, albeit in a community as large as the national one. Populism, too, originates from a contraposition between a part of society (the 'people', however defined) and 'the others'. The opposition of classes and social groups is of a different nature, arising from a conflict of interests over the distribution of income, wealth and power, and therefore presents itself on the level of economic rationality, and on that level can find points of equilibrium that vary according to power relations. Conflicts of interest are ineradicable; indeed, they can contribute positively to social dynamics, but they can also be disruptive; the outcomes, more or less positive or negative, depend to a considerable extent on the greater or lesser diffusion of social capital in the community, as well as the quality of the political leadership.

5.3 GREY NETWORKS: FROM AMORAL FAMILISM TO FREEMASONRY

The grey networks are the networks that are not illegal but whose primary purpose (in practice, though not formally) is the mutual support of members to the detriment of non-members of the network, with ideological covers that are more apparent than real.[9]

The two main examples of grey networks are amoral familism, in the broad sense,[10] and the varied array of masonic associations.

between realities distant in time, without taking into account what happened in the intermediate phases, can be misleading (Bagnasco, 1994).

9 The boundaries between what is legal and what is illegal depend, of course, on the law and may thus differ from country to country.

10 The term was coined by Banfield (1958), with reference to an entrenched ethos of maximizing the immediate material benefits of one's own household (and not the wider family clan, as is commonly understood today), assuming that everyone else behaves

In Italian culture (but not only there), it is common to claim that family ties come before the formal or ethical rules of fair behaviour towards a plurality of interested parties; in general, preferential treatment is often granted or demanded on the grounds of family relationships. (The terms 'prioritizing' and 'preferential treatment' underline the asocial element of these practices, which favour some and harm others.) Take, for example, the many cases of academic dynasties in universities, which are far more dangerous than favouritism towards own pupils.[11] Consider the widespread practice of pulling strings, direct or through intermediaries, for loved ones, in order to get a job, or a pass in exams, or preferential medical treatment.

Favouritism towards family members – either as active practice or supine acceptance – is a cultural phenomenon typical of a patriarchal society, which may conflict with the demands of a modern society. A distinction can also be made between a more or less normal and a pathological level. The former corresponds to a normal manifestation of family affection, within the limits determined by the need not to harm others. The latter occurs when the advantage of a family member amounts to a disadvantage for others. If I have my daughter win a competition for an unmerited professorship, I have damaged a more deserving candidate. If I get my mother to have a nuclear magnetic resonance scan ahead of her position on the waiting list, I have made everyone ahead of her wait an extra shift.

Love for the family is, on the whole, a commendable sentiment and is also one of the foundations of a modern society: consider the effort it takes to bring up children, or care for the sick elderly.

in the same way. Banfield sees amoral familism as the explanation for Southern Italy's backwardness.

[11] I must point out that I am the son, nephew, brother and father-in-law of university professors, but all active in different fields (respectively, Romance philology, chemistry, philosophy, physics), and none of us has ever lifted a finger in favour of the others, not even when one or the other has been the victim of the factiousness of others.

To give just one example, the Italian rule that spouses cannot work in the same university department is absurd, because it is not unusual for spouses to be active in the same field of research, perhaps having met at work: the separation of a family unit hinders the pursuit of positive family roles, while what must be combated head-on is the malpractice of favouritism. As can be seen here, when favouritism is so widespread as to require preventive intervention *erga omnes*, social inefficiency is created (only acceptable insofar as the amoral familism damage avoided clearly outweighs the negative consequences of preventive intervention, and there are no other ways to deal with it).

A different assessment must be made of the Freemasonry: more widespread and above all more robust than is often believed, it was originally a positive element of progress, when authoritarian governments made the open pursuit of political goals, such as national independence or throwing off the clerical yoke, impossible. In a democratic society, however, Freemasonry plays a purely negative role, as an opaque centre for the exchange of favours.

In fact, the characteristic feature of Freemasonry (and similar associations) is precisely that, in addition to the negative element of the exchange of favours, there is also the negative element of opacity. This implies the possibility of coordinated interventions in favour of some, therefore to the detriment of others, perceived only ex post by those who are harmed, with a serious deformation of professional competition. In the political field, the opacity of network connections – as, precisely, in the case of freemasonry – constitutes a heavily negative element; as Bobbio (2011, p. 99) observes, this 'is a problem that the academic literature underestimates'.[12]

[12] Insisting on the theme, Bobbio (2011, p. 6) quotes Kant's maxim: 'All actions relating to the right of other men, whose maxim is not susceptible to publicity, are unjust'. He then distinguishes between 'invisible power' 'directed against the state ... such as the mafia'; the power directed to 'gain illicit benefits' from public power, such as secret associations; and 'invisible power as an institution of the state: the secret services', perhaps necessary but 'to be controlled by the government, by the visible power which in turn is controlled by the citizens' (2011, pp. 8–9).

The Italian Constitution (Article 18, second paragraph) is clear: 'Secret associations and those that pursue, even indirectly, political aims through military-type organisations are prohibited.' Nevertheless, Article 1 of the Spadolini–Anselmi law passed to dissolve Italy's notorious P2 Lodge (Law No. 17 of 25 January 1982) limits the qualification of secret associations to those that 'carry out activities aimed at interfering with the exercise of the functions of constitutional bodies, public administrations … as well as essential public services of national interest.' Referring to this law, in the drafting of which he claims Freemason jurists participated, Grand Master Giuliano Di Bernardo concludes that 'an association [such as Freemasonry, we add] while having all the requirements of secrecy, if it does not plot against the organs of the State, is not secret' (Pinotti, 2021, p. 84). However, Freemasonry would fall under this definition of a secret lodge, albeit a restrictive one with respect to the perfectly clear intentions shown in the Italian Constitution, as soon as its members tried to influence public appointments and offices, which as we all know never happens … All in all, it would seem most appropriate that membership of Freemasonry should be strictly prohibited for magistrates, senior military officers, university professors and anyone holding political office.[13]

Associations such as the Rotary or Lions, which do not share with Freemasonry the element of opacity, but which often share with it the social base of professionals and leaders, have a positive function as long as they limit themselves to a socializing role and cultural or charitable initiatives (which is actually quite often the case), but they can hardly help also forming a network for the exchange of favours, even if their non-opaque nature makes them much less harmful than the Freemasonry.

[13] Apart from the P2 case, Freemasonry has been repeatedly involved in judicial investigations. Pinotti (2021, p. 109) reports that 'Falcone … had basically understood – as various enquiries would later ascertain – that Freemasonry represented [in Palermo, in lodges of the Ancient and Accepted Scottish Rite] the meeting ground between white-collar workers and organised crime'.

5.4 BLACK NETWORKS: P2

In addition to the negative characteristics of grey networks (support network and opacity), black networks are also marked by their dedication to illegal activities (thus constituting unmitigated criminal associations).

The main examples of black networks are criminal organizations such as, in Italy, the mafia, the camorra, the ndrangheta and the sacra corona unita. From the point of view of the power issue, an exemplary case is the P2, a 'covered' (i.e. secret) Masonic lodge, both in terms of the influence it has had and because – a very rare case – we have quite a lot of information about it, albeit incomplete.[14]

An episode too distant to be remembered by the youngest and too recent (and hot) to be taught in schools, the Propaganda Due (P2) lodge was founded in 1877 as a Masonic lodge of the Grand Orient of Italy, from the outset marked by reinforced secrecy; in 1975 Licio Gelli became its Venerable Master, having already been its de-facto leader since 1970. Since then, the P2 has been linked to various plot-like activities, with a strategy outlined in a so-called 'Democratic Rebirth Plan'. After the accidental discovery, in March 1981, of a list of 962 illustrious affiliates and the scandal that followed, a law of 25 January 1982 dissolved the lodge, making secret associations with similar aims illegal, in accordance with the Constitution (Article 18, paragraph 2), The Grand Orient instead limited itself to suspending Gelli without taking action on the lodge or its members, including ministers, political leaders, senior ranks of the army, navy, finance, police, carabinieri, journalists, top executives of state companies, diplomats and entrepreneurs (such as Silvio Berlusconi). Some politicians and various journalists even argued the innocuousness of the lodge, reduced to a quasi-legitimate centre for the exchange of recommendations and favours (grey network if not white!).[15]

[14] In what follows I take up part of my study on P2 economics (Roncaglia, 2012).

[15] It was not until 21 November 1996 that the Supreme Court issued its final ruling, confirming the secret and criminal nature of the lodge, while denying that it had

The Parliamentary Commission of Enquiry into the P2 Lodge, instituted in December 1981 and led by Tina Anselmi, carried out a precious and difficult task. Without the Commission's work, practically nothing would be known about the P2 lodge. Tina Anselmi's diaries, published by Anna Vinci (2011), help us understand the difficulties of an investigation obstructed by many, conducted amidst repeated attempts at disinformation, in an environment where it was difficult to establish whom to trust and whom not to. The Final Report is a compelling read, and is supported by an impressive body of documentation collected in 120 volumes of Proceedings. Nothing substantial has subsequently been added to the elements gathered by the Anselmi Commission, in particular on the background of the P2 lodge, on its Atlantic inspiration and on the role of its members. The hypotheses remain as they were at the time (concerning, for example, the use for political and economic blackmail of the old secret service files, which should have been destroyed, but were not, and ended up in the hands of Gelli; or the existence of a list of members even more important than the others, which remained secret; or indeed the direct involvement of the lodge and/or some of its members in coup and criminal activities)[16] – if we want to stick to the established facts, we must limit ourselves to the documents that the Commission collected, first and foremost among which the so-called Rebirth Plan (seized in July 1982 at Fiumicino airport).[17]

The political project of the P2, as it emerges from this document, is well known: control over society and, above all, the greater

carried out any conspiratorial activity as such. In 2020, however, the Bologna Public Prosecutor's Office concluded that leading members of the lodge, including Gelli, were among the instigators of the massacre at Bologna railway station on 2 August 1980 (85 victims, over 200 injured); further legal proceedings were blocked by the death of the suspects. Gelli had been convicted of aggravated slander (misdirecting criminal investigation) in connection with the same affair, with a sentence confirmed by the Supreme Court on 23 November 1995.

[16] On the secret service (Sifar) files, see the accurate reconstruction by Franzinelli (2010, pp. 23 ff.).

[17] Another important line of research concerns the economic influence of the lodge, through the presence of its members on boards of directors (interlocking directorships)

efficiency claimed in the management of public affairs, based not on a traditional type of dictatorship but on the constitution of a secret network of personal relationships and control over the mass media, and thus on a policy of cultural hegemony achieved with partially illegal methods. Efficiency – technology – is assigned supremacy over politics, with the claim that the choices made by a self-selected group of optimates are better than those resulting from free and open debate, which is absurd in the scientific field and undemocratic in the political sphere. The choices that affect the distribution of wealth and power are delegated to a control centre which, according to the Rebirth Plan, should have included a few politicians with instrumental functions alongside the heads of the judiciary, the army, state administration and the media. Priority is attached to controlling political parties, the press (including TV) and trade unions. In a country where 70 per cent of the population reads neither books nor newspapers (as Tullio De Mauro, 2010, points out), control of television is considered essential. As the Rebirth Plan states, newspapers and television constitute the instrument to 'control the average public opinion in the heart of the country'.

It is worth dispelling a misunderstanding that the Plan, and all the variants that subsequently appeared in Italian political life, were indeed mapped along conservative lines, but in a liberal spirit. Let us distinguish between political liberalism and economic liberalism. In the noble fathers of liberalism, from Adam Smith and John Stuart Mill to Hayek or Einaudi, the two cannot be distinguished: freedom of action in the economic field is in reality a simple corollary of the general freedom of action that must be recognized to the individual. As Smith (1759, p. 82) explains, 'Every man is, no doubt, by nature, first and principally recommended to his own care; and as he is fitter to take care of himself than of any other person, it is fit and right that it should be so'. The limits to individual freedom

and the related network of shareholding crossings. The findings arrived at by Lucarelli and Perone (2018) are striking.

of action are to be found in the damage that can be done to others; it is precisely on this basis that Smith, and many other liberal authors behind him, point to the need to place constraints on the economic freedom of action of capitalists, towards whom, indeed, Smith harbours a deep distrust. Freedom of economic action, the famous 'laissez faire, laissez passer' of Monsieur de Gournay and Turgot, is a progressive motto, in its limited reference to the economic field, only in an autocratic society such as France was in the mid-eighteenth century.

In the economic field, the freedom of action of the individual entrepreneur is (or rather, is believed to be) constrained by the existence of competitors: the price of the product cannot be set as high as one likes, because otherwise buyers will turn to someone else. Without this constraint, economic freedom turns into the freedom of oligopolists and monopolists. In the political sphere, individual freedom implies not only a system of rules and laws that are the same for everyone, but also the possibility of competing on an equal footing with everyone else in determining political choices; hence, the absence of networks of personal relationships that benefit one to the detriment of the others, all the worse if they are confidential or even secret networks, and the full availability to every one of the information available to everyone else.

This is a fundamental point, which Norberto Bobbio (1984) stressed with reference to the P2 experience. After recalling the distinction between political representation and representation of interests, typical of a neo-corporative state, Bobbio went on to underline the existence of an even more vital distinction: between a state based on powers visible to all, and a state based on invisible powers. 'The invisible state [Bobbio affirms] is the radical antithesis of democracy'; 'it is beyond dispute that the P2 Lodge ... constituted ... an accomplished organisation of occult power within, behind, below (or above?) the state'.

Another point of the Rebirth Plan deserves to be mentioned: the abolition of registered shares. Among the first measures carried out by the fascist regime immediately after seizing power (and seen at the time as a favour by the fascists to the Vatican), the abolition of registered shares is the main instrument to make progressive taxation of incomes practically impossible, or indeed fair taxation of assets or control over economic power networks or conflicts of interest. The Rebirth Plan, presented in aseptic form as a tool to achieve better management of public affairs, is in fact an illiberal programme, not simply conservative but decidedly reactionary.[18]

5.5 ORGANIZED CRIME

As we have seen, the black networks par excellence are those of organized crime: in Italy, the Sicilian mafia, the Calabrian 'ndrangheta', the Campanian 'camorra' and the Apulian 'sacra corona unita', although they have gradually spread from their regions of origin throughout Italy and into various foreign countries. Born as anti-state powers to control limited areas (control over irrigation in the countryside, as Sylos Labini recalled in 1965 in connection with the mafia; as a way to squeeze cash or resources from shepherds or small entrepreneurs; as an anti-power with respect to the public officials sent by the state to collect taxes, and so forth), in more recent times their main activities have been drug trafficking, squeezing local shopkeepers and businesses, exploiting public contracts obtained through collusion with political authorities, but also illegal disposal of toxic waste or trafficking in organs for transplants.[19]

In interpretations of the mafia as a phenomenon, there is a contrast between a 'culturalist perspective', which 'in the most extreme forms reduces the mafia to the culture diffused in the contexts in which it has developed', and an 'organisational perspective', which in

[18] See Sylos Labini (1995, 2001, 2006).

[19] For an accurate historical reconstruction of the birth and development of mafia, ndrangheta and camorra up to the Second World War see Dickie (2011). For the subsequent period see Arlacchi (1983), then Sciarrone (1998, 2009). Comparison between the three volumes shows the profound changes that the mafia phenomenon has gone through over time, and how fitting is the construction of a new legal figure, the mafia-type association: regularly criticized by the lawyers of the defendants, and sometimes

the most radical theses likens the phenomenon to organized crime, picturing the mafia 'as: bureaucracy, community, system, enterprise, network' (Sciarrone, 1998, pp. 21 and 65). With respect to interpretations that focus only on the internal structure of mafia organizations, however, we must not lose sight of the fact that 'without external relations, the mafia would not be the persistent and dangerous phenomenon we know' (1998, p. 29); the strength of these relations, on the other hand, also depends on control over the territory and the associated reputation of strength and impunity, which differentiates the mafia and its sisters from common criminal associations. The mafia is in fact 'a multidimensional phenomenon' (1998, p. 68): a secret society with bonds of loyalty and a hierarchy of command, active in the exercise of violence, which instrumentalizes cultural tradition and manipulates social and political relations (1998, p. 69).

In the initial phase, the political class of notables (landowners, professionals) can use the mafia but are not conditioned by it, at least not to the extent of being dominated by it, and for its part, the mafia avoids direct clashes with the political class. In a subsequent phase, control over the territory leads to control over sectors of the electorate sufficient to condition political life; shortly afterwards, the 'entrepreneurial mafia' arrives on the scene, marked by a change in mentality: the 'conversion of the mafia to the religion of accumulation' (Arlacchi, 1983, p. 105). Trade between electoral support and the concession of public contracts becomes systematic. Enormous profits are possible thanks to elusion of controls on safety in the workplace, the quality of the materials used and the regularity of the disposal of processing residues. Mafia entrepreneurs have the enormous advantage of murder and violence as new weapons in the competitive struggle, but can also count on systematic evasion of social security and insurance contributions, and non-payment of overtime

unapplied in court, taking reference from the outdated traditional conception of the mafioso with *coppola* and *lupara*. The reports and acts of the Parliamentary Commissions of Enquiry on the mafia are very useful, even though they are often scattered from the point of view of historical reconstruction.

(Arlacchi, 1983, pp. 115 ff.). The extra profits obtained in this way guarantee solid financial foundations, and can easily be transferred, in the absence of adequate controls over money movements, from the illegal sector to the legal sector of the economy, to the extent of conditioning the activity of important financial operators. The banker Sindona played an important role in this respect, opening a channel of communication between the Mafia economy and the legal financial circuits. In this situation, curbing the expansion of mafia organizations is a formidable challenge; in fact, the infiltration of mafia-type associations into the legal economy has major distorting repercussions on social and economic life.

The development of the entrepreneurial mafia did not lead to a development of the economy: rather, mafia enterprises substituted already active enterprises. There was thus a shift from 'a concrete, limited power of territorial and social governance' to 'the acquisition of an abstract, unlimited economic power' (Arlacchi, 1983, p. 181). The domination of mafia organizations (including the ndrangheta, camorra and similar formations) over the drug markets constituted another advantage, given the financial resources deriving from them, for the mafia-controlled enterprises operating in the traditional sectors of the economy and spreading through central-northern Italy and abroad, especially in the fields of commerce (including wholesale), construction, tourism and catering.

Between the end of the 1970s and the beginning of the 1990s, while the fight against red terrorism kept the best forces of the state busy, the mafia reached the peak of its power: it was in business with the Vatican, through Sindona and then through the Calvi-Marcinkus duo (at a time when the Vatican needed 'dirty money' to finance Poland's Solidarnosc revolt);[20] it had access to the highest levels of the government;[21] there were strong signs of collaboration with

[20] See Nuzzi (2009).

[21] Salvo Lima, the leader of Andreotti's faction of the Christian democrats in Sicily, became Undersecretary of Finance in the 1972 Andreotti government; Lima's

rogue intelligence services and the P2 lodge to fuel the strategy of tension; it reached the point of blackmailing the state (the bombs in Piazza dei Georgofili in Florence and various other emblematic sites), eventually giving rise to suspicions of state-mafia negotiations (trial in progress). What emerges in this phase is 'the intrinsically political character of the mafia, a criminal structure oriented towards the pursuit and exercise of power' (Sciarrone, 1998, p. 20). A sequence of 'excellent' assassinations put a long series of honest magistrates, politicians and police officers out of the way, until the Capaci massacre, when Falcone lost his life together with his wife and escort, and the assassination of Borsellino and his escort. The reaction of the honest part of the State, which seemed to come at the ninetieth minute, was partly a legacy of the work of some exceptionally valuable magistrates, like Falcone and Borsellino, and partly a last-minute burst of pride on the part of many when the situation was on the brink of collapse. The mobilization of public opinion played an important role in this, thanks, among other things, to the associations of the victims' families, although the persistent perverse relations between the Mafia and politics, extending from the local to the national level and all too often accepted for electoral convenience, continued to get in the way of real advance.

A milestone in the anti-mafia reaction had been set in 1982 with the Rognoni-La Torre law (Law 646 of 13 September 1982), which introduced the crime of 'mafia-type association' (Article 416 bis) into the criminal code for the first time and provided for the seizure of mafia assets. Between February 1986 and December 1987, on the basis of this law, a ground-breaking 'maxi-trial' was held in Palermo thanks to an anti-Mafia pool including Falcone and Borsellino, which used the evidence of some repented mafia bosses

proximity to Cosa Nostra is mentioned in various court documents. His murder by the Mafia, on 12 March 1992, took place after the failure of his attempts to obtain a reduction in the sentences of the so-called maxi-trial in Palermo, which sentenced many Mafia bosses to life imprisonment. Cf. 'Salvo Lima', online at: it.wikipedia.org (last accessed 5 May 2022).

like Tommaso Buscetta to bring to light the organizational structure and modus operandi of Cosa Nostra. The trial ended with 316 convictions, 19 of them for life. On appeal, the number and weight of the sentences were reduced, and they were partly reinstated by the Court of Cassation (30 January 1992) when several defendants, released from prison in the meantime, had been murdered in the mafia wars or had gone into hiding.

However, the Palermo maxi-trial marks a turning point with respect to the tradition that left many mafia crimes unpunished, both in the first degrees of judgment and with the repeated annulments of convictions in the Supreme Court.[22]

Weakened by the outcome of the Palermo maxi-trial, and by the continued application of Article 416 bis in other trials, the mafia has gradually returned to strength by operating under the radar. Moreover, compared to the traditional Sicilian mafia, weighed down by the relative rigidity of its pyramid structure, other mafia-type associations, in particular the ndrangheta and camorra, have grown stronger, characterized by a variety of smaller, more flexible and constantly evolving structures; control is often limited to restricted areas of territory. Overall, the phenomenon of mafia-type associations, characterized by intimidation and *omertà*, has spread. The judicial response is still uncertain; recently the profile of mafia-type association was recognized in the case of the Spada clan of Ostia, acknowledged in first instance and denied in appeal in the 'Mafia Capital' trial.

The mafia-type associations are no longer compact organizations under the government of a 'dome' (*cupola*, which existed only for a relatively brief period, and only for the Sicilian mafia), but a variety of criminal associations, characterized by 'mafia methods' which are now codified: the subjugation of counterparts through fear-mongering, reiterated by threats and, if necessary, by violence against

[22] Between 1861 and 1992, there were only ten life sentences for mafiosi in the Palermo district; in a much shorter period, from 1993 to 2006, life sentences rose to 430 (Sales, 2001).

those who refuse to submit, in order to arrive at the control of even relatively limited areas of territory; the corruption of public powers, and in particular politicians, also through vote trading, by now widespread, often intuitable from voting analysis, but very difficult to demonstrate judicially. These associations, which are constantly evolving, sometimes enter into relations with each other for specific purposes and limited periods of time.

The weight gained by the mafia is considerable; episodes such as the intertwining of mafia interests and those of the Vatican behind the Sindona case first and then the Calvi-Banco Ambrosiano case have left major after-effects and are indicative of an extremely difficult situation, in Italy as in the government of the Catholic Church. The intertwining of organized crime and neo-fascist extremism is evidenced by too many episodes to be ignored. Above all, from their territories of origin, mafia-type associations have created colonies in the centre and north of the country since the 1970s, partly accompanying migratory movements (and the numerous measures of forced residence), partly favoured by the experience accumulated in certain sectors of criminal activity, such as drug trafficking and the provision of protection services, and partly stimulated by the search for financial outlets for mafia capital.[23] Now the economic and social crisis resulting from the Covid-19 epidemic risks further weakening the state apparatus (many trials postponed, delays in many investigations) while favouring the spread of the economic power of organized crime and its grip on the territory.[24]

[23] See the last chapters of Sciarrone's important study in 1998, in particular pp. 330–444 on the case of Piedmont.

[24] Some recent analyses of the economics of crime are collected in a special issue of the *Italian Economic Journal* (vol. 6 no. 2, July 2020).

6 The State

6.1 THE BIRTH OF THE STATE (AND ITS DISSOLUTION?)

The nation state, as we now know it, is the result of a long process of creation and then of growth and development, which culminated in the mid-nineteenth century. Since the mid-twentieth century its powers have continued to expand in several respects (such as social welfare), but in other respects they have shrunk and have given way to new supranational power.

The modern state follows the rule of law, based on a set of rules made public (though not always strictly enforced) applicable also to politicians themselves. These are chosen according to preordained rules which can only be changed in certain ways and within limits preordained by higher-ranking rules, usually incorporated into a constitution. The political struggle for electing politicians concerns the control of institutions. At first glance political power can be identified with state power at a legal/institutional level.

There are several ways to interpret those characteristics that define membership of a state. Among these, ethnicity has a long tradition, and not infrequently terrifying applications. Fortunately, the dominant element today is legal: the state comprises a territory recognized, de facto if not de jure, by the international community, and the population residing therein, except as set out in its laws. The state is characterized by its own system of laws, and this also determines the way in which political competition occurs.

The modern state is not necessarily characterized by private property. A space for private property has always remained even in the strictest communist countries, where state ownership of the means of production is (or was) in force. At the other extreme, even in the most pro-market countries, the state occupies a significant economic space. The market plays a fundamental role as a countervailing power to that of the state, adding to the system of checks and balances that every modern country incorporates in its constitution and which – as Montesquieu teaches – are indispensable to stop it assuming oppressive forms for its citizens.

Compared to feudal society, in which power was exercised via a lord's direct rule over his lands and subjects, transition to the rule of law implied the affirmation (which increased as time passed) of rights of the individual, starting with private property. Machiavelli points to the integration between town and country as a central element in the formation of the nation state, together with the creation of an army. William Petty (1690) identifies another central element, namely the link between the different economic activities exercised by a set of autonomous subjects, in a regime of division of labour within the state territory. This latter aspect also marks a limit: although international trade exists, the variety of economic activities within a state are in principle self-sufficient. We thus have the concept of an economic system, upon which the development of Classical political economy is based, superimposed upon that of the nation state.[1]

Among the various theories concerning the origin of the nation state, Gellner (1983) argues that such origins correspond to the third stage of human development – the industrial stage, which comes after hunting and agriculture. Industrialization requires being able to communicate through interpersonal messages, including written messages, hence an educational system that favours increasing cultural homogeneity. The national spirit presents itself as a demand for congruence between the cultural community and the political community. The stimulation of this principle consequently leads to the birth of the nation state. In short, the transition to modernity generates the idea (and the spirit) of nationalism, and this is what creates

[1] See Roncaglia (1977, pp. 71–86).

nations. In this sense, nationalism has a positive function; further on (Section 7.3) we shall consider the totalitarian drift of nationalism.

For Gellner, therefore, the nation is not a fact of nature, but of culture. 'Two men are of the same nation if and only if they share the same culture ... if and only if they *recognise* each other as belonging to the same nation' (Gellner, 1983, p. 8).

Of course there is a great difference between the theoretical concept of the nation state and its actual manifestations. In theory the nation state is considered closed, while in reality the relations between different state entities are very important, especially in economics, but also at a cultural level. As we shall see later, this is fundamental to 'hold society together'. In theory, codified laws – or common law in the English system – reign unchallenged; actually, political and economic power have many forms (including direct influence upon the legal system) to escape these constraints. In many states there is a strong countervailing power of extra-legal if not outright illegal associations and various forms of organized crime, such as the mafia in Italy or the Yakuza in Japan or the drug cartels in Central and South America. In other respects, the countervailing power of hierarchies and religious organizations is strong: one need only think of the role of Opus Dei in Spain and elsewhere, the Vatican in Italy, and the religious basis of so many Islamic states.

Finally, productive interrelationships between different countries/economic systems have been strengthened more and more. In the most recent phase, with global value chains, manufacturing has been segmented into different areas of the world; finance now operates without recognizing state borders. The allocation of direct investment between countries, with its significant employment effects, involves competition between institutional arrangements (tax systems, environmental constraints, health and safety regulations, labour market rules and customs), with a downward alignment drive and powerful constraints on national economic policies. The spread of English as the lingua franca of the Internet and social media is moving in the direction of breaking down borders between states and regions of the world, with the development of a global culture. The number and role of supranational institutions and those of international coordination has increased; private international law (*jus mercatorum*) is gaining importance.[2]

We are not yet facing the dissolution of the nation state, but certainly a strong erosion of its autonomy: from the level of state authorities, power is moving downwards – towards the system of local communities – and upwards, with the increasing globalization of institutions, the economy and culture. It is difficult to predict how it will develop, but it is certain that its influence on the nature and distribution of power will remain enormous.[3]

6.2 WEBER: THE STATE AS A MONOPOLY OF LEGITIMATE FORCE

Among the many theories about the nation state, one of the most important is that of Max Weber. In a nutshell, his thesis is that the state, under the rule of law, is characterized by a monopoly of the legitimate use of force: both outwardly, through the army, and inwardly, through the police, the formation of laws and the administration of justice. According to Weber's famous definition, 'the state is that human community, which within the limits of a given territory ... demands for itself (successfully) the *monopoly of legitimate physical force* ... it is the only source of the "right" to force'.[4]

This definition can only be the starting point of our analysis. To simplify, we can distinguish three different aspects: what processes

[2] See Mazzoni and Malaguti (2019). An international private association based in Italy, Unidroit, seeks to promote coordination between the different national legal systems, especially as regards commercial law, including the stimulation of treaties on specific issues of great economic importance.

[3] 'The nation state is becoming too small for the big problems of life, and too big for the small problems of life ... in short, there is a mismatch problem' (Bell, 1987, p. 14).

[4] Weber (1919, p. 48; see also p. 55). An earlier, less precise definition was published posthumously in *Economy and Society* (Weber, 1922b, p. 53). For Weber, force is not the normal means of the state, but its specific means. Note also that Weber's definition insists on the *legitimacy* of the use of force, and only subsidiarily on *legality*, which can take a variety of forms.

lead to the formation of a state? What forces hold it together, or rather ensure that a complex society, full of conflicts and contradictions, does not implode? And under what conditions can a state prosper, stagnate or decline?

The story giving rise to the birth of the modern state concerns the economy, with the development of the market economy and the birth of capitalism. Culture played an important part with Protestantism nurturing a form of mind favourable to concrete commitment and individual initiative, to calculating risks and keeping them under control as far as possible in a long-term perspective; hence the development of capitalism, which in turn favoured the dominance of reason over passions,[5] and hence acceptance of the rule of law; the development of institutions which, from the *jus mercatorum* and the subordination of the countryside to the cities, led to a single body of rules. This, together with the rationalization of economic and social life, favoured the calculability of the outcomes of choices, and in particular economic choices.[6]

Around this notion revolves interpretation of the nature and tasks of the state: in constant evolution, characterized by a twofold tendency towards consolidation and disintegration. The development of technology and bureaucracy works in the first direction, allowing for increasing control over social life. In turn, this leads to the growth of a political-bureaucratic apparatus, within which political power plays a dominant role in principle, but with its weight varying according to circumstances. It derives its democratic legitimacy from the electorate, so it should have a function of guidance and control over

[5] See Elias (1939) on the 'civilisation process' and Hirschman (1977) on the interrelationship between passions and interests and the transition from the dominance of the former in feudalism to the latter in the modern era. Of course, the process of civilization proceeds at different rates and in different ways in different countries; for example, Elias emphasizes the relatively greater persistence in German culture of warrior values and the aristocratic code of honour, together with traits of contempt or undervaluation of the virtues of tolerance and willingness to compromise.

[6] For the most recent phase, characterized by an acceleration of change, Beck (1986) notes an opposite trend, towards incalculability and thus towards a 'risk society'.

bureaucracy; however, increasingly, the technical (and in particular legal) skills required for legislative and governmental activity tend to endow the top echelons of the bureaucracy with autonomous and directly political power. Thus, bureaucracy has a systematic tendency to expand, and in some phases can acquire considerable autonomy from the political apparatus, thus increasing its power.[7]

The political apparatus has the task of managing and directing the legal/institutional structure of the state; at the same time it organizes and channels a majority consensus 'from below' towards political and legislative choices. This requires a political class for which Weber saw a 'vocation' for the common good as the appropriate motivation.[8] However, as it grows in size, it seems to refer increasingly to itself alone, with a motivation that mainly aims at acquiring resources and defending its status as *princeps* within society. Yet, it must be recognized that 'for the politician ... the aspiration to power is the indispensable instrument of his work' (Weber, 1919, p. 102).

Today, this self-referentiality, along with the desire to 'keep one's seat', is manifested, among other things, in the ever more frequent recourse of political leaders to opinion polls and *spin doctors*: instrumental in continuously adapting to the electorate's orientations, renouncing at least in part the traditional active role of the political leader, of guiding public opinion based on the leader's own convictions. Compared to electoral competition between parties and leaders with different and clearly recognizable positions, an electoral market seems to prevail, based on the adaptation of political

[7] See the lively and at times impassioned account of an anonymous senior bureaucrat on the role of ministerial heads of cabinet, indicatively titled *Io sono il potere* (*I am power*), edited by Salvaggiulo (2020). Schmoller (1914) argues that civil servants, together with the self-employed, constitute a third social group other than capitalists and workers and can therefore pursue common interests, or at least remain outside the frontal opposition between the two classes on which Marx focuses.

[8] This does not mean that politicians should not be remunerated for their work: 'The government of a state or party by means of people who live exclusively for politics ... and not of politics, necessarily entails a "plutocratic" recruitment of politically leading categories' (Weber, 1919, p. 59). The problem is complex, and Weber discusses it at length in the essay 'Politics as a Profession' (in Weber, 1919, pp. 45–121).

personnel to the preferences of consumers/voters. These preferences are often volatile, based on an approximate knowledge of the issues and open to the influence of lobbies, which can influence popular orientations through advertising methods and the use of social media.

Not only (or not exclusively) do the growing costs of this apparatus – political and bureaucratic – of state management and the self-referential drift of the political and bureaucratic classes work towards disintegration, but also (and especially) the elements of globalization of the economy and culture already mentioned, to which we will return later on. We can thus see evolution towards a multilevel public power. The state is very often directed towards a federal model, with a downward delegation of tasks and powers. This is towards local authorities, from regions to local councils, and towards autonomous institutions with specific tasks and skills, such as central banks or the various authorities. Additionally, a complex series of supranational and international institutions intervene to condition and in some cases constrain state choices: from the United Nations to the World Trade Organization, and associations of states, the most powerful and most structured of which is the European Union.

This system of multilevel institutions was at least partly created to limit the use of force by the state, both externally and internally. Thus, for example, conflicts between Catholics and Protestants in Northern Ireland have been contained with the abolition of the border between the Irish Republic and Northern Ireland, thanks to their common membership of the European Union (which are now in danger of exploding again with the exit of the United Kingdom from the Union, which also makes the threat of the secession of Scotland from the United Kingdom topical again). At least to a certain extent something similar has happened in South Tyrol in Italy, the Basque Country and Catalonia in Spain, and the tensions between Flemish and Walloons in Belgium. Czechoslovak entry into the European Union has greatly facilitated its peaceful division into two independent states, the Czech Republic and Slovakia, which nevertheless find themselves with a basically single economic system, no borders, and a common set of rules.

As for international conflicts, the UN's power to contain them is limited but far from non-existent, as the intervention of UN peace-keeping forces has shown on several occasions.

Even within the limits of international treaties, the armed forces (external defence), the police forces and the judiciary (internal defence) are subject to national political authorities; the same applies to legislative powers except, in the case of EU countries, for the powers attributed to EU bodies, whose directives (but not regulations) must, however, be transposed by each country into their own legal system through specific legislative acts. Moreover, the state remains an essential point of reference in the cultural field: both because of the persistence of a widespread sense of national belonging (in peacetime manifested, for example, in sporting events), and because – very importantly – the organization and operation of the school and university education system remain within its competence. It also plays a role in guiding cultural orientations, through sector regulations, public appointments and a complex system of subsidies and funding.

6.3 SOCIAL CONTRACT AND TACIT CONSENT

What holds a state together? First of all, as Weber explained, a monopoly upon the legitimate use of force. Secondly, the acceptance by the citizens of this monopoly, for different personal reasons, utilitarian and idealistic, usually combined, linked partly to tradition and partly to culture.

The latter has been variously interpreted: in Rousseau's theory (and elsewhere) as a binding original covenant (a social contract); in the theory of Hume and others, as a non-binding but sufficiently strong cultural bond, based on the notion of tacit consent, more flexible than that of the social contract, such as may derive from the historical narrative (sometimes spiced with fantastic elements) of the glories of a nation or of its origins and growth.

The thesis of an original social contract from which civil society arises was formulated in different ways by various authors between the seventeenth and eighteenth centuries.[9] The common element is the idea that the obligations deriving from belonging to a civil society arise from an original agreement between the members of the society, which makes it possible to pass from a primitive society, characterized by all against all (*homo homini lupus*), to a society governed by rules of coexistence accepted by all, which make it possible to channel the efforts of each individual in the pursuit of the common good.

An original agreement (contract) may be explicit or implicit, relating to all or almost all aspects of life associated with it, or only a few basic elements. Here we shall focus on what can be considered the most extreme version, due to Rousseau (1762). He speaks of a 'general will' as the founding element of the social contract, thus referring to something that is beyond – above – each individual. Only those who adhere to all the elements of the social contract, that is, those who share the 'general will' with others, can be considered citizens: the beliefs, starting with religion, traditions and life practices that characterize a society. An example of this is Calvin's Geneva, where a city dweller dissenting from fellow citizens cannot be considered part of the community and is consequently expelled, if not condemned to be burned at the stake.

What Rousseau has in mind is a society that has the merit of being cohesive, but at the same time the defect of being closed to all differences, inimical to variety of opinion. It is not by chance that Rousseau was to be Lenin's reference for building the notion of the

[9] However, this is a much older idea. A beautiful example is the oath of allegiance to the sovereigns of Catalonia and Aragon from the twelfth century: 'We, who are as good as you, swear to you, who are no better than us, to accept you as our king and sovereign lord, provided you observe all our liberties and laws; but if not, not' (*Nós, que valem tant com vós, per separat, i junts més que vós, us investim sobirà i us jurem llialtat per tal que ens protegian, i traballeu per nostre progress; i si no, no*). Both the text and the English translation are taken from https://anglophone-direct.com/i-swear-catalan-oath. There are various texts of the oath, each slightly different, used in different periods, but always referring to Catalonia.

dictatorship of the proletariat:[10] in both cases, an organic aim dominates individuals, regulating and directing their life choices.

An important critique of Rousseau's social contract is provided by Mills (1997) with his notion of the 'racial contract'. While Rousseau (and, as Mills remarks, most other political theorists) assume a basically homogeneous society, Mills argues that Western societies are systematically founded on a social contract distinguishing between a superior and an inferior race (the whites and the blacks, the whites and the natives in North and South America or in Australia, and so on), and concerning as a matter of fact only those belonging to the superior race. Recognition of the 'racial contract' is a necessary step for any attempt at improving the situation by overcoming the racial dichotomy: a process that may require a long time (decades if not centuries, rather than years) but which is under way, as we may see by comparing the situation powerfully described by Mills with the contemporary situation. (As Mills remarks, something analogous may be said about a 'gender contract'.)

A much less rigid idea than Rousseau's of the presuppositions of social coexistence was proposed by Hume, who speaks of 'tacit consent', which is considered necessary only for certain basic aspects (for example, and significantly, not with regard to religious beliefs). Tacit consent can be seen as the fruit of an implicit and limited social contract, but it can also be seen more simply as the consequence of a tendency to seek the coexistence of human beings whose nature is that of 'social animals' (as a long tradition, from Aristotle onwards, and as Hume's friend Adam Smith also argue).

Hume observes that there is no contract to enforce contracts, nor would the law be sufficient without a widespread ethic to minimize violations, that is, a tacit consensus on the need to comply.[11]

[10] Cf. Colletti (1969, pp. 195 ff.).

[11] Hume (1752, pp. 465–87) (*Essays*, 'Of the original contract'). This position is taken up by Polanyi (1968, p. 74), who emphasizes the role of public authority in maintaining a sufficient degree of tacit consent: 'The function of power is to insure that measure of conformity which is needed for the survival of the group: as David Hume showed, its ultimate source is opinion'.

Tacit consent is an elastic notion; its greater or lesser extent corresponds to a greater or lesser cohesion in the society in question. A society in which only one religious belief prevails is more cohesive, to the extent that the few 'out-groups' do not necessarily arouse feelings of hostility or rejection, rather curiosity; the same applies to the few foreigners in a mono-ethnic country that has not experienced substantial migration flows for a long time.

A society with good cohesion is not necessarily preferable to one with greater internal diversification. Especially when uniformity (ethnic or religious, for example) has been achieved through policies of closure or expulsion, internally eliminated tensions can reach unsustainable levels externally, leading to wars, as has happened so many times in the past.

Tacit consent need not (cannot) embrace every aspect of associated life. There will be parochialism, supporting another football team often but not always related to parochialism, preferences for different types of music, different political orientations, different sexual orientations – all of which will add to the distributive conflicts inevitable in any market economy.[12] Thinning of the tacit consent may be brought to breaking point when various elements of tension come together: for instance, when political hostilities find support in racial or religious hatred.

The flexibility provided by a notion of tacit consent with limited scope is important insofar as it is compatible with the freedom of personal life choices, particularly in the sphere of sexual orientation. The risk of an all-pervasive mass culture can be countered not

[12] Huntington (2004) emphasizes the importance of citizens of a state recognizing their national identity, assigning it a high value in the context of the many types of identity that characterize each, of which he provides an indicative list: '*Ascriptive*, such as age, ancestry, gender, kin ..., ethnicity ..., and race; *Cultural*, such as ... language, nationality, religion, civilisation; *Territorial* ...; *Political*, such as ... interest group, ... party, ideology ...; *Economic*, such as job, occupation, profession, work group, ... class; *Social*, such as friends, club, team, colleagues, leisure group, status' (p. 27). Identities are 'overwhelmingly, constructed' (p. 22), so their relative importance can vary over time; the greater or lesser importance attached to national identity helps determine the strength of a state.

only by building a culture that is more open to differences (as well as rejecting legal rules that claim to sanction private choices), but also by defending the right to privacy as a matter of principle, which in this sense is an important element of freedom.[13]

For this reason, multi-ethnic or multi-religious societies are at the same time richer in cultural stimuli but also, inevitably, less cohesive and subject to a greater risk of disruptive tensions. Public support for a culture open to diversity, aiming at promoting coexistence and integration rather than the affirmation of identity (for example, as already mentioned, by giving preference to state schools over private schools), thus takes on real importance.

Obviously, different ideas about the foundations of civil coexistence have different implications for the nature and scope of the state's tasks, which in the case of a Rousseau-style social contract will be more comprehensive and incisive, whereas in the case of the Hume-style tacit consent may be more circumscribed and less binding. Neither conception, however, has logical consequences for the form economic institutions should take. Other later theories of the state focus on these.

6.4 THE STATE AS AN INSTRUMENT OF CLASS POWER, AS A LEGAL CONSTRUCTION OF THE MARKET AND AS A SPONTANEOUS ORDER

The Marxian view of the state recognizes it as an instrument of power of the ruling class,[14] the state of the bourgeoisie or, alternatively, the

[13] The point is well illustrated by a classic of liberal thought, John Stuart Mill (1859, pp. 68–9): 'Society ... practises a social tyranny more formidable than many kinds of political oppression, since, though not usually upheld by such extreme penalties, it leaves fewer means of escape, penetrating much more deeply into the details of life, and enslaving the soul itself. Protection, therefore, against the tyranny of the magistrate [i.e. political and judicial authority] is not enough: there needs protection also against the tyranny of the prevailing opinion and feeling; against the tendency of society to impose, by other means than civil penalties, its own ideas and practices as rules of conduct on those who dissent from them.'

[14] Bobbio (1976, pp. 21 ff.), in denying the existence of a Marxist theory of the state, refers to a different aspect: the absence of an adequate theoretical reflection on the

dictatorship of the proletariat. History is seen as the history of class struggles; the notion of the common good is rejected.

These theses found an ample following, but are less widespread today. In fact, they constitute an opposite extreme to the organicist theses that assert the existence of a higher purpose of society to which individuals must bend their behaviour. Like all extreme theses, the Marxian theory contains some truth, precisely in its opposition to the opposite extreme: social conflicts are endemic to any social organization, and to deny them under the pretext of the existence of a Rousseau-like 'general will' leads ultimately to a dictatorial society. However, wanting to deny any element of 'common good' seems equally wrong. In the terms of game theory, it would be tantamount to assuming that the coexistence of different interests always implies a zero-sum or negative-sum game, whereas in reality positive-sum games are possible, indeed very frequent. In these, depending on the decisions taken, the situation can improve for everyone. In other words, the societies in which we live are complex realities, in which elements of conflict coexist with elements of common interests; political choices can direct institutions towards positive-sum games rather than negative-sum games, even if the sign remains difficult to assess, also because the choices generally have a redistributive effect that for some classes or individuals can outweigh the overall positive or negative effect.

The thesis that the resolution of conflicts should be entrusted to the regulatory power of competitive markets is a feature of the dominant neo-liberal conception. According to this view, the distributive variables (income, wages, profit rates) express, under competitive conditions, the relative scarcity of the respective production factors (land, labour, capital); the response of these variables to the interplay of supply and demand should therefore ensure an

forms that a socialist state can take. Since it is considered a transitory form, destined to disappear with the (utopian) realization of the communist society, the dictatorial solution seems acceptable to Marxist theorists without much discussion.

optimal equilibrium with the full employment of available resources. Deviations from this optimal situation depend on the presence of elements hindering competition (such as trade unions), on errors of economic policy, or on unexpected shocks that would be more or less rapidly reabsorbed. However, apart from the fact that these deviations are systematic, the neo-liberal theory does not take into account the destructive criticism of the myth of the invisible hand of the market[15] and the fact that in any case the original distribution of resources is taken as given).

Within the neo-liberal conception, we can distinguish two streams with distinct characteristics: the ordoliberal (Eucken, Roscher and others) and the Hayekian.[16]

The first orientation, which looms large in German culture, emphasizes the importance of the institutions that underpin the functioning of the market. These legal institutions must be actively constructed. Moreover, they must be robust, to ensure both regular trade (in particular through a clear allocation of ownership of property rights)[17] and competitive markets, despite a spontaneous tendency towards the formation of monopoly power. The state has the right/duty not only to build such institutions and organize them into an adequately comprehensive and efficient legal system, but also

[15] For an illustration of the contemporary debate in economic theory see Roncaglia (2019).

[16] Both streams include differentiated individual positions. We then have a third, important, neo-liberal stream, namely Friedman and his Chicago colleagues, who take a position similar to Hayek's as regards the nature and role of the institutions governing the market economy.

[17] The issue of the attribution of property rights is certainly not new. As early as the second half of the seventeenth century, William Petty underlined the usefulness of the institution of a land register (which at that time only existed in Holland) in order to make certain the private ownership of land, which for centuries had been at the centre of an infinite number of disputes, often decided arbitrarily by political power. On Petty, see Roncaglia (1977), p. 74. Not by chance, the first known vernacular text in Italy (the so-called Placito Capuano, dated 960) concerns a land dispute: '*Sao ko kelle terre, per kelle fini que ki contene, trenta anni le possette parte Sancti Benedicti*'. (I know that those lands with those boundaries were owned for the past thirty years by Saint Benedict' monks).

to defend them against the continuous pressure of economic and political potentates to bend them to their interests.[18]

The ordoliberals share with the marginalist theory of the Chicago monetarist school or the Austrian Hayek school a belief in the invisible hand of the market, provided that the competitive nature of the market is preserved. It is in this confidence, common to all neo-liberal orientations, that their limit can be seen.

The point of theoretical and political disagreement between the ordoliberals and the Austrian and monetarist schools (which led to an albeit partial break within the Mont Pélerin Society, the association founded by Hayek and which played an important role in coordinating the various streams in a common effort for the cultural rise of neo-liberal thought) concerns the need for active anti-trust policies, advocated by the ordoliberals, initially only partly shared by Hayek, who on this essential point ended up siding with the Chicago school, which tends to view public intervention in the economy as negative in any case.[19]

Another point of disagreement concerns the creation of the institutions that guarantee the smooth functioning of the market. For Hayek (who sees his major contributions precisely in the field of

[18] A theme that the ordoliberals do not dwell on, despite the experience of Nazism (which most – but not all – of them opposed) concerns the importance of a strong civil society, open to political debate and diversity. Together with the belief in the myth of the invisible hand of the market, this constitutes a major limitation for their theory. Those who – like many authoritative Italian jurists such as Irti (1998) – have developed certain aspects of their conception (the importance of market institutions and anti-monopoly policy) but not others (the myth of the invisible hand of the market, a conservative if not authoritarian political conception) should not be identified with them.

[19] Van Horn and Mirowski (2009, p. 162) attribute to the Chicago school 'a repression of overt considerations of power, both within economics and in neoliberal political theory'. Under the direction of Aaron Director (Friedman's brother-in-law), the Free Market Study group set up at the University of Chicago with the support of a conservative foundation, the Volker Fund (on whose activity see Van Horn and Mirowski, 2009) went far beyond Clark's (1940) interpretation of competition as 'workable competition', and came to regard anti-trust interventions as statist intrusions into free private activity. The 'old' Chicago school (Knight, Simons, Viner) considered a serious anti-trust policy necessary.

analysis of the formation of complex orders), the development of social institutions follows a selection process in which the best institutions assert themselves. This is not a Darwinian process, with the selection of individuals based on their innate characteristics, but the spontaneous formation of institutions and customs, rules and laws. Spontaneous social order can facilitate adaptation to changing conditions, and moreover, change that occurs in unforeseen directions.

Hayek was opposed to 'constructivist rationalism', that is, the idea that it is possible and appropriate to construct social institutions from above, according to the precepts of impersonal and objective reason: an idea that in his view inevitably generates authoritarian tendencies. The *taxis* (made order) is thus contrasted negatively with the *cosmos* (grown order).[20]

The idea that the spontaneous formation of institutions leads to optimal results, or at least to efficient and adequate institutions, is a replication on a larger scale of the faith in the invisible hand of the market, or in this case in an invisible hand that guides individuals belonging to a society towards optimal outcomes not only at the economic but also at the political, cultural, legal and institutional level. As in the case of the invisible hand of the market, this faith does not rest on adequate theoretical foundations, but is essentially a matter of begging the question.[21]

The ordoliberals are 'constructivist rationalists', to use Hayek's terminology. In their view, as far as institutional arrangements are concerned, market economies tend to move away from competition, which must therefore be guaranteed by appropriate anti-monopoly institutions. The facts – the concrete evolution of market economies – have borne out their thesis, rather than Hayek's,

[20] Hayek (1973, p. 37).

[21] Begging the question the other way round could lead to asserting that the evolution of the state tends towards dictatorship. Onfray (2019) points out this danger in today's situation; it would be arrived at through 'seven main stages: destroying freedom; impoverishing language; abolishing truth; suppressing history; denying nature; propagating hatred; aspiring to empire'. On the path to dictatorship, Onfray attaches great importance to 'Big Brother' who acquires a mass of private data on our lives.

with the continuous formation and strengthening of concentrated economic power. However, Hayek and Friedman's theses eventually predominated, both within the Mont Pélerin Society and within the variegated group of neo-liberals, because of the decisive advantage they bring in international competition between institutional systems. In fact, the freedom of movement of capital between countries ensured by the rules of the international game after the collapse of Bretton Woods favours countries with a 'small state' (less welfare state; more limited environmental or workplace, health and safety constraints; constraints on free bargaining in the labour market and the consequent strengthening of employers' bargaining power; lower taxation, especially on corporate profits). The result is a growing diffusion of neo-liberal institutions on an international scale.

We owe a particular version of the thesis that interprets the allocation of political power as a market game to Schumpeter (1942) who identifies electoral victory (and not the realization of a better society, albeit understood in the most diverse ways) as the objective of politicians, who consequently choose strategies to maximize consensus, however obtained, that leads to the desired result. This thesis is based upon a pessimistic view of human nature, and in particular of politicians, who are considered to be devoid of idealism. Choosing to be a professional politician is assumed to be opportunistically motivated. Gradually, this view seems to have influenced the selection of politicians (which to a considerable extent is self-selection), all over the world and in particular in Italy, with a distinct decline in moral qualities compared to the immediate post-WWII Liberation.

6.5 INTERNAL ORDER AND THE ADMINISTRATION OF JUSTICE

Since the birth of political economy, economists have stressed that internal order and the efficient administration of justice are essential to the smooth functioning of the economy. Adam Smith, who assumes a society mostly made up of sufficiently honest individuals, nevertheless considers the administration of justice and the police to be essential for maintaining civil coexistence in a society based on the division of labour. According to a more pessimistic but probably more realistic view of the moral standard of citizens (the 'Sylos Labini rule': '10% very good, 10% very bad, and the rest adaptable'), much depends on a rigorous and efficient administration of justice that can tip the scales, that is, the orientation of the intermediate band towards one side or the other. A similar, important role can be played by a more or less widespread civic culture of legality.

Here our reference is to Italy, but much the same considerations apply to many other countries.[22] Breaking the rules is extremely widespread. The most common infringement, tax evasion (especially if we add tax elusion, often linked to poorly drafted rules suggested by powerful lobbies),[23] robs the public budget of huge sums, amounting to several percentage points of GDP. Corruption also causes enormous damage: when a bribe puts construction of a bridge into the hands of a dishonest firm, another bribe avoids checks and the bridge – built with shoddy materials – then collapses, the damage does not amount to the bribe or to the extra profits of the criminal firm, but exceeds the total value of the order. If the disposal of toxic wastes ends up in the hands of criminals, the health damage can be incalculable (as the case of Terre di Fuoco teaches us); simply cleaning up illegal dumps can cost enormous sums of money.[24]

The spread of crime (especially in the case of organized crime) can lead to actual forms of territorial control. In the suburbs of large urban agglomerations, drug dealing adds up to blackmailing of shopkeepers, illegal occupation of houses, covering up of robberies and

[22] Italy ranks 52nd out of 180 countries in the Corruption Perceptions Index 2020 (Transparency International, 2021).

[23] An impressive example is provided by the events in the Italian oil sector recounted by a great magistrate, Mario Almerighi (2006).

[24] To give just one example of an issue I have had occasion to study (cf. Roncaglia, 1989; Pease et al., 1989; Darvas et al., 1991), I am opposed to the construction of nuclear power stations not because of their theoretical danger – which for new-generation power stations is practically zero – but because of the risk that the construction of the safety infrastructure will be entrusted to corrupt hands that use poor quality materials or skimp on controls.

burglaries, and illegal recycling of toxic waste. In their day-to-day operations, police forces are often forced to come to terms, to turn a blind eye to minor offences in exchange for a few tips on the occasional more serious crimes. At times, political extremism or organized football supporters create underworld links that can influence political and economic power centres. Those black networks mentioned in Chapter 5 have electoral strength, can infiltrate high finance and make alliances with certain political forces and important religious circles. The game of blackmail between the controlled and the controllers can be so widespread as to foster acquiescence rather than social rejection on the part of the people involved.[25]

Both the police and the administration of justice are thus absolutely necessary. At the same time, they constitute a use of force by the state. Thus arises the problem we set out in the previous section: insofar as the state is run in the interests of the ruling class, the police and the administration of justice play a role in ensuring its persistence in power. In fact, in dictatorial regimes (such as fascism in Italy) the judiciary and the police operate as instruments for the repression of dissent.

In order to understand the distribution of power in society, it is therefore necessary to study the way the administration of justice and the protection of law and order function in practice, including the level of independence from political interference, the selection mechanisms for recruiting staff and careers, and the various management and control bodies and mechanisms. In principle, the neutrality (and hence autonomy) of the judiciary and the police vis-à-vis the political power should be ensured in a democratic system, but without turning them into autonomous centres of power, and avoiding making them a caste, a counter-power without democratic legitimacy. The problem of ensuring accountability, neutrality and efficiency at the same time does not and cannot have perfect solutions, but this does

[25] 'The ultimate tragedy is not the oppression and cruelty by the bad people, but the silence over that by the good people' (Martin Luther King).

not mean that it need not be addressed; the voice of a free press and in particular of good investigative journalism are, from this point of view, essential.

Judicial institutions are different in different countries. A comparative analysis can help assess the merits and demerits of each. For example, the direct election of magistrates ensures direct control by the citizens but not a meritocratic selection based on in-depth knowledge of the law; it may therefore be suitable for a customary legal system (*stare decisis*) such as the English system but much less so for a system based on a broad and articulated body of written law. In the USA, federal judges are appointed by the Senate; state judges may be elected. In the European countries meritocratic rules are preferred both for the selection and the career of judges. As regards sanctions, promotions and appointments, self-government is tempered by a co-participation of political authorities, as in the case of Italy with the Consiglio Superiore della Magistratura, which includes members elected by (and among) magistrates and members appointed by Parliament (with a qualified majority of two thirds) and by the president.[26]

Judges are called upon to apply laws, not to formulate them. It is therefore mainly laws, passed by parliaments, that guide society in a conservative or progressive direction. However, even with a system of written laws, there remains a margin of interpretative discretion that magistrates can make ample use of. Among the three powers (legislative, executive and judiciary), judges have the final word concerning the behaviour of citizens, public functionaries and economic agents; thus, their influence on society is quite strong. Tendencies to judicial self-restraint and to activism are both present, with different strength over time and in the various fields of social action, in both cases with important potential negative effects.

Above all, the 'Sylos Labini rule' referred to above (a few very good, a few very bad, and the rest…) also applies to the magistrates.

[26] A clear and detailed picture for Italy is provided by Consiglio Superiore della Magistratura (2015).

The resulting problems are exacerbated by a practice of 'revolving doors' between the judiciary and political offices, as well as by the appeal of media notoriety, which sometimes leads to establishing privileged relations with the world of information. The right balance between respect for the individual rights and political citizenship of the magistrates and the need to ensure mutual independence between the judicial and political spheres is hard to achieve; in Italy, the rules, as well as the decision-making practice of the Consiglio Superiore della Magistratura, are constantly coming under debate, often prompted by controversial episodes.

Delays and malfunctioning of justice have very high costs for the economy and for social cohesion, as well as for the transparency of political events.[27] The excessive length of trials – in too many, even important cases, being time-barred – is due both to insufficient commitment to their work on the part of various magistrates, in the absence of strict controls, and to baroque procedures. Among the causes of the latter, besides the desire for impunity of the political class or part of it, which in the last three decades have led to a series of 'guarantee' laws, often *ad personam* but with obviously general effects, the corporative resistance (also on the part of lawyers, much more numerous in Italy than in other countries) to measures to streamline trials, in particular to the use of telematic tools, should be noted.[28]

[27] Historians in the future will hopefully be able to analyse in depth a specific but very important case in Italy, the events of the Court of Rome, for a long time nicknamed 'the port of mists'. In the immediate post-war period, this was partly connected to the very timid epuration of fascist magistrates (as in the absolution of the instigators behind the assassination of Giacomo Matteotti: cf. Franzinelli, 2007, pp. 187–231) and to the impact of the Cold War. I can bet right now, however, that in addition to the undue influences of Italian politics, the exchange of Masonic favours and cross blackmail, an important role will have to be attributed to pressures from 'beyond the Tiber', the Vatican curia. One episode about which all too little, but something, is known is the theft (of confidential documents, among other things) in the vault of the bank in Piazzale Clodio, where the court is located, by a notorious underworld figure with a far-right background, Massimo Carminati (see Abbate, 2017).

[28] In some cases we can even speak of defence against the trial, i.e. stretching it out to reach the statute of limitations, rather than within the trial, on the merits.

In the administration of public order, the police (and in particular cases the army) play an essential role. Here too, there are a number of problems, from low-level corruption (unpaid traffic fines, the blackmailing of shops, restaurants and bars, etc.) to the violence that is easily used in difficult environments and dangerous conditions. In the United States and in several developing countries with dictatorial regimes, police violence goes as far as murder unjustified by any immediate danger, and is only rarely punished. There seems to be a positive correlation between right-wing orientation of governments and the use of violence by the police.[29] Police officers, carabinieri and traffic wardens are also human beings, for whom the 'Sylos Labini rule' applies, and thus with a substantial importance of rules and controls, which can steer the majority in the direction of good or evil.

As regards both the administration of justice and the protection of public order, technological change entails (or should entail) the systematic updating of operating methods. For example, a structural use of IT, which has so far been only partially adopted, would be very useful for speeding up trials.[30] As regards the protection of public order, IT developments should favour the collection and cross-checking of information (to be facilitated also at international level, especially for economic crimes).[31] A problem of privacy protection arises here, which may require, for instance, an absolute ban on collecting information on political orientations, unless racism or terrorism are involved. These new technologies can greatly help the war against the illegal and criminal economy: a decisive war for the survival and development of a civilized state, in which the citizens feel both free and safe.

[29] In this regard, the cases of repression of political demonstrations in Reggio Emilia, 7 July 1960, or in the Diaz school in Genoa on 21 July 2001 are worth mentioning.

[30] Even for citizens called to testify, sometimes in cities other than their own, the use of telematic connection would be a huge time saver. The same would hold for lawyers, were they able to request and deposit documents electronically.

[31] Sanctions, such as punitive tax treatment for economic transactions involving them in any way, should be foreseen for countries that refuse to provide the information requested by magistrates.

6.6 DEFENCE AND MILITARY POWER

The transition from mercenary armies to national armies was an important step in the construction of the nation state. Control of the army has always been essential for control of the state and in many cases has been decisive in contests for political power.

An important change was the transition from an army of professional soldiers to a conscript army, extended to all citizens fit for military service. In this way, the loyalty of the army to democratic institutions is assumed to be ensured from below. However, the increasing technical specialization required in the army (linked to technological developments in armaments) gradually led to the formation of a professional army, and thus to the abolition of the conscript army.

In older democracies, fears of coups have almost disappeared, although fears of secret service deviations persist, especially in Italy.[32] The influence of the high command is considerable, however, especially in the United States where a 'military-industrial technostructure', as Galbraith (1967) called it, has taken shape since the Cold War: a concentration of political and economic power, based on the interactions between military spending, public research and industrial production of armaments, which exerts considerable influence on domestic and foreign policy strategies, on the choice of candidates for public office, and – through sponsorship and funding – on electoral results.[33] Moreover, the formation of a military alliance

[32] In Italy, fears of a coup d'état made themselves felt in the 1960s and 1970s at times of real or apparent strengthening of the reformist left, with an instrumental function to impose conservative positions. Let us recall General De Lorenzo and the Piano Solo of 1964, which together with the (questionable: cf. Salvati, 1967) severely restrictive monetary policy adopted by Guido Carli's Bank of Italy helped to curb the reforming impulses of the first centre-left government; the attempted coup d'état of Junio Valerio Borghese in December 1970. With regard to the deviations of the secret services, we can recall Sifar, the strategy of tension, Gladio, the various hypotheses of pollution of investigations such as those concerning the Piazza Fontana in Milan or the Bologna railway station massacres, the use of information files for blackmail purposes. See Franzinelli (2010).

[33] The role of military expenditure in research is emphasized, among others, by Mirowski (2002, pp. 153–231). Retired military officers occasionally become well-paid consultants, even to the Pentagon, or – more often – to defence contractor companies, even joining their boards of directors.

such as NATO was and still is, after the fall of the Berlin Wall, an important constraint on the national foreign policy strategies of member countries.

Military strength is indeed an important, often decisive, element in the relations between countries. The foreign policy of alliances may at best reduce the importance of this element in the larger countries, while for smaller countries it remains decisive. The possibility of resisting a superior military force by means of guerrilla warfare techniques, as seen in Vietnam, has probably been superseded by new technologies, and in particular the use of drones. The possibility remains for non-conventional forms of warfare fought through terror, such as that waged by ISIS (which, however, had military supplies, logistical support and considerable financing during the early stages, when in Afghanistan it fought against the Soviets. In all likelihood, this was also true later among the fundamentalist circles of Saudi Arabia).

One element to be taken into account is the participation of top leaders of the armed forces and secret services in Freemason-type networks. This aspect, more than frontal threats to democracy, involves a heavy corruptive pollution of political and economic life, generally in a conservative sense. The importance of these phenomena is pointed out, for example, by Bobbio (2011), whose condemnation of 'hidden powers', given his scholarly credentials, certainly cannot be attributed to 'conspiracy mania'.

Intelligence services are essential in dictatorial regimes for retaining control of a situation, through activities ranging from the physical elimination of dissenters to disinformation, which can also be used against democratic countries to influence their political affairs.

Finally, in the balance of terror resting on the presence of nuclear weapons, the great powers tend to intervene in limited areas of conflict (as in operations against terrorism) and preferably indirectly, by supporting the war effort of smaller contenders.[34] Moreover,

[34] A typical case of 'war by proxy' is that of Libya. In the recent invasion of Ukraine by Russia the menace of a nuclear war was utilized by the invaders in an attempt to limit support to Ukraine by Western countries.

the international confrontation of power is increasingly entrusted to instruments other than traditional weapons: cyber-attacks (whose paternity can be denied); duties and other regulatory interventions in the case of commercial, financial and technological conflicts; and financial support for anti-government organizations within the adversary country. Finally, the space race retains military implications, but cannot be reduced to this. In essence, it can be said that the new frontiers of international conflict – cyber-attacks and the space race – take military conflict onto a new terrain.[35]

6.7 THE STATE AS A COUNTERVAILING POWER TO ECONOMIC POWER

Since the fall of the Berlin Wall, centrally planned economies have practically disappeared and the economic systems in which we now live are considered market economies, even if the presence of the state is commonly quite strong. Public expenditure and public revenues are around 50 per cent of GDP and sometimes exceed it; economic activity is regulated by a set of laws and subject to the control of regulatory bodies; public economic policy has a key role in determining the trend of production and income and, through more or less coherent systems of incentives and disincentives, in steering it in the direction of certain sectors and technologies rather than others.

In the private sector of the economy there is a strong tendency towards concentrations of power, as already mentioned in Chapter 4. The dominance of increasing returns to scale, both static and dynamic, leads to the growth in size of firms and drives towards oligopoly if not monopoly regimes (in important sectors such as infrastructure networks: transport, telecommunications, etc.). The

[35] Let us also recall (although beyond our scope here) the debates among military strategy experts on the relative importance of the air force or the navy, of military land bases or aircraft carriers, and the like, which are the basis of important strategic choices, to be constantly revised in response to the evolution of technology and the geopolitical situation.

greater gains possible when acquiring market power drive in the direction of concentrations of power even in cases where the impulse of increasing returns does not come into play.[36]

Concentrations of power in the economic sphere stimulate the formation of alliances of convenience between representatives of the public and private sectors. It is therefore necessary for the state to act as a countervailing power, hindering the formation of concentrations of power in the private sector and/or limiting their effects.

Let us consider three aspects of the Italian case (but there are others, which are also important): anti-trust legislation; labour market regulation; and the role of monetary authorities.

In Italy, since 1990, anti-monopoly legislation has led to the establishment of a Competition and Market Authority, charged with actively intervening in cases of use of market power to the detriment of consumers. Interventions do not usually concern the limitation of market power per se but rather its use to the detriment of consumers: we thus have ex post rather than ex ante interventions. When they do address market power, they do so by focusing on one indicator, the market share of the firm under examination in the relevant market; in this way much depends upon the definition of the relevant market, which entails a large margin of discretion. Moreover, after an initial preparatory stage in which the focus was on substantive economic aspects, the Authority's work has been channelled into purely legal terrain, with advantages in terms of substantial revenue for various law firms. However, this system has limited effectiveness, as it finds it difficult taking account of constant technological changes and restricts the scope of intervention to established cases. Ex ante interventions may block mergers between companies when they threaten to result in an excessive share of the relevant market.

There are various other sectoral authorities (from the Transport Regulatory Authority to the Communications Authority and the

[36] Let us recall Breglia's (1965) distinction between 'subtraction profits', obtained through the exploitation of market power, thus to the detriment of other economic agents, and 'addition profits', obtained through technological or organizational improvements, with at least potential benefits for all.

Authority for Energy, Networks and the Environment) who, with different duties and powers, regulate private activity in the areas for which they are responsible, in some cases by controlling tariffs.[37]

Labour market regulation is a central aspect of market economies, to which we shall return several times. What needs to be stressed here is the importance of the active intervention of the state in the balancing of powers between workers and employers. A legal measure such as the Workers' Statute (Law No. 300, 20 May 1970), which we shall return to later in Section 11.1, has brought about a substantial modification of the power relations between workers and employers, by sterilizing a series of mechanisms that increased the power of the employers. Subsequent amendments to the Statute, in particular regarding firing for just cause, have once again increased the employers' margins of manoeuvre; the growth of 'precarious employment' worked in the same direction.[38] The degree of efficiency of public control over compliance with health rules and working conditions is also important.

The supply of legal tender is of course controlled by the monetary authorities, through various types of operations, in particular open market operations (the sale and purchase of securities on the market, which, through the choice of securities on which to operate, also influences the yield curve), and through the direct financing of banks, which must hold with the central bank a compulsory reserve commensurate with their assets.[39]

The central bank also acts as lender of last resort for the banking system, with the aim of avoiding systemic financial crises.

[37] In many cases, the authorities may themselves be influenced by private operators in the sector concerned (what is known as 'capture' of the regulator). This influence often takes the form of 'revolving doors', whereby former managers of companies in the sector are appointed to the regulatory authorities and sometimes return to the same companies once they have completed their term of office.

[38] In principle, fixed-term employment contracts should be disincentivized (e.g. through higher pension contributions) in favour of open-ended ones, but the opposite is the case.

[39] The central bank can also vary reserve requirement ratios. This type of manoeuvre has now taken a back seat to the setting of minimum thresholds for equity capital, which are established taking into account the riskiness of the various asset classes.

This function intersects with the (preventive) function of supervising the smooth functioning of financial institutions and with the (ex post) function of orderly management of possible crisis situations. The supervisory function often implies interventions that can steer the financial system towards one power structure rather than another.[40]

For several decades after World War II, partly as a consequence of the bank failures following the Wall Street Crash in 1929, the banking system was almost entirely in public hands. Since the 1990s, privatization has led to a situation of public/private control in which even public shareholders (the foundations) operate on a substantially private basis. The supervisory function exercised by the Bank of Italy (and for years now by the European Central Bank for the largest banks) helps to guide concentration strategies in the sector, especially but not only during crises and bailouts.

Regulations also affect its size in various ways. For example, promoting private insurance against illness and to guarantee an income in old age helps to expand the share of the financial system in the economy. Tax regulation can have an important influence; for example, the establishment of a tax on financial transactions (the 'Tobin tax') would have a substantial effect in discouraging 'high-frequency' financial speculation activities (such as those run by computer programs), thus reducing both the size and the systemic fragility of the financial system.[41]

[40] Let us recall, for example, the clash between 'secular' and 'Catholic' finance in Italy, on the occasion of the crisis of the 'Sindona system' and then of the 'Calvi system' between the Vatican Bank and Prime Minister Andreotti on the one hand, who pressed for the rescue of first Sindona's Private Bank and then Calvi's Banco Ambrosiano, and Baffi and Sarcinelli's Bank of Italy on the other hand, who were willing to manage the closure procedures of the two banks in an orderly manner but not to burden public accounts with the cover-up of speculative operations involving serious irregularities. Among the many contributions on these issues see, in particular, the Commissione parlamentare d'inchiesta sul caso Sindona (2005), Lombard (1980) and Stajano (1991).

[41] For those who accept the theory of efficient financial markets, and in general for those who accept the myth of the invisible hand of the market that would ensure continuous, rapid and automatic rebalancing in the face of unexpected shocks, the idea of

Strict regulations would also be necessary for the rapidly expanding cryptocurrencies, now more or less totally unregulated: both because of their role in favouring the criminal economy (already recalled above, in Section 4.6) and because of the serious risk of potentially devastating systemic financial crises.[42]

6.8 WELFARE STATE AND TYPES OF REGULATION

This brings us to the system of public intervention in pensions and health care. An analysis of comparative economic systems contrasts two models: the social-democratic welfare state, and the liberal model, which entrusts family savings to the private management of investment funds, insurance companies and other financial institutions. According to a more moderate version of liberalism, state intervention is permissible in support of the poor and for health care for the weak, while the social-democratic view sees the welfare state as a right of citizenship; health care in particular must be universal. The liberal solution is usually accompanied by incentives (in particular, tax deductibility for private savings set aside in regulated financial funds). These two models should then be complemented by a consideration of the role of the Third Sector, made up of non-profit associations active on the various fronts of social care: a role that may vary in strength in the various countries and show different characteristics, for example in terms of the share of religious associations.

There is no end to the analyses, both theoretical and applied, of the merits and demerits of the two models and the role of the

systemic financial fragility is totally alien. Even many central banks had excluded it from their horizon, encouraging the deregulation of financial markets and the growth of the financial sector until the bloodbath of the 2008 crisis. Thus the Swedish central bank, which awards Nobel prizes for economics, has stubbornly neglected the leading theorist of systemic financial fragility, Hyman Minsky.

42 The debate on cryptocurrencies is wide and quickly expanding. Neoliberal economists favour them, seeing them as the realization of the Hayekian dream of private monies (cf. Roncaglia, 2019, pp. 83–7); Keynesian economists stress their role in increasing systemic fragility (cf. e.g. Kregel, 2022). In the theoretical debate, their role as means of payment for the criminal economy is too often forgotten.

Third Sector. Such analyses are often tainted by conflicts of interest and logical errors. For example, when calculating returns on private pension funds, the cost to the state of tax incentives is sometimes not taken into account; funds that disappear from the survey due to bankruptcy (which is important given the long duration of pension investments) are not considered. The risks of failure of private pension fund managers are, of course, in the long run much higher than the risks of failure of the state.[43]

In the case of public health care, account should be taken of the lower administrative cost of universal cover, which does not require verification each time of the patient's insurance coverage or willingness to pay, or of the complex control mechanism required in the case of tax deductions. Additionally, competition within the private health system is vitiated by the fact that patients do not have the necessary knowledge to assess the value for money of the services offered, and by their willingness to pay stratospheric amounts of money to improve their chances of survival in health.

On the whole, public health care systems appear to guarantee, for the same income, a longer life expectancy and a lower level of infant mortality than those based on private systems. With all its distortions, the state pension system guarantees a certainty of income (although not necessarily of its precise level) that is decidedly higher than private systems; when the management of pension funds is entrusted to the same companies, it can happen that the worker loses both his/her job and his/her pension payments simultaneously, with the bankruptcy of the company (as happened in the United States in the case of the Enron Corporation, which went bankrupt in 2001, leaving 29,000 employees destitute).[44]

[43] For a comprehensive and balanced discussion of public pension systems and their rationale, see Lindert (2004).

[44] Sustainability of a public pension system for the state budget naturally requires certain conditions, for instance that the retirement age be increased in the face of rising average life expectancy. From the point of view of a public pension system, what

The welfare state can be more or less extensive. Besides health care and the pension system, which constitute its core (and the main share of expenditure), we have different forms of support for lower incomes, unemployment benefits and interventions of various kinds (e.g. for the training of unemployed workers). In a broader sense, the public and (at least for primary and secondary education) the free education system can also be included in the welfare state system, accompanied by measures such as school meals and free textbooks (and now, in some cases at least, subsidies for digital reading devices).

A large welfare state system corresponds to a greater diffusion/lower concentration of power, inter alia by making the level of income and wealth of each individual/family less important, since some basic benefits are universally provided. Of course, the presence of the welfare state and its specific organization affect the micro-division of power in various ways, with the attribution of power to a bureaucracy that manages a system necessarily endowed with ample resources and a reduction in power for insurance companies, private doctors, owners of private health care facilities, and so on.

The welfare system, together with the institutional characteristics of the labour market, helps to define 'types of capitalism', for which there are several possible classifications. We can thus speak, for example, of the 'Scandinavian model', characterized by an extensive welfare system accompanied by substantial measures in favour of the unemployed and the poor and by a certain flexibility in the labour market (so-called flexicurity) – ease of hiring and firing accompanied by effective support measures for those who lose their jobs; of the 'US model', characterized by limited welfare, limited support measures for areas of poverty, high labour market flexibility; and of the 'Southern European model', with high welfare expenditures, low labour mobility, limited assistance for those who lose their jobs

counts is macroeconomic sustainability: the consumption of goods and services by pensioners must find room in a current production of these goods and services that exceeds the consumption of the rest of the population.

and for the area of poverty. Definitions can be further specified, for example, by taking into account the dichotomy between guaranteed and precarious workers, or by combining welfare types and labour market characteristics with the type of political regime. Above all, the situation in different countries may change over time, although the underlying characteristics seem relatively stable. These classifications can then be used for a comparative analysis aimed at establishing which types of capitalism are most appropriate for ensuring the country's economic growth, social cohesion and international competitiveness.[45]

Taken together, these analyses can be seen as part of an institutionalist paradigm, which contrasts with traditional economic theories that take little account of the variety of welfare state systems and their institutions. The importance of the variety of capitalisms is, in fact, fundamental for examining the distribution of power, in its multiple aspects, within contemporary societies and – as might be expected – for outlining possible strategies of intervention.

The debate on 'types of capitalism' constitutes in several respects a response to the 'end of history' theses that became so widespread after the collapse of the Berlin Wall and the dissolution of the Soviet Union, in the wake of Fukuyama's book (1992) from which, to tell the truth, several commentators seem to have taken up only the title.

Fukuyama starts from acceptance of Hegel's thesis: there is a direction of travel in the path of history, and he sees the ideal of liberal democracy as the point of arrival, never fully attainable, of this path. Therefore, not the market economy as such, since 'authoritarian states oriented towards a market economy' are possible (1992, p. 17): Fukuyama cites Franco's Spain and Brazil under military rule as examples, while today the case that stands out is that of China.

[45] See, for example, Esping-Andersen (1999) and the contributions collected in Hall and Soskice (2001), Iversen and Soskice (2019) and Trigilia (2020). Comparative analyses of this kind also make it possible to assess the importance of elements such as interpersonal trust or the role of small towns and urban self-employment traditions for economic development; on these issues Paci (2013, pp. 367–9) recalls the work of Bagnasco (1996) and Trigilia (1992).

With respect to the ideal end point, Fukuyama also recalls the presence of 'injustices or serious social problems' (1992, p. 9) even in the main contemporary democracies. The 'end of history' is therefore far from being reached with the victory of market economies over planned economies, which is nevertheless a very important step along the path of history. Of particular concern is the decline of community life: 'liberal democracies are not self-sufficient: the community life on which they depend must come from a source other than liberalism' (1992, p. 339).[46]

It is certainly not possible here to enter into the debate on the Hegelian conception of history, except to recall that these are controversial theses. What we can point out, however, is Fukuyama's underestimation of the economic aspects: social solidarity is certainly not fostered by high unemployment or growing distributive inequalities, while it is supported by institutions such as the welfare state.

In this respect, the main distinction between types of capitalism appears to be the one proposed by Milanovic (2019) between 'liberal meritocratic capitalism' and 'political capitalism' (which essentially corresponds to Fukuyama's 'market economy-oriented authoritarian states'). The former is characterized by meritocratic equality, that is, careers determined by talent (at least in principle) and correctives aimed to ensure high intergenerational social mobility, for example inheritance taxes and free education. In the second type of capitalism, the political control exercised by the ruling group favours the intergenerational transmission of power and its concentration.

In Russia as in China, in the transition from communism to a market economy, the concentration of political power remained and with privatizations favoured a concentration in a few hands of

[46] Fukuyama laments the decline of the religious spirit and its accompanying ethics (1992, p. 339), but looks forward to the existence of 'inexhaustible reservoirs of idealism', of which he cites Donald Trump and George Bush, along with the climber Reinhold Messner, as examples.

private control over productive activities.[47] However, political power has retained its supremacy over economic power. In China this has happened without any major external repercussions, whereas in Russia the links that the oligarchs have established with the Western financial system have made the interventions of political power more blatant.

Milanovic points to the rapid development in recent decades of China, but also of Russia and India, to underline that the real challenge for the future lies between these two types of capitalism. And it is a challenge, we add, that is played out in the field of institutions and economic policies, and that liberal democracies certainly cannot win by relying on the myth of the invisible hand of the market. Not least because the season of neo-liberalism and financialization has favoured a growing polarization in income distribution and a reduction in intergenerational social mobility, which jeopardizes basic social cohesion that, despite the inevitable presence of conflicts, is crucial for the efficient functioning of liberal democracies.[48]

[47] The privatizations carried out with the system of vouchers distributed to the citizens, promptly subject to exchanges that favoured their concentration in a few hands, recalls some historical precedents, such as the distribution of Irish land after Cromwell's invasion in 1652: William Petty, who had overseen the topographical survey of the land to be distributed to English soldiers, came out the owner of an entire county (cf. Roncaglia, 1977, pp. 9–15).

[48] Milanovic (2019, p. 11) notes 'a movement towards the creation of a self-perpetuating upper class and polarization between the elites and the rest, that represents the most important threat to the longer-term viability of liberal capitalism'. He also considers the possibility of a convergence between the two models, which could be favoured by the strengthening of the 'plutocratic features in today's liberal capitalism' (p. 217). 'The objective of political capitalism is to take politics out of people's minds, which can be more easily done when disenchantment and lack of interest in democratic politics are high' (p. 218).

7 Culture and Power

7.1 PUBLIC DISCOURSE AND ITS REQUIREMENTS

In this chapter we will – very briefly – deal with only a few aspects of a vast and complex theme: the influence of ideas (culture in the broad sense)[1] on the power structure of society and its evolution. In the next section we will recall the opposing positions of Marx and Weber on the culture-power relationship, and Gramsci's concept of hegemony. We shall then look at the debate on the role of the masses and the relationship between civil society and the state, followed by some considerations on the role of religions. Another aspect, in itself very complex, is the role of technocracy in the social power structure, especially in the formation of elites, and the related theme of the relationship between the two cultures, the humanistic and the scientific. Finally, a highly topical issue is the role of the new media, both in its positive aspects of increasing social participation in political and cultural debate and in its negative aspects of corrupting public discourse.

These themes concern both the structure of power at a given moment and its evolution over time. The latter is determined by the dialectic between the stabilizing force of tradition and the intrinsic drive for change, which underlies the themes discussed in the following sections. At the end of this introductory section, we will recall the requirements of public discourse which sees cultural confrontation.

The power of tradition (customs, habits, procedures conforming to norms) is considerable, and manifests itself both in the masses and

[1] Culture in the broad sense consists of ideas and beliefs, and the institutions that foster their dissemination, lifestyles and habits and conventions in society. Culture in the narrow sense is the body of knowledge with specialist content, the possession of which defines the category of intellectuals.

in the political and cultural elites as a desire to exploit acquired and internalized knowledge, or not to run the risk of change.[2] Tradition has a fundamental manifestation in religions, which include not only metaphysical convictions regarding the existence of God and the afterlife, but also prescriptions of behaviour ranging from general rules (such as the Ten Commandments) to specific norms (ritual fasting, participation in ceremonies, and so forth). The result is an ethos of behaviour that favours the stability of social arrangements. Many other types of cultural, political and social associations, whether institutionalized or not, prescribe or at least encourage codes of conduct that are persistent over time.

In terms of technology, too, tradition plays a major role. In the context of the division of labour, traditional work procedures cannot be changed by individual workers: each change usually affects several segments of the work process and thus requires coordination from above, as well as the need for the workers involved to learn new operations. The same is true in the field of productive services and public bureaucracy: procedures and regulations cannot be changed by individual employees or users; adaptation can take a long time. Conflicts of interest may often arise; for example, possible improvements from the user's point of view imply a reduction in discretionary power and/or a greater burden of responsibility for the bureaucracy. Changes are therefore relatively infrequent. The importance of these areas in everyday life in itself promotes a mindset that is conducive to stable behaviour.

Conversely, technological innovations, large and small, impose changes in both lifestyles and mindsets. The mind goes, for example, to the IT and telecommunications revolution and all its implications: from the new social media to the use of computer archives in scientific research, from distance learning to the reduced constraints of territorial location for friendship networks, and so on. Change is

2 The strength of tradition is a commonplace for historians, emphasized as early as Herodotus (*Histories*, III, 38).

favoured by phenomena like youth rebellion, or the desire to *épater les bourgeois*, to break out of the chorus. Schumpeter (1942) emphasizes the role of universities and research: these stimulate the method of internal criticism in their own fields of work, then turn the weapons of criticism against the constituted powers, against the passive acceptance of customs and traditions.

The outcome of the dialectic between tradition and change depends to a large extent on the tendencies present in public opinion, and so on an ongoing debate concerning specific choices of conservation or change rather than the choice between the general principle of tradition or progress. Cultural institutions independent of centres of political, economic and cultural power are essential for progressive policies, both in defining the objectives and the instruments for achieving them, and in forming an active consensus around them.

Rational reflection and open public debate are indispensable for an ever-changing society. While the tradition of utilitarianism, still dominant in the economic field, leads to the assumption of individual preference systems as given, the real role of active politics (which all too often today is limited to managing what already exists) consists precisely in stimulating and directing change, creating a favourable climate, primarily in the cultural field, for what can be considered progress.[3]

The public discourse consists first and foremost of the statements of political parties and their representatives, but also of the participation of intellectuals in the debate and the mediation of journalists and the world of communication in general. Indirectly, but no less importantly, those who produce culture in the broadest sense of the term, from novelists and poets to writers and musicians, from

[3] 'Instead of looking at politics as the *aggregation* of given preferences, one can argue that the essence of politics lies in the *transformation* of preferences, through public and rational debate' (Elster, 1982, p. 294). Elster also recalls Habermas's thesis: 'multifarious individual preferences do not constitute final authority, but only idiosyncratic needs that must be shaped and purified in the public debate on the public good' (1982, p. 294).

film and theatre directors and actors to architects and urban planners, participate in the public discourse. The street demonstrations too, with their slogans, constitute participation in the public discourse.

Public debate thus takes over various different facets, which, in their uncoordinated and at times confused complexities, play an essential role in specifying strategies for social change or conservation and their underlying motivations, and in seeking consensus around them. Rational and open discussion therefore plays an essential role in the smooth functioning of a democratic system.

Effective public discourse requires certain conditions. First, the willingness of politicians to illustrate their ideas and choices, both strategic and tactical, as clearly and precisely as possible: a willingness that can also be useful in clarifying for oneself the meaning of what one is doing. Secondly, the willingness of the 'transmission belts' of the media to provide unbiased accounts of the different points of view on the field and possibly reasoned criticism. Thirdly, the willingness of all citizens to devote time to acquiring political information, with sufficient readiness to revise their starting positions if necessary. Fourthly, and crucially, the presence of a robust reverse transmission chain, from citizens – who must consider themselves and be considered an active part of public discourse – to professional politicians. In this respect, cultural institutions active at different levels, from political and cultural associations to local party branches and recreational clubs, play an important role.

Decisions – which are inevitable and necessary in any social context – are more likely to be effective if they are taken in accordance with the majority principle and after open debate, and do not arouse the active opposition or delaying tactics of opposing minorities. In any case, maximum respect for minority views (and willingness to compromise when possible) is another important requirement of open public discourse.

Seen in a negative light, these conditions imply that politicians do not use public discourse for demagogic purposes, for the mere pursuit of electoral consensus or to stimulate the worst feelings of the masses;[4] that the media do not use their role to distort the news, favouring, even before their own convictions, their own interests (and it should be remembered here that the media have property and advertisers to answer to); that the public retains a critical and self-critical sense, rejecting easy slogans and convenient preconceptions in favour of a serious search for information and a method of critical reasoning open to debate.

These requirements obviously refer to an optimal situation, which is very difficult to see realized in practice. However, they are a reference point for the adoption of rules and regulations, for example with an extended (and prompt) use of the obligation to rectify false statements, and to stimulate a stricter attitude towards the moral responsibility of the politician, which cannot be reduced to criminal liability alone, often very slow and in any case very difficult to use in cases of violation of the optimal standards of public discourse. These are difficult issues, but they should be explored further, also in relation to the growing importance of the new social media.[5]

7.2 THE NOTION OF HEGEMONY

The notions of domination and hegemony were introduced by Gramsci in the *Prison Notebooks* (*Quaderni*) precisely as tools for analysing power, or more precisely, the alternation between phases of stability and phases of change in power structures. Gramsci notes that the traditional notion of power (state-military) is only one aspect. The other pillar of the control of a political/social class over the population is the influence exerted on people's way of thinking: the underlying values, religious beliefs, ethics, opinions on basic

[4] An example that is likely to become a classic is Trump's speech to protesters about the 'stolen' election before the attack on the US Congress on 6 January 2021 (https://apnews.com/article/election-2020-joe-biden-donald-trump-capitol-siege-media-e79eb5164613d6718e9f4502eb471f27).

[5] For example, one could consider the advisability of an arbitration panel, with members appointed by the President of the Republic and the top echelons of the judiciary, or similar bodies, within qualified categories, which could condemn the most blatant violations of the optimal conditions of public discourse; for example, sexist or racist attacks on rival politicians, nowadays considered a normal part of public discourse.

political orientations and what generates a solidarity of behaviour for small and large social groups as well as for society as a whole.[6] It is on the hegemonic capacity of a political/social group (what Gramsci calls 'intellectual and moral leadership') that the conquest and then the preservation of political power is based, also through a policy of alliances: conquest of power by a new group is only possible if the old dominant group has lost its hegemonic character.[7]

In another part of the *Quaderni*, in the context of an examination of the differences between Croce and Gentile, the dichotomy between hegemony and domination takes the form of a dichotomy between 'civil society' and 'political society',[8] where by 'civil society' (a definition to which we will return later, in Section 7.4) Gramsci indicates whatever in culture, institutions and instruments of social consensus formation is not included in 'political society'. The two pairs of concepts must be kept distinct: in a dictatorship with a broad popular base, political society may be both dominant and hegemonic with respect to civil society (as in the case of Nazism in the late 1930s), whereas in an efficient democracy the opposite may be true.

The dichotomy proposed by Gramsci is different from the Marxian one between structure and superstructure. For Marx,

[6] Even a regime like Nazism, which made extensive use of violence and terror as elements of its rule, availed itself of a control of mass culture that was decisive for the conquest and preservation of power (cf. Mosse 1974, 1980); precisely for this reason it can be considered a totalitarian regime, not simply a dictatorial one, insofar as it tended to control all aspects of life, with the limit claim of creating a 'new man'. The debate on totalitarianism is wide-ranging, the best-known contribution being Arendt (1948).

[7] 'The supremacy of a social group manifests itself in two ways, as "domination" and as "intellectual and moral leadership". A social group is dominant over the adversary groups that it tends to "liquidate" or subdue even by armed force, and it is the leader of related and allied groups. A social group can and indeed must be the leader even before it conquers governmental power (this is one of the main conditions for the very conquest of power); afterwards, when it exercises power and even if it holds it firmly in its grip, it becomes dominant but must also continue to be "leader"' (Gramsci, 1975, pp. 2010–11; my translation).

[8] 'Croce wants to maintain a distinction between civil society and political society, between hegemony and dictatorship ... Gentile ...: hegemony and dictatorship are indistinguishable; force is consensus without question' (Gramsci, 1975, p. 691).

changes in power structures have their deep roots in changes in technology understood in the broad sense as developments in the division of labour: what Marx calls 'the forces of production'. These changes constitute a dynamic element of progress, which generates increasing tensions in the static element of conservation, constituted by the 'relations of production'; that is, the set of institutions and customs within which economic activity takes place. The force of inertia of the relations of production is in turn linked to the political, legal and cultural 'superstructure'. The dynamic element – the forces of production – is destined to unhinge the structure of the relations of production and the superstructure in a revolutionary phase. Then comes transition to a new set of production relations (to a new 'mode of production', in Marxian terminology: from feudalism to capitalism, and from the latter to socialism and then communism), with a corresponding upheaval of the superstructure.[9]

Marx's historical materialism consists precisely in seeing the economic structure as the *primum movens*, which informs the superstructure of institutions and culture. 'It is not the consciousness of men that determines their being, but it is, on the contrary, their social being that determines their consciousness.'[10]

In contrast to Marx we have Weber ('the Marx of the bourgeoisie'), who re-evaluates the fundamental importance of institutions and culture in the overall structure of society. Thus, for example, an essential contribution to the origins of capitalism comes from the Protestant Reformation, with its culture in favour of concrete commitment in society (as opposed to the asceticism of mediaeval Catholicism or the Counter-Reformation) and the active role entrusted to the individual (in the reading and interpretation of sacred texts as well as in social action). The development of capitalism itself is seen as a process of general rationalization, accompanied by the bureaucratization of public administration and the

[9] The exposition of Marx's theses is drawn from Roncaglia (2001, p. 261).
[10] Marx (1859, p. 5).

management of companies, and thus by the growth of the clerical and technical middle classes.

It must be stressed that both Marx and Weber's positions are more complex and nuanced than those taken by the more extreme historical materialists, such as Engels, or by earlier and later idealist philosophers: a mutual influence between the two spheres is recognized, and the opposing views essentially concern their relative importance. In fact, both Marx, in his historical writings, and Weber, especially in his posthumously published lectures on *Economic History* (1923), tend to construct multi-factor explanations of concrete historical change.

Gramsci's position is influenced by the previous debate. Gramsci basically agrees with Marx in considering changes in the forces of production as the engine of historical evolution, but he attributes a central importance to the element of 'intellectual and moral direction' for both the conquest and the preservation of power. Gramsci, therefore, does not question the Marxist thesis of the inevitable transition from feudalism to capitalism and from this to socialism first, and then to communism: in essence, the Hegelian-derived thesis of an intrinsic rationality of history. His attention is focused on the problems of the immediate political struggle: the reasons for the rise of fascism, the possible ways of overcoming it, the role of intellectuals and party organization in the political struggle, and particularly in the struggle for hegemony.[11]

In this respect, it is interesting to note Gramsci's (1975, p. 1591) rejection of a bipolar vision of society, and his recognition of the complexity of the alliance strategies necessary for the conquest of hegemony: 'Hegemony undoubtedly presupposes that the interests and tendencies of the groups on which hegemony will be exercised are taken into account, that a certain balance of compromise is formed'. Intellectuals are attributed a dual role of support for the ruling class

[11] Much has been written on Gramsci's conception of hegemony. For a concise exposition and critical interpretation, see Paci (2013, pp. 85–108).

(or, conversely, the emerging class): cultural and technical support for political action; and as a transmission belt for the political strategy of the ruling class vanguard (thus with an educational function, but a biased one: no neutrality of intellectuals in class conflict is conceivable).

The dialectical relationship between culture and power can therefore be illustrated by resorting to a simplified and partially deformed version of Gramsci's dichotomy between domination and hegemony: domination can be defined as the control of culture (and society) by political and economic power; hegemony, on the other hand, can be identified as the influence that culture, in the broadest sense, exerts on political and economic power in various ways, conditioning its choices and strategies.

The active exercise of hegemony is entrusted to the political leadership of civil society, which in Gramsci's view takes the authoritarian form of the centrally directed political party, and to the vast class of intellectuals. With respect to them, Gramsci (1975, p. 1591) speaks of a 'very great extension of the notion of the intellectual, but only in this way is it possible to arrive at a correct approximation of reality'. In fact, they are entrusted not only with the role of elaborating and organizing hegemony but also with the role of using hegemony for domination, through their role in state administration, including the administration of justice. 'Intellectuals are "clerks" of the dominant group' in charge of ensuring the 'spontaneous consent given by the broad masses … and for the apparatus of state coercion'.

The role of transmission belt thus attributed to intellectuals (like that later attributed to trade unions by both Soviet and Western communist parties) must be understood in the context of the situation Gramsci was facing: the fascist dictatorship on the one hand, Stalin's Soviet Union on the other. The guiding role is attributed in both cases to the political ruling group. In today's Western democracies, the situation is significantly different; the role of political direction in the broad sense, and therefore also cultural, attributed to the party is today, so to speak, dissolved, and above all fragmented in the composite world of politics, culture, journalism and university research. By definition, liberal democracy guarantees the plurality of ideas, lifestyles and political positions: the role of political leadership is attributed to the majority and its representatives, but with the constraint of respect for minorities.[12] In this scenario, power takes on a varied range of colours: hegemony is not a monolith but is dispersed throughout reality. Indeed, there can be different forms of hegemony: different cultures, not necessarily of classes or social classes, but of groups that are more or less cohesive and in other respects diversified within themselves. The influence of culture on power may concern the formation of ideas, the creation of a favourable terrain for their dissemination (particularly through teaching, but also through literature or music – as with popular songs – up to the use of atypical means such as murals or, in another era, satirical verses posted on the statue of Pasquino in Papal Rome); support for the formation of a critical consciousness and its dissemination. We shall return to these aspects in various contexts.

So far, we have considered the role of culture in conditioning the conquest and conservation of power. Let us now consider the conditioning exerted by economic and political power on culture. It is evident, but only in extreme conditions of totalitarianism can it be all-pervasive. It mainly involves the control of communication media, from newspapers to books, from radio and television to the modern social media (which we consider, albeit briefly, below). But it also flows through the rules of selection of researchers and teachers, especially in the field of the university, and can affect both their selection and the dissemination of ideas.

More generally, we can distinguish three levels in the power structure governing the cultural debate: those who decide what is discussed (agenda setting), those who determine how it is discussed (framing), and those who have the necessary influence to propose solutions (solving).

[12] See Mill (1859).

Conditioning is present at all three levels: it is strongest in fields of direct interest to economic and political powers. In the public sphere, an obvious example lies in the importance of appointments to state-controlled radio and television, museums and superintendencies, and a thousand other such positions, or the funding for cultural events in the broadest sense. In the private sector, the same applies to the control of newspapers, magazines, publishing houses, radio and television networks and new media, but also to the financing of research and conferences. Profit-driven media, competing for advertising revenues, may also be conditioned, but can also exert an active role, especially on specific issues that may arise the interest of readers; thus the path of hegemonic influence differ in societies according to the greater or lesser role of profit-driven media.

Obviously, those who have more resources have a louder voice. In the field of politics, this allows dominant groups to give their opinions wide circulation, extolling their own successes and criticizing the failures of others. Distortions in the debate, which are increasingly frequent, may occur when systematic defamation of opponents and the most absurd fake news are resorted to. The loss of ethical tension and professional commitment on the part of professional politicians and journalists alike favours the worst aspects of these trends.

In the field of economics, the very fragile theoretical foundations of the neo-liberal mainstream have been obscured by a *conventio ad excludendum* with respect to those parts of the debate (theory of capital, Keynesian theory of decisions under conditions of uncertainty) that highlight these fragilities.[13] Thanks partly to the elimination of the history of economic thought from the scene, the mainstream has even come to support the thesis of one single possible scientific approach, rejecting which is considered equivalent to Holocaust denial.[14] In Italy, lecturers in corporate

[13] For a review of economic theory debates from the post-World War II period to the present, see Roncaglia (2019).

[14] See Tabellini (2018) and Cahuc and Zylberger (2016) (the title is *Denialism in Economics*). In this respect, Corrado Guzzanti's line seems appropriate: 'There is only

economics who retained their jobs after the fall of fascism heavily conditioned the selection of their successors,[15] although they did not manage to prevent gradual openings to modern theories; then there was, largely thanks to Fulbright grants, a growth in the influence of US economic culture, which limited the extent of the break with the marginalist tradition through the compromise of the 'neoclassical synthesis' or defended its cornerstones through Chicago monetarism. More recently, there has been recourse to decidedly biased criteria for evaluating research, albeit to different degrees in different countries. In Italy, ANVUR (the agency in charge of evaluating research) adopted unbalanced criteria in the field of economics according to research fields and orientations, with the result of ensuring a 'barrier to entry' for critical orientations and, even worse, of encouraging the spread of opportunistic behaviour among researchers (exchange of signatures in articles and of citations).[16]

7.3 THE MASSES

However wide the circle of intellectuals, who have the driving role in defining a hegemonic culture, the traditional Marxist conception shared by Gramsci (and by many others, both conservatives and progressives) attributes an essentially passive role to the 'masses': not immobile, but moved from the outside, and endowed with a considerable force of inertia. This conception goes back in some respects to Mosca and Pareto, with the theory of a 'political class', an active elite that directs the course of events by drawing in the passive masses, and is perpetuated by co-opting. Still, the mobilization/activation of the masses was important for the rise to power first, and its

one answer … and it is wrong!' On the importance of research funding in distorting the debate between different orientations, see D'Eramo (2020).

15 To take just one example, let us recall the scandalous rejection of Sylos Labini in his application for a professorship in 1956.

16 Among the many works on these topics, see Corsi, D'Ippoliti and Lucidi (2011), Heckman and Moktar (2018), D'Ippoliti (2020, pp. 62 ff.) and the various contributions published on the Roars website (www.roars.it).

preservation later, of fascism and nazism, as De Felice and especially Mosse have shown.[17]

This theme had been addressed, right from the initial phase of the fascist dictatorship, by Ortega (1930). Ortega saw in the masses the superseding of social classes (the mass standing for the average person), thus of political life as class opposition. He proposed a libertarian-elitist view, according to which individual rights are guaranteed (in particular the right to dissent), but the leading role is entrusted to an elite of individuals who manage to place themselves outside and above the choir, and counteract the passivity of the masses. In contrast to class-based analyses, historical events are accounted for primarily by the broader culture that elites manage to disseminate among the masses, rather than by economic interests (with what Marx called 'false consciousness', distinguishing between the 'class per se' based only on the structure of production relations, and the higher level of the politically conscious 'class in itself').[18] Beyond his theses, the aspect Ortega emphasizes is important: studying the role of the masses in actual cases makes it possible to find a mediation between analyses entirely based on class structure and those entirely focused on ideology.

As Mosse (1977, p. 39) observes, those who adopt the point of view of modern parliamentary democracies overlook 'the fact that for millions of people, taking part in political life means not just a vote every few years, but mass gatherings, mass marches, mass myths and symbolism', and repeatedly emphasizes the role of associations and sporting events.[19] Certainly in dictatorships the cultural context is

[17] Cf. De Felice (1969, 1975) and Mosse (1974, 1980).

[18] An example of 'false consciousness' proposed by Marx, in a long letter to Sigfried Mayer and August Vogt of 9 April 1870 on the Irish question (Marx, 2020), is the racism of English workers against Irish immigrants, functional to (and instigated by) English industrialists.

[19] On the role of the gymnastic associations see also Mosse (1974, pp. 186 ff.). Mosse (1974, pp. 149 ff.) also emphasizes the role of music, in particular the works of Wagner, in creating the national feeling (the *Volk*) that was so important for fascism and nazism. In the Italian Risorgimento, Verdi had played a somewhat similar role, with the Nabucco choir 'Va pensiero sull'ali dorate' (1842) utilized as a sort of clandestine national anthem in Austria's Pope's and Borboni's governed territories.

different: Mussolini or Hitler 'glorify struggle as a way of life' (1977, p. 46); 'fascism proposes a myth, the myth of a happy and healthy world, the myth of the new man (in Germany the myth of the master race) and tries to translate it into reality' (1977, pp. 147–8). De Felice (1975, pp. 40–1) points out that it was precisely the 'mobilisation and participation of the masses' (in particular, as various authors point out, of the petit-bourgeois classes) around the task of 'transforming society and the individual in a direction that had never been tried or achieved' that made fascism 'a revolutionary phenomenon', different from the many dictatorial regimes (such as that of the colonels in Greece or Pinochet in Chile), which tended rather towards the 'demobilisation of the masses'. These regimes tend to defend and not to modify the pre-existing power structure, hitting those centres (such as trade unions or progressive or revolutionary parties) that aim to change it; fascism and nazism, on the other hand, want to modify society (nazism to bring back the rule of the aryan man, unchanging over time).[20]

Of course, the nature of nationalistic sentiment changes over time. Gellner (1983) emphasizes its positive role in the emergence of nations, which respond to a systemic need in the transition from the agricultural to the industrial stage (see Section 6.1). In the initial phase of state building we can distinguish (following Anderson, 1983, p. 119) a 'popular nationalism', generally centred on common reference to a vernacular language (and this is the nationalism on which Gellner focuses his attention), and an 'official nationalism' representing the response of the monarchy and aristocracy; after World War II, 'the last wave' of nationalist movements that spread

[20] In this sense, it is wrong to reduce fascism (and nazism) to merely a reaction against communism (as Croce and other conservative liberals who supported – or at least did not oppose – its rise to power in its crucial initial phase maintained). See also De Felice (1969, pp. xiii, 24–6). De Felice (1969, p. xvi) also underlines the difference between the national-socialist regime, 'based on the total pre-eminence of the party over the state', and the fascist regime, 'which pursued the clear and programmatic subordination of the party to the state', with a much lower degree of totalitarianism. On the difference between fascism and Peronism see Germani (1971).

throughout Asia and Africa constituted 'a response to the new models of global imperialism' (Anderson, 1983, p. 108). Forging a national sentiment means not only stressing common elements, such as language and a cultural tradition, but also overcoming and forgetting the elements of fracture present in the history of a people, such as the Crusade against the Albigensians and the expulsion of the Huguenots in France (Anderson, 1983, p. 153). As Anderson points out in the very title of his work, nations are 'imaginary communities', even if national sentiment has an objective force that cannot be underestimated: the mother country is not chosen, but one may be ready to die for it (1983, p. 115). It is precisely for this reason that the instrumental role that nationalism has taken on in the construction of dictatorships and totalitarianisms is an ever-present risk, which has been reproposed in the most recent phase in sovereign ideologies, with their appeals to identity (religious or ethnic, for example) in opposition to 'others'.

The theme of the role of the masses has been since taken up by many, in particular by Elias Canetti (1960). *Masses and Power* is the title of his wide-ranging essay, the result of a long research project, which constitutes a fundamental reference point for this aspect of our work, as well as for the theme of power in general.

First of all, Canetti distinguishes between 'open mass' and 'closed mass', and defines as 'bursting' 'the sudden transformation of open mass into closed mass' (1960, p. 19), from relatively passive to ready for action. The tendency of masses to be stationary may last a long time, but the upheavals are then sudden and revolutionary. The density of the mass can be an element of reassurance, and therefore of strength, at the moment of change. When the mass is attacked, it tends to react with greater compactness, which strengthens it. On the other hand, if the aggression comes from within, a dangerous situation is created: simultaneous aggression from within and without generates a sense of persecution, inducing people to see enemies everywhere. This can lead to a situation of 'panic', which corresponds to the 'disintegration of the masses' (1960, p. 31).

Canetti proposes some laws of behaviour of the masses: '1. The mass always wants to grow ... 2. Mass loves concentration ... 4. Mass needs direction' (1960, pp. 34–5). Of course, there are various types of masses. Canetti recalls the 'invisible mass' of the dead, but also non-human masses (which can be used as metaphors for human masses): fire, sea, rain, river, forest, wheat, wind, sand, piles of stones, treasure. Even masses of limited size can be used to describe a human mass in action by means of metaphors: pack of hounds, patrol, ... (1960, pp. 109 ff.). Power over the masses is also evident from the physical positions assumed by rulers and subjects: the elevated position of the throne; standing (the conductor, the speaker in front of the listeners, but also subjects in front of the king sitting on the throne) or sitting or prone or kneeling.

What interests us here is the social mass, the characteristics of which may differ from country to country. In order to summarize these different characteristics we can use 'mass symbols': the army – the marching mass – for the Germans, the revolution for the French (1960, p. 199). The clash between two masses is war. Of course, when a mass gets moving the power structure is bound to change; moreover, change is difficult to control, given the inertia of the movement of a large mass. It is more difficult to establish what can set the masses in motion; this requires a guiding action from outside, from a leading or potentially leading group; however, to be convincing the stimulation must be able to capture some motive forces (interests, culture) within the masses.

Compared to the period between the two World Wars, the growth in income, the increasing specialization of production roles and, above all, the spread of higher levels of education has changed the power relationship between the ruling classes and the masses, creating a fragmentation of interests and cultures within the latter and less static positions. Indeed, the populist movements that are widespread in contemporary politics show a reversal of the relationship, in which the 'many' must react to the overwhelming power of the 'few', denying their superiority ('one is as good as another').[21] In the political field, this principle has an ethical value, corresponding to the reaffirmation of the values of liberal democracy. The further step taken by demagogic populism consists in extending this principle to the fields of culture and science, replacing it to meritocracy, with the result of giving space to bizarre currents of thought, from flat-earth to no-vax and the like, with serious effects on the rationality of political debate and disastrous consequences on the practical level, as in the spread of the Covid-19 pandemic well beyond the inevitable.

7.4 CIVIL SOCIETY AND THE STATE

Partly coinciding with the theme of the relationship between elites and masses and partly distinct from it is that of the relationship between the state and society. This relationship is obviously influenced by the form of government. In dictatorships, often a part of the so-called civil society (in particular the intellectuals, the educated classes) forms the basis of the opposition to the regime. Here we shall focus on democratic governments.

First of all, by civil society we mean the set of institutions (legally structured cultural associations, parties, media, religious organizations; but also culture in the broader sense of individuals, families and other various forms of association) that are not necessarily opposed to the state (indeed they may even draw funding and support from it for their activities) but exist separately from it. Thus understood, civil society includes individuals belonging to different classes and strata; consequently, it may be affected by social conflicts, and it is not possible to attribute a specific political identity to it.[22]

[21] The different aspects of the opposition between the 'few' and the 'many' have been illustrated by Urbinati (2020).

[22] The term 'civil society' has in fact been given different meanings over time. For example, it has been identified with the 'Third sector': non-profit associations considered to be outside the public and private sectors, in Italy mainly Catholic, considered to be ethically deserving, for which favourable tax treatment is therefore required. In fact, not everything that falls under this definition deserves positive ethical judgement.

Civil society has a fundamental role in guiding the political choices of the community. It can also play an important role in directing citizens' actions towards the common good, prioritizing it over the selfish pursuit of self-interest regardless of the repercussions such actions have on others.

As regards the first aspect, civil society acts towards the state not only at the time of general elections, when its influence on voting (or not voting) determines the choice of political representatives; but also in inter-electoral periods, through the increasingly frequent use of opinion polls or the traditional instrument of street protests or the new instrument of the social media, which often have a steering function but which in some spectacular cases can change the course of political choices.

For the second aspect, it is necessary to consider the constantly changing balance between the different motivations (passions and interests) of human action.[23] The culture (*stricto sensu*) of a country determines the orientation of civil society, and so aspects like the spread of corruption, the more or less demagogic orientation of rulers and voters, the spread of favouritism, that is, the priority given to group interests over the interests of the community. Cultural dynamics, and the forms of its influence on civil society, are thus very important for a country's welfare, as well as for the efficiency of its economy – or in the opposite direction. It is usually a slow, gradual process, but one that can show sudden acceleration in change. To mention just a couple of examples, England in the early eighteenth century, before Pitt the Elder, was one of the most corrupt countries in Europe; Sweden, at the end of the nineteenth century, was considered among the most bigoted. In such cases, it is often the role of a few individuals, endowed with extraordinary character and personality, that can bring about significant changes – for

Rather, the attribute 'civil' can take on a positive connotation if used in the sense of a person who respects the rules of social coexistence and is attentive to the well-being of others (a bit like the English expression 'a decent human being').

23 On the origins of this debate see Hirschman (1977) and Rothschild (2001).

better or worse. But also the ethical attitude of those who operate in the various channels of transmission of ideas counts for a lot: in particular teachers and journalists, but also clergy, writers, actors, publishers and so on.

7.5 THE ROLE OF RELIGIONS

Religions may play a significant role in shaping society and its evolution.[24] To begin with, there is their role in forming the 'spirit' of a society, as in the thesis of Weber (1904–5) and others on the role of Protestantism in the birth of capitalism (or in the opposing thesis of Chafuen, 1986, on the role of Catholicism in the same direction). Then we have the role of religions as an instrument of control and domestication of the masses (religion as the 'opiate of the people' according to Marx, 1844, p. 126). Note that, although apparently opposed, these two theses can coexist: a religion that has contributed to the cultural foundations of a social formation such as capitalism may well be useful in shoring up its stability. In general, religions exert an important influence on the political orientations of the masses and on the cultural background of the ruling classes themselves.

The differences between the various religions are fundamental in this respect. An organization like the Catholic Church, with the intermediary role attributed to the clergy, allows for a greater top-down control of the culture of the masses than Protestantism, which gives the faithful a direct role in the search for the divine. While many religions are oriented towards ritualism and tradition, and in general towards control over all aspects of life, some (such as Islam and Orthodox Judaism) are more so than others; less so are religions such as Shintoism and Buddhism, which tend to be private cults centred on the family. Hinduism and Confucianism

[24] A less superficial treatment of the subject would entail comparative analysis of the different religions: their anthropological roots, their philosophical and ethical doctrines and the doctrinal debates within each of them, their diffusion over time and their influence on lifestyles and politics in different parts of the world. The literature on these topics is boundless.

convey, in different ways, a hierarchical conception of society (while Christianity and Islam tend to be egalitarian). The tensions, seen everywhere, between respect for religious traditions and the rights of individual self-determination are accentuated by the evolution of social customs driven by the growing cultural connections between different parts of the world.[25]

All monotheistic religions have a basic absolutist orientation ('thou shalt have no other Gods before Me'). However, this element lost power over time, starting with the Enlightenment and the progressive secularization of the state.[26] The fundamentalist extremism of the era of the Crusades and religious wars survives only in minority fringes of the various religions (ISIS, although important for its terrorist methods, is a small minority within the Muslim world). Economic and cultural globalization generates a drive towards integration, or perhaps better, towards coexistence, albeit full of tensions, with occasional outbreaks of violence. Although suggestive and useful in many respects, Huntington's (1996) thesis on the clash between religious traditions seems to grasp only one element, however important, within a multipolar world in which the economic-political-military confrontation between the United States and China and the varied positioning of the other main countries play an even more important role.

The integration of immigrants into traditions different from those of the countries they come from, in particular, requires the dissemination of a spirit of coexistence that allows for recognition of differences without absolutizing them. State education, as an alternative to denominational education, is a decisive means for spreading this spirit of coexistence: pupils become accustomed to dealing with

[25] Issues like gender equality, mixed or imposed marriages, teaching of religion in schools, presence of religious symbols in public buildings and schools, divorce, abortion, euthanasia, respect for different sexual orientations and sexuality outside marriage, do not necessarily imply a dichotomy between believers and non-believers.

[26] On the crisis of religious authority and the consequent political and intellectual emancipation initiated by the Enlightenment, see Israel's ponderous essay (2006).

teachers and other pupils with different religious views, to understanding their backgrounds and finding ways of coexisting with what is alien to their own family traditions. Coexistence in the classroom can indeed stimulate curiosity about the origins (not only religious, but also social and ethnic) of ways of thinking different from one's own, helping mutual understanding.

Defence of denominational schools by religious hierarchies does not contribute to spreading the spirit of coexistence. To their great credit, though, it should be pointed out that the spiritual leaders of the three major monotheistic religions – Catholics, Jews and Muslims – have attempted to provide an example of fraternal coexistence in diversity, concelebrating religious rites on some important occasions.

7.6 TECHNOCRATIC KNOWLEDGE AND THE ROLE OF ELITES

With the development of the division of labour, specialized knowledge becomes increasingly important. This contributes to the growth of a middle class of researchers, technicians, professionals and communication workers, who can aspire to representing the intellectual elite.[27]

What legitimizes this claim? As D'Ippoliti (2020, pp. 85–6) observes, in all fields of scientific research, the selection of insiders (*input legitimacy*) is done by co-optation, as are the choices for career advancement. Following this path is inevitable: it cannot be up to a neurosurgeon, a tram driver or a computer scientist (the general public) to assess the abilities of a philologist, or vice versa, which hinders legitimation from below. *Output legitimacy* poses complex

[27] This is somewhat different from the 'professional-managerial class' on which the Ehrenreich and Ehrenreich (1977) focus their attention: it is not characterized as 'labor necessary for the reproduction of capitalist social relationships' (p. 10) – on the contrary, it can have an oppositional role in raising criticisms against capitalism, as Schumpeter (1942) stresses – but rather as labour indirectly necessary for productive activities, to be characterized by the specific role played in the division of labour (simultaneously determined by technological and social elements).

problems of evaluation;[28] through the choice of appropriately unbalanced criteria it can be used – as has been the case in Italy and other countries in the last decade in the economic field – to favour certain orientations and fields of research over others. There remains what D'Ippoliti (2020) calls *throughput* legitimacy, that is, the legitimacy that can come from an open debate, recognized as an ethical obligation, between researchers working in the same field but supporting different theses.

The problem of the qualifications required for the task at hand also concerns the political class. In a democratic system, the political class is not selected on the basis of professional preparation; rather, the politicians must have the ability to select technically prepared and professionally honest advisors and to understand and evaluate the different opinions that may be offered to them. Meritocracy is an appropriate method of selection within the various fields of professional specialization, not for a 'profession' such as that of the politician – of which one should rather ask above-average ethical rigour, without any lapsing into any form of demagogy.

The need for high-level vocational training for certain professions automatically leads to the formation of technocratic elites. The risk is that an uncritical way of thinking will form within them, the conviction that they have the 'Truth' in their pockets (which Feyerabend, 1975, p. 180, equates with the pretension of the religious fanatic to hold the 'One True Religion'). The negative consequences are at least twofold: that the servile adhesion to the set of scientific knowledge available at a given moment blocks the exploration of new, potentially fruitful paths (the aspect on which Feyerabend insists in all his works, and not only him); that theoretical certainties end up imposing themselves, without the necessary mediations, even in concrete political choices, which often require more general evaluations.

[28] For example, if neurosurgeons were rated according to the percentage of successful operations, many would refuse to operate on patients in desperate conditions.

Let us take one example, namely nuclear power. Physicists and engineers can vouch for the fact that the latest generation of generators are much safer than their predecessors, but they seem immune to the consideration of problems such as the possibility of the construction of containment structures being outsourced to mafia-affiliated companies using substandard materials. In the case of bitcoin (or in general 'private crypto-currencies' based on blockchain technology), computer scientists enthusiastic about the development of the new technology – which is truly fascinating on an intellectual level – seem not to realize that it encourages the formation of opaque financial networks that are in fact used for trafficking drugs or human organs for transplant. When people claim to be able to carry out checks simply by registering who enters the network, they forget the systematic use of front men in the criminal economy. In essence, technocracies that specialize in a given field of work often fail to take into account the imperfections of the society in which they live, compared to a utopian ideal standard of comparison. Precisely for this reason, political evaluation of their analyses and policy proposals is necessary; the technicians themselves, when they have tasks of public importance, must be open to the consideration of aspects that are not within their direct competence, but which are relevant to the choices under consideration.

The growing role of specialist knowledge now makes it possible to consider the presence of a technocratic elite alongside the elites of economic and political power. In the next section we will consider the differences between technical culture and humanistic culture – the issue of the two cultures – which further complicates the picture.

Knowledge provides power. Hence, the smaller the circle of people who share it, the greater their impact on the economy and society. This power runs in two directions: towards political power, and towards the ordinary citizen.

For the latter, take the example of the power of doctors in general, and of the few really good doctors in particular, over the seriously ill; or of the power of teachers over students. Power of this kind is limited by the power of money: the specialist sells his/her skills on the market, and in it the power of the principal, which is given by his/her ability to pay, depends on the unequal distribution of income and wealth.

There is a dialectical relationship between technocratic and political power: normally, it is political power that selects trusted technicians to surround itself with; however, there may be circumstances in which social malaise or situations of political chaos lead to technicians being entrusted with political roles. Technicians consulted by politicians retain their autonomy of judgement, and to some extent help to specify political strategies. Politicians, on the other hand, have the problem of distinguishing, in the variety of positions often presented by technocratic elites, those that are more reasonable from those with less solid scientific foundations.

The relationship between politicians and technocratic elites is particularly complex where economists are concerned. Keynes argued that economics is an art: the art of choosing between various theories (after scientific scrutiny) and deciding which apply to the situation at hand. Differences of opinion are therefore legitimate and recurrent. However, a dangerous situation can arise when some political movement decides to pursue a strategy full of contraindications, and to support its validity enlists second-rate technicians, willing (whether convinced or not) to defend the untenable in order to gain a place in the sun.

In economics, one choice in which technicians played a major role was the creation of the euro. The political choice – to strengthen European unity through monetary union, in order to counterbalance the weight of German unification after the collapse of the Berlin Wall – left economists with the task of outlining the specific institutions and operating rules for the single currency. And here, almost as a counterbalance to the pressure for monetary integration that Germany had had to endure, German fiscal rigour prevailed, encouraged by the spread of ordoliberal and neoliberal doctrines among economic experts. The Central Bank was thus entrusted with the sole objective of containing inflation, neglecting unemployment, which was essentially entrusted to the invisible hand of the market; strict limits were set for financial policy; looser limits were assigned to excessive balance of payments surpluses, essentially placing the burden of adjustment on the countries in deficit, forced to adopt restrictive policies (whereas it would have been wiser to require countries in surplus to adopt expansionary policies, contributing to the overall growth of the European Union). In this way, the sum of the political element (Germany's bargaining power) and the technical element (the spread of a neo-liberal economic culture) have contributed to the construction of a single currency that tends to act as a brake on economic growth.[29]

7.7 SPECIALIZATION AND GENERAL CULTURE: THE DEBATE ABOUT TWO CULTURES

Technocratic elites are fragmented according to branches of knowledge. In some cases, modern forms of freemasonry provide meeting points and links between the different specialties: legal, medical, financial, and so on. In this way, they facilitate the selection of experts to be called upon if the need arises (the choice of a lawyer by a doctor, the choice of a doctor by a lawyer and so forth); however, in the case of appointments, political or otherwise, they can favour a 'network' selection over a meritocratic selection.

The diversity of the fields of specialist knowledge, of the forms of more or less meritocratic selection within them, of the types of power involved, emerges strikingly in the contrast between humanistic and scientific culture. This is a long-debated topic (if not before, at least since an essay by Snow in 1956 in the *New Statesman*, later developed in Snow, 1963) and one of considerable importance. The dialectic between the different types of culture can be made more complex by distinguishing within the humanities between literary

[29] On these issues see D'Ippoliti et al. (2020).

culture and social culture, as proposed by Lepenies (1990); over time, the relationships of proximity and differentiation between the three poles evolve, with social culture maintaining a median position, perpetually oscillating between literary culture and that of the natural sciences. The presence of interdisciplinary links (such as the use of chemistry by art historians, geology by archaeologists, or mathematics by demographers, economists, and now also sociologists) does not eliminate the underlying problem, which arises, for example, in the contrast between different methodologies (such as the experimental method in the natural sciences, the logical-deductive method in mathematics, the method of text and context verification in philology).

The criteria of truth or, in less bombastic terms, the criteria for validating theories, vary from case to case, ranging from pure abstract logical reasoning based on the principle of non-contradiction in the case of mathematics to the construction of theoretical models that can be verified through experiments in the case of physics or chemistry, or through observation of actual behaviour of appropriately selected cases in the case of ethology or psychology, to the identification, analysis and interpretation of available documentation in the case of historiographical reconstructions. In the field of the humanities, what has been called (among the first, by Adam Smith, 1795, followed in contemporary times by a philosopher of science like Feyerabend, 1975) the method of rhetorical comparison dominates, which is in fact also used in the field of natural sciences: a procedure analogous to that of the trial debate, in which arguments, both logical and factual, are brought to support or criticize the various theses.

The criteria for validating theories, which vary from discipline to discipline and may vary over time, are essential for establishing the rank of scientists, hence their relative power within their discipline (provided meritocratic criteria and not network powers prevail). However, the increasing recourse to collaboration in research groups, together with the need for funds to finance the research itself (especially in the case of experimental research), generates a level of power distinct from that of individual success in research activity: the power to obtain funding and valid collaborators; the control of research bodies, evaluation agencies, bodies (from foundations to ministerial directorates) that make research grants; participation in academic networks that favour the career of one's collaborators or relations with journals and publishers to facilitate the publication of research. In this way academic power intersects with political or economic power.

7.8 NEW MEDIA AND THE CORRUPTION OF PUBLIC DISCOURSE

The tools of public discourse are the subject of a large body of research by communication scholars. McLuhan (in McLuhan and Powers, 1986) emphasizes the link between technology and culture that passes through the form of communication: a first phase, 'tribal', dominated by oral communication; a second phase (the 'Gutenberg galaxy') dominated by written communication; finally, a third phase (that of the 'global village') dominated by radio and television. Before him, Innis (1950) had proposed a new perspective, stressing how communication technology determines the form of power, with epochal changes in the passage from stone to papyrus, then to paper, and finally to printing. Furthermore, Innis identified two types of communication tools: those oriented to duration in time (such as written texts, whatever their medium, but also memorization) and those oriented to diffusion through space (radio, TV, newspapers, which transmit messages that are ephemeral by nature): the former support the constitution of societies that tend to be stable, the latter characterize societies that are constantly changing. In retrospect, these reflections allow us to fully grasp how revolutionary the development of the Internet and the new social media can be today.[30]

[30] Heimans and Timms (2018) speak in this regard of 'new power', right from the title of their extensive illustration of the topic.

As a new instrument of both public and private discourse, the Internet is a real revolution. Its birth and initial development stemmed from the intersection of basic research (CERN in Geneva) and the importance of communications for the military field; its subsequent rapid expansion owes much to the libertarian culture spread in scientific circles, with the widespread use of open-source software, not patented by its creators and therefore freely available to all.[31]

Different interests and cultures revolve around the Internet: the community of computer scientists who work on its technical development and oversee its smooth operation; entrepreneurs interested in the multiple value creation possibilities offered by the new tool; the community of users, which is varied, vast and rapidly growing, with beginners gradually acquiring new skills; and, finally, hackers.

The latter are characterized by an extreme libertarian culture, concerning both the new software and its use for information gathering, and the value placed on technical skills: the display of skills in using the network sometimes becomes an end in itself.[32] At least originally, hackers were keen to distinguish themselves from 'crackers', who use their skills for not only illegal but also criminal purposes: gathering information for espionage (especially industrial) or blackmail; cyber-attacks to create malfunctions in network nodes, now also used as a military weapon. Compared to the initial stages of IT, the situation is now progressively worsening, so much so that the distinction between hackers and crackers disappeared in practice.

For the community of users, the main advantages of the Internet are twofold: the construction of a wide network of contacts, which can ignore geographical distances;[33] the availability of a huge mass of information (Wikipedia, computer libraries, etc.). Contacts become more frequent, even if somewhat less intense; the search for

[31] A lively history of the early developments of the digital world is Ciotti-Roncaglia (2000); on the importance of open-source software for the rapid technological development of the sector, see Castells (2001, pp. 47 ff.).

[32] See Castells (2001, pp. 49–59).

[33] 'Networks replace places as the medium of sociality' (Castells, 2001, p. 125).

information can cover a much wider ground, even if at least occasionally at the cost of being more superficial. Other developments in the use of the Internet include role-playing games (now the Metaverse) and home automation, which are spreading rapidly, and – as we saw during the Covid-19 pandemic – distance learning and smart working. The latter in particular is likely to retain importance after the end of the pandemic; the implications in the field of education are wide-ranging, in large part still to be verified.[34]

Among new communicators more than among the new forms of communication we can include the think tanks: research centres established in the form of foundations, companies or associations, dealing with the most diverse topics, usually in the political and economic field. In principle, they are self-financed through the sale of their own research products, but in reality they are often supported by external funding that directs their work as part of a lobbying activity. Although biased, in many cases their output is serious and worthy of consideration.[35]

The distortions of public discourse enabled by media control frequently stem from lobbies, pressure groups organized to support some interest, usually economic. Without going as far as corruption (which is also abundantly practised, often in the minute form of small favours and gifts), lobbies operate as advocates of specific points of view, organizing the favourable elements in a pleasant form and criticizing the unfavourable ones, providing political staff with appropriately selected material, going as far as preparing speeches, interpellations, parliamentary bills. Their function is in this respect similar to corporate marketing, which highlights the positive qualities of a product while actively silencing or downplaying its negative side. As with marketing, we can say that lobbies have a positive aspect, due to the sometimes hard-to-find information they make

[34] 'We need a new pedagogy, based on interactivity, personalisation and the development of autonomous learning and thinking skills' (Castells, 2001, p. 258).

[35] The University of Pennsylvania publishes an annual *Global Go to Think Tank Index Report*, available at https://repository.upenn.edu/think-tanks.

available, and a negative aspect, due to the systematic distortion inherent in that information, which is one-sided even when it is correct, and which obliges (or should oblige) those who use it to be extremely cautious.

Important, too, is the fact that most of the world's publishing groups are controlled by industrial and financial conglomerates; pure publishers themselves, given their position as entrepreneurs, often tend to put up a common front with the former.[36] The influence on public opinion comes through omission of some issues, emphasis on others, selection of who to let speak in debates.

The diffusion of new social media (first the Internet and email services, then Facebook, Twitter, WhatsApp, Instagram and the like) changes the nature of communication due to their characteristics of speed and increasing diffusion, but also to some aspects of their technology: the high initial fixed costs and the very low marginal costs favour the tendency towards concentration of users on certain platforms, which often finance themselves not by selling their services but through advertising inserts, which, thanks to the use of big data collected on Internet users, can be targeted at individual users. This leads to three main consequences. The first, positive, is the enormous enlargement of the audience of participants in the debate. The other three are negative: the tendency of each participant in the debate to respond immediately and to intervene on multiple fronts leads to downplaying serious documentation and meditated reflection; new social media (Twitter, WhatsApp, etc.) often impose brevity, hence simplification of reasoning, replaced with slogans; the formation of 'bubbles', groups of people with common interests and opinions who, by interacting with each other, escape open debate and tend to adopt extreme positions, with a segmentation of identities.[37]

[36] Antitrust rules should be stricter in the case of information media than for other economic sectors. In particular, there is a need to define strictly the markets for which the degree of concentration should be assessed: for example, sports and generalist newspapers should not be considered together as belonging to a single market.

[37] See G. Roncaglia (2018).

The fact is that the choices to be made in social life can never, ever, be reduced to binary choices (yes/no, this or that). When faced with complex choices, which also imply gradual margins in their adoption, simplification is often a source of error. In fact, simplification encourages what Hirschman (1991) calls the rhetoric of reaction: policies aimed at changing the status quo have negative effects, are ineffective, and jeopardize achievements already made. In fact, any incisive policy has negative effects (for some subjects and/or for some aspect), but it also has positive effects that can more than counterbalance the negative ones; it is ineffective, if this means that it can never lead to a utopian perfect solution, although it guarantees an improvement in the situation; it can be counterproductive, if badly formulated – the details are crucial.[38] Another rhetorical technique often used to stimulate a negative attitude towards reforms is 'TAMITOE' (there are more important things on earth): there are more important problems than the one being addressed – as if addressing one problem prevents us from addressing another (this can happen, but rarely, and would need to be demonstrated).[39] The rhetoric of reaction, used in an organized way and with adequate financial support, can affect public opinion and shift electoral support.

Another area in which the simplification of political discourse has serious negative effects is that of online voting, smuggled in as an example of direct democracy, considered more 'pure' than representative democracy. Beyond the representativeness of the voters, who generally constitute a small and distorted sample of potential voters, online voting implies that the questions put to the vote are clear-cut, devoid of nuance. As a result, the very way in which the question is

[38] 'According to the perversity thesis, any action aimed at improving some aspect of the political, social or economic order only serves to exacerbate the condition it is intended to remedy. The futility thesis asserts that attempts to transform society will be in vain … Finally, the jeopardy thesis argues that the cost of the proposed change or reform is too high because they jeopardise some valuable prior achievement' (Hirschman, 1991, p. 14).

[39] The mind goes, for example, to those who claim that it is pointless to fight individual income tax evasion while success is lacking in the fight against tax avoidance on the part of businesses (or vice versa: two outlandish justifications for doing nothing).

formulated inevitably constitutes a stretch: a subtle, or not so subtle, pressure to vote one way rather than another.[40] It follows that the systematic use of online voting constitutes a denial of open political discourse and is therefore deeply undemocratic.

The issue of fake news is very serious. As we have already said, social media can be used by organizations offering services of repeated messaging to audiences that are vast and highly selected. The purchasers of such services are companies interested in marketing their own products (and sometimes also in casting their competitors' products in a bad light), but more and more frequently they are entities (political parties or their supporters, or foreign governments) interested in spreading – under the cover of anonymity – partisan slogans, slander and false news, with the aim of conditioning the orientation of public opinion, especially during elections. There is evidence, or at least there are strong indications, of active interventions of this kind to influence the referendum on Brexit in the UK, Trump's US presidential campaign, and elections in other European countries including Italy. Alongside the dissemination of fake news, or the repeated hammering out of personal criticisms towards certain politicians, the use of trolls (computer programs that send out messages) has been reported to clog up the accounts of political opponents. In addition to all this, there is a relatively new social phenomenon (perhaps always latent and made more incisive by the new technology): haters, who under the cover of anonymity with personal attacks and threats are able to affect the lives of prominent personalities negatively. Interventions of this kind can focus on marginal electoral areas, where a modest shift in public opinion can determine election results. The supranational nature of the Internet, and of social media in general, makes it possible to operate from foreign countries and to escape the controls of the countries towards which the intervention is directed.

[40] The importance of framing (the way alternatives are presented to choose from) has been widely recognized by behavioural scientists; nudge, which earned Thaler a Nobel Prize, is seen as a tool for public policy as well as corporate policy (marketing). On framing, see Kahneman and Tversky (1979); on nudging, Thaler and Sunstein (2008).

Additionally, the messages transmitted are calibrated to the sensitivities of the recipients, identified through the 'big data' that Internet users make available almost without realizing it (credit card purchases, websites visited, personal data given, and so on), so as to have maximum effectiveness. The development of information technology makes it possible to easily obtain and quickly process these enormous masses of data and to extract what is needed for targeted interventions on specific groups of the public (such as swing voters). We have now entered the world of the Panopticon, the ideal prison designed by Bentham (1791) and organized in such a way that the guards could always monitor the inmates on sight. Pervasive control over others gives enormous power (even to the point of blackmail) to those who are able to use it.

Defending democracy means blocking fake news, which comes up against the opposition of not only those who use it and the powerful companies that control the new social media, but also of the ultraliberals who see any restriction on freedom of speech as an attack on freedom itself. However, just as a democratic government can adopt restrictions on freedom of movement in the face of a pandemic, so too should a democratic government be able to intervene on the spread of dangerous falsehoods: freedom of speech is one thing, to be defended against totalitarian regimes that seek to constrain it; intervention by a democratic government, therefore in principle representative of all and subject to public scrutiny of its actions, to prevent the serious damage to social coexistence that can come from the distorted use of new social media is quite another.[41] Of course, great caution is needed when dealing with any constraints on free speech. Faced with the distortions of public discourse and the difficulties of ad hoc

[41] Let us recall Popper's 'paradox of tolerance' (1945, vol. 1, p. 265): 'Unlimited tolerance must lead to the disappearance of tolerance'; one cannot be tolerant towards the intolerant, who otherwise would end up prevailing. On the importance of new social media and fake news in the power struggle, see Heimans and Timms (2018); they point out, for instance, that advertising space sold by Facebook to Russian-backed operators had reached over 150 million Americans (p. 156).

interventions, the main channel of reaction remains educating the public to a serious, informed and conscious political debate. State education and public cultural institutions can play an essential role in this respect.

We can distinguish between education and training policies. The latter are concerned with the acquisition of vocational qualifications and thus influence the distribution of income and power. Education policies, which conservative culture regards as secondary to vocational training policies, are concerned with the acquisition of the general cultural basis, including the ability to learn, collect and process information. Alongside primary, secondary and university education, there are institutions of continuing education: public libraries, museums, cultural centres and associations that provide tools, meeting places and stimulation for the general public. These institutions are central to the defence of open, uncorrupted public discourse: hence, to making the democracy we live in less imperfect.

8 The Spatial Dimension of Power

8.1 SPATIAL LEVELS OF POWER

One aspect to be considered in the analysis of power is its spatial extension. In general, the power relationship is all the stronger, the closer the active and passive elements of the relationship are to each other. In primitive societies, this is absolutely true, because of the absence of relationships beyond a fairly limited perimeter: a caveman may dominate within a cave, may have a limited influence on other cave-dwellers within walking distance, but cannot have any relationship, power or otherwise, with cavemen far away.

In modern societies, spatial distances can easily be overcome, but they retain some importance. Military power is now omnipresent, but intercontinental ballistic missiles are only available to a few major powers. Economic competition from products of other countries is increased by the reduction of transport costs, but these may remain important. Modern means of mass communication allow the exercise of cultural influence – up to a situation of hegemony – between countries and even between different continents; language barriers may limit (but not completely block) this type of influence but even in this case, direct relations, favoured by proximity, exert a stronger influence.

We can therefore think of a series of concentric spheres, extending from small groups of people to the whole of humanity. The nuclear family, then the extended family, constitute an initial nucleus, with an internal glue that weakens very gradually in the course of history, at a faster pace as the mobility of young people increases and the stability of the relationship diminishes.[1]

[1] Transition from the patriarchal family to the modern family, which has been going on for decades now, cannot, however, be said to be fully completed, especially if we

Then comes the local community: the village, the city district, the circle of families that gather around a parish or a school or a cultural centre, a pub or a club. Here too, the bond is weakening, though not disappearing, with technological and social developments, which extend – for example, via the Internet – the range of relations of each individual. However, the local community level is still very important for consensus building. Tools such as newspapers, radio, television and the new social media, often have – perhaps even increasingly – a local dimension.

Then we have cities, whose importance has grown enormously with the rapid process of urbanization that in almost all countries has accompanied the growth of state functions and the service sector. In some cases, large cities act as centres of attraction for metropolitan areas that can reach the size of a small state. In all cases, the economic and social structure of cities, especially the larger ones, has distinctive characteristics. On the other hand, city institutions have often remained unchanged for decades and today may present problems of functionality.[2]

Mid-way between these levels and the state level is the regional level, whose importance varies over time and from country to country. Its importance is highest where the dominant ethnic group in the region differs from the dominant ethnic group in the state of which the region is a part. Examples include Catalonia, the Basque Country, Scotland, Chechnya, Flanders and Wallonia, South Tyrol, the Armenian diaspora, Russians in the eastern parts of Ukraine, the Uyghurs and many others; in these cases there can be separatist tensions, such as those that led to the division of Czechoslovakia into the Czech Republic and Slovakia or to the break-up of Yugoslavia.

consider not the residential units but the significant persistence of a 'family culture' that concerns more the traditional than the modern nuclear dimension. For a long time the extended family included slaves and servants or *clientes*, as in ancient Rome; a similar extension had the Scottish clans, which for centuries represented the main element of segmentation of that people.

[2] As Bagnasco (2013, p. 190) notes, in large cities social problems accumulate and aspects of social polarization manifest themselves more strongly.

Even greater tensions can arise in cases where there is not even a reference state reality, as in the case of the Kurds or the Palestinians, the Uyghurs or the Rohingyas.

The next sphere is the nation state with its legal structure. As we saw in Chapter 6, this is a sphere whose importance grows in the course of the modern age, only to gradually lose weight, although the glue of the political and legal superstructure remains very strong. In the case of the European Union, nation states have ceded part of their sovereignty, initiating the transition to a federation, which requires further important steps to be taken.

Finally, in defining the great regions of the world, geography counts, but history and culture count even more (as in the case of Australia and New Zealand, which are more closely linked to Europe and America than to Asia). As we shall see later, a very important element is constituted by religions (which Huntington, 1996, considers preponderant in defining rival areas on a world scale: the 'clash of civilisations', with its 'fault lines' marking the imprecise boundaries between different religious orientations). Another constantly evolving element is the relationship between the North and the South of the world (between countries with different levels of economic development) and the markets for raw materials, whose importance varies over time, also in relation to changes in technology. The North–South divide also includes the problem of migration, which to a large extent involves population flows from poorer to richer countries, although the immediate trigger is often crises within the countries of departure (as with Syria and Ukraine).

The game of international relations leads to more or less long-lasting, more or less close and more or less wide-ranging alliances. It has its own autonomy, albeit partial and limited: the temporary predominance of one political faction over the other within various countries can lead to changes in the lines of connection and the intensity of relations, which are therefore always evolving. At a national level, politics dominates the economy, but to a decreasing extent as globalization takes hold, so that international economic constraints can now also be decisive for national politics, particularly in times of crisis.

As we shall see later, the rules of the international economic game have changed over time. The foundations of the new postwar international economic order were laid at the Bretton Woods conference in 1944. A fundamental aspect of this new order, the system of fixed exchange rates, collapsed in 1971: public powers were weakened in favour of private ones; the uncontested freedom of movement of financial capital became established, even in the short and very short term, which favoured globalization dominated by a few major financial centres and players.

8.2 FAMILY AND FAMILY CLAN

Distribution of power within the family is one of the most widely studied themes. This is from both the point of view of historical evolution and of the differences between various peoples and cultures.

As regards the first aspect, technological and environmental factors influence the dominant but not universal trend towards the monogamous family; exceptions are also interesting, such as polygamy, present in areas and periods of war where male mortality is high.[3] The transition from the extended to the nuclear family seems to accompany the transition from predominantly rural to industrialized economies, which are characterized by a higher territorial mobility of workers. Culture often follows the economic impetus for evolution only belatedly; family favouritism (cf. Section 5.3) often concerns the extended family even when the nuclear family dominates and is the sign of opposition by the extended family, of ancient origin, to the state and its laws, of more recent origin: a long-lasting cultural persistence. In addition to being a direct source of inefficiencies that are costly for society as a whole, family favouritism implies an a-social mentality in which respect for the rules

[3] See Cairncross's (1974) reconstruction of the case of the Munster republic in Germany in the mid-sixteenth century.

of civil coexistence loses importance. In particular, corruption and mafia-type criminal associations tend to be more present in countries where nepotism is more widespread.[4]

The second aspect, differences in the family between peoples and cultures, seems to be losing importance in the age of globalization. The tendency is for the monogamous nuclear family to prevail. The distribution of power within the family, though, continues to be marked by significant differences, often reaffirmed as manifestations of identity, for example with the contrast between traditional Islamic culture and the equal families that are spreading in the Western world. At one end of the spectrum we have the power of the *pater familias* (somewhat reminiscent of the alpha male of various animal species), often accompanied by matriarchal power in the internal management of the family unit, while the male is assigned the role of representative of the family to the outside world. At the other extreme we have the modern family, characterized by increasing (though far from complete) gender equality, an ideal type that has now gained cultural hegemony in Western countries, but not among all classes and geographical areas. One-person families, non-traditional families and simple partnerships are also increasing.[5]

Changes taking place in the family institution are part of the gradual but profound evolution of customs, characterized by the development of individual rights and above all by the process of rebalancing gender roles. Very slow in Islamic countries, much faster

[4] Recommendation can also be considered a form of corruption (Zinn, 2001, p. viii), although 'on the whole, recommendation is part of a wider network of emotional relationships' (p. xi); it has various forms, in which the figures of 'mediator' and 'patron' appear (p. 38). The widespread habit of accompanying (or following up) a recommendation with a gift makes this practice very similar to bribes, paid to obtain an unfair or illegal advantage. Very dangerous for the vitality of democracy is clientelism in the political field, with the exchange of votes for favours; even more dangerous are the links that clientelism can create between politics and organized crime (not only in the south of Italy). In the next section we shall return to the importance of what Putnam (2000) calls 'social capital'.

[5] On a cultural level, one can point to the spread, still at an early stage, of 'queer theory', i.e. the existence – and legitimacy – of a variety of sexual orientations that cannot be rigidly classified. See Jagose (1996).

in Western countries, this process experienced a strong initial push when, during the Second World War, women massively entered the world of work to replace workers and employees who had left for the front. Encouragement to stay in work after the end of the war came from the parallel spread of artificial contraceptives and household appliances, which greatly reduced the family workload.

Women's activity rates are still lower than men's, with significant differences from country to country, but they tend to increase everywhere. At the same time, the proportion of women completing secondary school and graduating from university is tending to level off with that of men, even in scientific faculties. This trend is being followed by the spread of women into various jobs, including those traditionally regarded as male prerogatives, from engineers to the police. Even more gradually, but with perceptible progress, there has been an expansion of the proportion of women in managerial and top positions in the various professions. Differences in income for the same job still persist but are being reduced over time. For working women, there is still a large difference in daily working time when taking into account work within the family. If we look at the achievements compared to the starting points, we are indeed facing epochal changes. But if we look at the persistent inequalities, which are still considerable in all these respects, we must recognize that there is still a long way to go, and that the pace of change can be considered insufficient. Although this is a decisive issue of civil progress, it is not possible to address it here beyond these brief remarks; there is a vast literature on the subject, to which we refer.[6]

8.3 LOCAL POWERS

Local authorities par excellence are the local branches of the state: in Italy the governing bodies of cities, provinces and regions. Very different in size and therefore also in problems (ranging from

[6] For a recent wide-ranging collection of contributions on various aspects of the topic and various perspectives of investigation, see Berik and Kongar (2021).

regional to small town councils where everyone knows everyone else), they are commonly governed by the same set of rules, which in democratic countries include free electoral competitions to choose administrators.

The choice of local leaders (especially mayors of large cities or regional presidents) is part of the broader process of selecting a national political class. The quality of the political class depends on the selection mechanisms: both those of initial co-option and those of internal circulation from less important to more important positions (and vice versa, perhaps temporarily following electoral defeats, or as a form of gradual retirement from political activity). Both the electorate and party bureaucrats that select candidates play a role in selection.

Voter activism, both at local and national level, seems to have declined over time. After a high level of public participation in elections immediately after the Second World War, there has been a gradual decline in participation, while still contradicting the theorems of public choice theory that argue that it is irrational for individuals to vote, since the utility/importance of an individual vote is lower than the cost of time required to cast it.[7]

Alongside local communities, a multitude of smaller bodies collectively play a significant role in the lives of citizens and in the formation (or disintegration) of the social fabric. Strongly positive outcomes are possible, where cooperation develops in mutual help, or strongly negative outcomes, where differences of opinion on decisions to be taken turn into systematic opposition and deep-rooted

[7] If, in the context of a utilitarian conception of individual choices, one compares the negative element of the time wasted in going to the polls with the practically nil weight of the individual vote in determining the electoral result, voting appears irrational: cf. Downs (1957). Simon (1993, p. 160) comments: 'The 'paradox' of voting (the fact that people go to vote) is a paradox only in the absence of altruism', in the sense of interest in what happens in society. What also counts is the desire for active participation, to concretely manifest one's adherence to a political position. Fortunately, participation in politics is often guided by ideals (the most diverse, from individual to individual) and not by immediate personal interests.

hostility. Examples are apartment block management, departmental councils in universities, or class and school councils in schools.

Cultural, political, religious or sports associations are of a different kind. Although their members are self-selected because they are united by a common purpose, all too often they become a battleground for management selection and control (especially when they are used as a launching pad for political careers). The initial impetus that leads to their establishment and to providing a useful contribution to the life of the community can be lost along the way with the passage of time, especially but not only in the inevitable occasions of generational change; the good reputation acquired can make the company name attractive for a distorted use of individual power. Such transformations are not the rule, but neither are they uncommon.

8.4 THE CENTRALIST STATE AND THE FEDERAL STATE

Thousands and thousands of pages have been written on the forms of organization of the state. Here we can only briefly mention some of the main aspects.

Firstly, there is a clear distinction between the centralist state and the federal state. The former, the classic example being Napoleon's France, considers local authorities as mere administrative articulations of the state administration. The second, for which the USA is a typical example, envisages wide spaces of autonomy, including legislative autonomy and self-government for local communities. These are different cultural traditions, crystallized in different constitutions.

In this regard we can recall the contrast between the centralist statesman Camillo Cavour and the federalist Carlo Cattaneo on the organizational form to be adopted for the nascent kingdom of Italy. The prevalence of the centralist-authoritarian form, partly due to the influence of the French model (and the French army), crystallizing in the constituent phase of Italian unity in the second half of the nineteenth century, conditioned the development of civic culture in Italy.[8]

Transition to a confederal form, with the granting of extensive autonomy to regions, took place gradually in the three decades after the Second World War and the proclamation of the Italian Republic, although the institution of the regions was immediately included in the Constitution. The subject is still topical, linked to the issue of the transfer of resources between the richest and poorest areas of the country, while most recently the Covid-19 pandemic has re-proposed the issue of the division of tasks and coordination between the various decision-making levels.

The organizational political form is important: parliamentary or presidential democracy, first-past-the-post or proportional representation, and so on. Each form has its pros and cons, and the debate is too wide-ranging to cover here.[9]

In parliamentary democracies with a party system, the organizational form of the parties themselves is important. After the 'democratic centralism' of the Italian Communist Party (PCI) and the system of competing factions of the Christian Democrats (DC) and the Socialists (PSI), we now have in Italy a variety of forms, from traditional parties to personal leaderships. The role of parties can be more or less important in the selection of the political class: a predominantly bottom-up selection in parties of the old type dominated by internal factions; a mixed selection in parties characterized by democratic centralism, where selection is guided from above but on the basis of the skills demonstrated in grassroots work; a top-down

[8] The federalist thesis was taken up by Carlo Rosselli, who stressed the importance of communal autonomy (2020, pp. 256–7): 'Without communal institutions, a nation can give itself a free government, but not the spirit of freedom. … The most serious error of the democratic conception that sprang from the French Revolution was to believe that the *state and the individual were the two sole poles*, and to fear that individual freedom, conquered with such difficulty, would soon be annulled if other freedoms were recognised alongside it.'

[9] For an introductory overview, see Pasquino (1997).

selection in Caesarean parties and political movements; now occasionally also telematic consultations among members (being a very small minority of the voters) on a telematic platform. In the absence of a strong ethic of responsibility of professional politicians (Weber, 1919), each of these paths has important drawbacks.

8.5 MULTINATIONALS

The relative power of states depends on a number of elements: absolute population size, absolute (GDP) and relative (GDP per capita) economic strength, military might, technology, influence and cultural attractiveness.

The role of the economy has been widely discussed. In addition to the power of states, there is the power of large transnational corporations, which contribute (over and above their economic strength as measured by GDP) to the power of their countries of origin. Transnational corporations are companies, or groups of companies, whose activities take place in several countries at the same time. The overall strategy, including investment decisions in the various countries, is decided at the centre, by the parent company; transfer prices between the major subsidiaries are also decided at the centre, thus determining the amount of tax paid in the different countries and favouring those with the lowest tax rates. For example, an oil transnational may have crude oil extracted in Nigeria by a local affiliate, transported by tankers of a Panamanian affiliate, refined by an affiliate in the Virgin Islands, with gasoline sold by an Irish affiliate, following an overall strategy devised by the parent company in the United States. The result is that tax payments by oil transnationals are generally less than 1 per cent of profits.

Consequently, thanks also to their size and control of technology, which contribute to their bargaining power – often reinforced by the power of the state hosting the parent company – transnational corporations, together with the major financial institutions, are an important component of neo-colonialism, that is, the power exercised not only economically but also politically by the richest countries over the poorest ones.[10]

Connected to but distinct from the topic of transnational corporations is that of so-called global value chains, that is, the relocation of the production and final assembly of the components of a product to different countries (see Section 3.7). Local producers of components may in fact be enterprises independent of the enterprise that organizes the chain and sells the final product; only if they are not, does the global value chain fall within the case of the transnational enterprise.

The power of large transnational corporations has been criticized on several occasions, particularly after Pinochet's coup in Chile (1973).[11] The United Nations launched the New International Economic Order programme in 1974, and in 1975 set up the United Nations Center on Transnational Corporations (UNCTC). This was followed in 1976 by the adoption of the OECD Guidelines for Multinational Enterprises, which outlined a kind of code of conduct both for companies and for the countries of the parent companies and those hosting the affiliates (e.g. the latter were to avoid nationalization of local affiliates without adequate compensation, and the parent companies were to avoid intervening with bribes or otherwise to influence the policies of the affiliates' host countries).

Subsequently, the revival of neo-liberalism led to a change of course, with widespread adherence to the doctrines of the Washington Consensus and the launch in 1999 of the Global Compact as a partnership between UN agencies and large transnational corporations. Recently the issue of tax avoidance, which reduces corporate tax revenues to an insignificant trickle, has returned to the centre of

[10] Among the many works on the subject, we recall one of the earliest, Hirschman (1945).

[11] For example, ITT, which in 1970 bought the Chilean telephone company (the CTC), whose nationalization was threatened by the newly elected Chilean president Allende, intervened heavily in support of the Chilean right-wing opposition, including through pressure on the US authorities and the CIA. See Sampson (1973).

attention; in the face of attempts to tackle it, it is increasingly clear that transnational corporations constitute a strong countervailing power to that of states.

8.6 CONFEDERATIONS AND ALLIANCES

In an increasingly interconnected world, structured relations between states are becoming more and more important: confederations, such as the European Union; military alliances, such as NATO; free trade treaties, such as the UMSCA (formerly known as Nafta, composed of the United States, Mexico and Canada); and agreements such as the Treaty on the Non-Proliferation of Nuclear Weapons, or the one that gave rise to the World Trade Organization (WTO), or the Paris Environmental Agreements on global warming.

As Hirschman (1945) points out, international economic relations are used as an instrument of national power politics, through the use of quotas, tariffs, exchange controls, capital investment and other instruments, including the choice between systems for regulating international trade. To avoid the risks arising from economic nationalism, Hirschman (1945, pp. 79–80) states, 'The exclusive power to organise, regulate, and interfere with trade must be taken away from the hands of single nations. It must be transferred to an international authority able to exercise this power as a sanction against an aggressor nation.' Almost eighty years later, Hirschman's goal has only been partially achieved; economic nationalism is gaining ground again and with it international tensions.

For almost half a century after the end of World War II, the Cold War bipolarity between the United States and the Soviet Union dominated the world stage. In the decades following the break-up of the Soviet Union in 1991, Russia, while remaining the world's second nuclear power, gradually lost economic ground (its GDP is now smaller than that of Italy). During the same period, China's economic and military strength grew rapidly. The United States, while remaining the world's leading nuclear and technological power, experienced a gradual economic decline (in relative terms: China's GDP is expected to overtake that of the United States within a few years). The European Union has considerable economic clout, but has no common army and in fact no common foreign policy; other free trade areas, such as Asean, are elements of partial regional cohesion.

The United States is therefore gradually losing its role as the world's leading power, and is increasingly dependent on a network of more or less close, more or less structured, relations with other countries and groups of countries: a network of relations that was put to the test in the four years of the Trump presidency, with its sovereign/isolationist line summed up in the motto *America First.* Surpassing Russia, China is now the second world power, thanks also to a shrewd policy of expanding foreign economic relations, especially in Africa, which accompanies domestic growth in a targeted manner, ensuring supplies of raw materials, including rare metals, outlets for exports and for a growing presence of Chinese capital abroad, particularly in the transport infrastructure sector.[12]

We shall not consider here, but they are important, the military strategies of the major powers, such as the importance to be given to navy, air force, land army, special corps (and within these to the various types of weapons, e.g. aircraft carriers or submarines); the presence with air or naval bases in the various theatres of operation, the new role of drones and of cyber war: on these topics there is a vast amount of literature.[13]

As we can see, the subject of international power relations has a multiplicity of aspects, which we can only touch on here. We can recall the 'realist' theories, stressing sheer power relations between states, with special attention to military force; on the opposite side, 'liberal' theories built on the role of economic interrelationships

[12] See Kalantzakos (2018) on China's rare earths procurement policy. The topic of US hegemony and its gradual decline has been discussed extensively since the 1970s; see the bibliography cited by Strange (1987), which critiques the decline thesis. For more recent assessments, see e.g. Milanovic (2019) (discussed above, in Section 6.8).

[13] See for instance the reports on the subject by the Institute of International Affairs, available at www.iai.it.

connecting nations in a web that conditions them all. Keohane and Nye (1977, 1987) take an intermediate position, stressing the role of different aspects in international power relations, that may also limit the role of the state in world politics; they also develop the notion of 'international regimes', defined as 'governing arrangements that affect relationships of interdependence' (1977, p. 19), by favouring repetitive patterns of interaction that through reciprocity may induce cooperative behaviour. We have then Susan Strange's (1987) thesis of 'structural power', according to which there are four dimensions to be considered: security (military force and alliance policy), production (economic force), finance and knowledge (technology, universities). These elements help to identify where hegemony is located in international relations, making it possible to influence the institutions that regulate these relations (the meta-power to change the rules of the game) or to control their functioning.

Nye (1990) makes another distinction, between hard power and soft power. Developed as a counterpoint to the 'clash of civilizations' thesis to be discussed in the next section, this dichotomy aims to emphasize the importance of culture, values and institutions as a force of conviction for achieving and defending a position of hegemony in international relations (while hard power consists of the dimensions of the state: population, territory, natural resources, economic size, military strength and political stability). Nye emphasizes the tendency towards a diffusion of international power: growing economic interdependence, transnationals, diffusion of technologies and nationalist sentiments in weaker countries. While hard power allows a state to impose its will on other countries, soft power consists in bringing other countries to share its objectives.

8.7 THE CLASH OF CIVILIZATIONS

In considering the theme of the international distribution of power between states, we can recall in extreme synthesis three theses: that of the 'end of history' (Fukuyama, 1992), that of the 'conflict of civilisations' (Huntington, 1996) and that of the dichotomy between 'liberal meritocratic capitalism' and 'political capitalism' (Milanovic, 2019). In Section 6.8 we have already dealt with the first and third theses; the latter is the most recent, the one that seems most adequate to represent the dualism between the United States and China likely to constitute the dominant theme in the years to come. Let us now focus, albeit briefly, on the second thesis.

If read in a simplified way, Huntington's 'clash of civilisations' seems to divide the world into two opposing camps, the Christian West and Islam. The real world and Huntington's text are, however, much more complex. Above all, his thesis intends to signal a change in the definition of the forces in the field, attributing to the religious (and cultural, more generally) context of international politics in the era of globalization a decisive importance that had not been attributed to it until now.

Huntington uses this thesis to define the 'fault lines' of an increasingly complex interaction between and inside countries. The old tripartition of the world into Western bloc, Communist bloc and Third World countries, which focused on economic structure (market economies, planned economies, backward economies) and related political culture, has been followed by a phase in which the Christian world (including both the United States and Russia) has appeared to be under attack by an Islamic fundamentalism that is far more widespread than it appears if one looks at its territorial roots. The wars that followed the break-up of Yugoslavia, attacks such as that on the Twin Towers in New York or the subsequent ones in Paris and other European cities, also indicate that this confrontation does not follow traditional lines: economic competition, the arms race and diplomatic negotiations/tensions. Rather, we are faced with an oblique cultural/religious confrontation with ubiquity, which eludes diplomatic relations and measures military strength in terrorist actions. Opposition between Shiites and Sunnis in the Muslim world complicates the situation, as does the continuing opposition between the United States and Russia, with the inclusion of China as a new power, but one that is also beset internally by ethnic and religious tensions.

The case of Syria is an example of the complexity of these fault lines. Assad's dictatorship, supported by Russia, faced a popular rebellion that began in 2011 in the context of the 'Arab Spring'; the Shiite (Alawite) Assad, although a dictator with secularist tendencies, was supported by Shia Iran, against a largely Sunni Syrian population; the United States from the outside, then more directly and through Turkey, supported the rebellion, while Russia continued to support Assad. In the chaos that followed the uprising, an ISIS 'state' was formed within Syria, a fundamentalist base for Islamic terrorism around the world. The war against ISIS prompted alliances, albeit transitory, between historical adversaries such as the Kurds and Turkey, Russia and the United States. The war and the harshness of Islamic fundamentalism have driven a substantial proportion of Syria's population, around 6 million out of around 20 million, to flee; the defeat of ISIS and Trump's decision to withdraw US forces from the area have given way to a resurgence of attacks by the Turks against the Kurds, with a push for an alliance between Turkey and Russia (even while Turkey adheres to NATO). The war in Ukraine raises new interpretative issues: it may be seen as a renewal of the East–West confrontation, but with the Russian Federation looking backward to the orthodox catholic czarist Russian empire rather than communist Soviet Union. As is evident, the notion of a 'fault line' between Christians and Islam is of little help in understanding these events: once again, the multiplicity of factors at play must be acknowledged and their interrelationships taken into account.

8.8 MIGRATIONS

Migration waves, such as that of Syrian refugees and, more recently, Afghan and Ukrainian refugees, are nothing new in world history. But the memory of barbarian invasions certainly does not serve to reduce concern about today's problem. The character of contemporary migrations is, however, different: they are not invasions of entire populations moving to conquer new territories, but a significant and persistent flow over time, with economic motivations but also to escape from wars, dictatorships and civil chaos. Climate migrations (e.g. from the coastal areas of Bangladesh) are also likely to acquire a growing importance. Compared with previous decades, migration is strengthened by the development of communications and a greater awareness of the wealth and security differentials between countries and geographical areas, as well as the development of a sector of illegal economic activity involving the transport of migrants from one country to another.[14]

For both receiving and sending countries, migration brings both advantages and disadvantages. The main advantage for receiving countries (such as those in Western Europe) that are experiencing a demographic decline, is the influx of young people of working age, who are willing to take up jobs that are no longer attractive to the national workforce (agricultural and construction workers, carers, nurses, etc.); if they are regularly employed, their social security contributions can be crucial in covering the pensions of the elderly. Disadvantages include competition with national workers in the low-skilled labour market, the possible expansion of petty crime in the case of irregular immigrants, and the social tensions that may arise in the case of non-integration.

For the sake of simplicity, let us distinguish between three strategies for dealing with immigration. Actually, it will be possible (and perhaps preferable) to adopt mixed strategies. The first is the closing of borders. The second is multiculturalism: immigrants preserve their culture of origin by forming homogeneous groups within the country of arrival, often with the establishment of housing enclaves. The third is integration between immigrants and natives.[15]

[14] This aspect should not be underestimated: the fight against migrant smuggling is necessary both to achieve a minimum of control over migratory flows and to combat the spread of organized crime in a branch of activity that presents interrelationships (economies of scale and scope) with other branches of criminal activity, such as trafficking in drugs, arms and human organs. Blocking legal immigration means stimulating illegal immigration, thus favouring organized crime.

[15] Huntington (2004, pp. 128–9) distinguishes three types of assimilation: 'melting pot' ('society with a new culture produced by the amalgamation of peoples on its shores'),

A fundamental tool in this regard is state schools, which become a meeting point for different affiliations (among students as well as teachers) in a spirit of shared learning and collaboration.

Isolationism is basically impossible in the modern world, however many walls one may build at the borders. Multiculturalism – that is, the coexistence of different cultures with the reaffirmation of each one's own characteristics within it – involves tensions that repeatedly lead to episodes of rupture with the risk of dramatic escalations of violence. The third strategy, integration policies, is therefore preferable, provided that it is not interpreted as the absorption of different cultures within a dominant culture, but as the acceptance of a basis of common rules of coexistence, in particular the 'secular' rule of respect for individual rights. This implies, for instance, the possibility for young people to refuse arranged marriages.[16]

Faced with high-intensity migration flows, the geographical location of the countries of potential immigration close to the countries of emigration constitutes an element of weakness, which should be recognized in European and international cooperation agreements.[17]

Support for integration policies may come from a phenomenon characteristic of the modern world, the multiplicity of affiliations (on

'tomato soup' ('immigrants add ingredients that enrich and diversify taste, but are absorbed into what remains essentially tomato soup') and 'salad' ('cultural pluralism'). Among immigrants he distinguishes two types: 'Ampersands have two national identities, diasporans one transnational identity' (2004, p. 276) and adds that 'The central focus for diasporans is their homeland state' (p. 277).

[16] Collier (2013) provides a balanced reference point for this debate: migration has both positive and negative aspects for both countries of arrival and departure; positive aspects prevail over negative ones as long as migration flows do not become too large, rapid and uncontrolled. Integration policies are the best response, but they must be accompanied by control (agreed between countries of departure, transit and arrival) to contain the scale of migratory flows; if these policies fail, there is a progressive impoverishment of the countries of departure, to the point of their collapse, and explosive social tensions in the countries of arrival.

[17] The Dublin Agreements (1990, then amended in 2003 and again in 2013) require that immigrants be taken care of by the countries of entry into Europe. This implies a highly unequal commitment for EU countries, in fact linked to geographical location – they should therefore be amended, as quickly as possible.

which Amartya Sen has insisted so much, in contrast to Huntington):[18] every human being, apart from being born in a certain country, may have his or her own religious conviction, but at the same time may prefer a certain sport (and support a certain team), classical music or rock, chess or bridge, and so on, and may attach great importance to each of these affiliations, with intersections of the various cultures. Bauman (2003, p. 23) recalls a poster on a wall in Berlin: 'Your Christ is a Jew. Your car is Japanese. Your pizza is Italian. Your democracy is Greek. Your coffee is Brazilian. Your holiday is Turkish. Your numerals are Arabic. Your alphabet is Latin. Only your neighbour is a foreigner.' And again Bauman (2003, p. 58), quoting Peyrefitte, speaks of a 'new and unprecedented freedom of self-identification'.

8.9 THE INTERNATIONAL MONETARY SYSTEM

For a quarter of a century after World War II, the international monetary system was governed by the agreement reached at the Bretton Woods Conference in 1944, based on a series of mainly US and British proposals: fixed exchange rates, with a small margin of fluctuation (with changes, in the case of persistent balance of payments imbalances, to be agreed with the International Monetary Fund [IMF]); convertibility of the dollar into gold, but only for central banks, at US$35 an ounce; establishment of the IMF, which acts as a bank for the central banks (these hold a portion of their foreign exchange reserves with the IMF, in proportion to which they can receive loans) and facilitates international payments, acting as a clearing house, so as to create a multilateral payments system that facilitates trade. Subsequently, the IMF also issued limited quantities of Special Drawing Rights.

A central point of the agreement, which Keynes had fought for as the head of the British delegation, should have been coordination between the governments of the member states, with the aim

[18] Sen's criticisms of Huntington are varied: from the misclassification of India as a wholly Hindu civilization to the widespread importance of the multicultural model. See Sen (2006).

of making international flows of private financial capital consistent with national macroeconomic balances, so as not to oblige countries with balance-of-payments problems to take deflationary measures and/or competitive devaluations, as had happened after the 1929 crisis. The purely voluntary nature of the coordination imposed on the Agreement by US big business prevented effective control of private financial capital movements from the outset, which would have required the active cooperation of the Agreement countries. In the absence of symmetrical rebalancing mechanisms, another point of the Keynes plan that was not adopted, exchange rate tensions could only be contained by the deflationary measures that were originally intended to be avoided and that were imposed by the Fund as a condition for its loans.

In this context, even the fixed exchange rate system was not destined to last. As Triffin (1960) shows, a growing international economy would necessarily have had to be accompanied by an increase in the quantity of the reference currency, the dollar, held abroad; but this would have required a constant deficit in the US balance of payments. At the same time, the gold convertibility of the dollar would have required that the larger amount of dollars held abroad be guaranteed by an increase in US gold reserves, which would not be possible with a balance-of-payments deficit.

In fact, in the wake of a series of US balance-of-payments deficits, largely linked to military spending on the Vietnam War, distrust of dollar convertibility forced Nixon between 1971 and 1973 to abandon first convertibility and then fixed exchange rates. The huge balance of payments imbalances that followed the 1973 oil crisis and then the 1978–79 crisis would have required strong international coordination, managed by the Fund. Again, the interests of international finance, aided by the growing hegemony of neo-liberalism, stood in the way of that solution whereby the so-called recycling of petrodollars was managed by an increasingly liberalized private finance. The trail of financial crises, both local and general, that has since affected most countries has accompanied a financial globalization whose scope has no historical precedent.

Without going back over the history of the last half century, we can observe that the world economy has experienced a slowdown in growth and growing instability, both in financial markets and in economic activity. As will be mentioned below, the severity of the Covid-19 crisis seems to be encouraging some, as yet very timid, steps towards rethinking the international economic order. Still deeper and more complex rethinking appears necessary in the wake of the war in Ukraine.

8.10 THE EUROPEAN UNION

The European Union deserves a separate discussion. Its origins can be traced back to the Europeanist drive after World War II; we can recall the Ventotene Manifesto (Spinelli and Rossi, 1944), the Frenchmen Jean Monnet and Robert Schuman, and the Belgian Paul Henry Spaak. The formation of the European Economic Community (with the Treaty of Rome of 25 March 1957) was followed by a gradual process of enlargement (from the initial six countries to the current twenty-seven) and deepening (the Maastricht Treaty of 1992, the Lisbon Treaty of 2007, the birth of the euro in 2002 preceded by the creation of the European Central Bank; an increase – still partial – of the powers of the European Commission and the European Parliament compared to the Council that gathers the governments of the individual states).

The euro originates from an exchange, agreed between Kohl and Mitterrand in 1989, between the acceptance of the abandonment of the mark by the Germans, despite inflationary fears, and the acceptance of the unification of Germany by the French and other European countries, despite fears of the overwhelming power of a 'big Germany' in the centre of Europe. This agreement can be considered as a classic example of a positive-sum game, making German unification and a decisive step forward in the European unification process possible at the same time. Those in favour were aware that the agreement constituted in several respects a risky leap forward, given the persistent differences between the various economies of the area and in economic policy traditions. However, the single currency should have acted as a stimulus to further steps towards economic policy coordination and political unification: the fragility of the monetary construction would have been overcome by a conscious effort that on the geopolitical level should have anchored the German colossus in Europe, eliminating the root causes of so many tensions and repeated wars.

Two factors worked against this design. First, there has been a major enlargement of the Union, with the entry of Eastern European countries, made necessary after the dissolution of the Soviet Union to overcome the situation of geo-political uncertainty on the Union's eastern borders. The result was an increase in the differentiation between the economies of the EU countries; moreover, the centrality of Germany was reinforced, further enhanced by Brexit. In the new enlarged Europe, nationalistic parties and movements have grown stronger, coming to government in some countries: the unanimity required for changes in the political constitution of the Union has substantially blocked the deepening process.

Second, construction of the euro took place on the basis of a neo-liberal/ordoliberal ideology. The ECB's monetary policy is limited to pursuing price stability alone, in the belief that the invisible hand of the market would automatically ensure convergence towards optimal levels of output and employment.[19] This same belief constitutes a constraint on the use of countercyclical fiscal policies. Moreover, again in the wake of a neo-liberal orientation in favour

[19] As a consequence of these statutory limitations, Draghi as ECB president had to present his actions to preserve the stability and the very existence of the euro as justified by excessively low inflation and the need to preserve monetary policy instruments aimed at controlling inflation: a justification that did not convince the German Supreme Court, but was fortunately considered satisfactory by German political leaders (who were thus able to avoid questioning the basic rules of the euro, as it would otherwise have been inevitable in the face of the precipitating crisis). The resurgence of inflation in the most recent phase of rapid post-pandemic economic recovery and especially with the war in Ukraine now risks exploding contradictions: a monetary tightening would in fact risk generating a fiscal crisis in some states and a general financial crisis.

of reducing the public presence in the economy, the prohibition of unfair competition, which is at the heart of so many regulations on product quality and state aid to companies, has not been extended to the elimination of tax havens within the Union (Luxembourg, Holland, Ireland), with the consequence of a substantial and growing limitation upon the taxing power of the individual state. These constraints risk becoming fatal when, after the end of the pandemic and the war in Ukraine, the problem of a public debt that has grown considerably will have to be tackled. So far, the pressure of the crisis has made it necessary to make choices even against EU rules; but the rules themselves will have to be amended, and above all the underlying neo-liberal culture will have to be abandoned. The exit of the United Kingdom from the EU, namely a country that has always been an obstacle to the deepening of the Union, and above all the need to respond to the economic and social crisis generated by the pandemic and by the war in Ukraine, could lead to new steps forward, possibly through the mechanism of enhanced cooperation that would make it possible to involve a more limited group of countries initially, overcoming the vetoes of nationalists and Eurosceptics.[20]

[20] See D'Ippoliti, Malaguti and Roncaglia (2020).

PART II Ethical Assessments and Policy Perspectives

9 The Ethics of Power between the Common Good and Equality

9.1 THE INDIVIDUAL AND SOCIETY

This chapter, unlike the previous ones, does not deal with the elements that determine the distribution of power within society, but with the ethical background of the strategy of reforms, that is, of interventions aimed at reducing inequalities in the distribution of power, which will be the subject of the next two chapters. Here we shall touch briefly on some of the issues: the dialectic between the individualistic spirit and the social nature of human beings, the concepts of the common good, justice and freedom, and the distinction between reasonable and fanciful utopias.

When considering the relationship between the individual and society, two traditions stand in contrast. The dominant one in today's economic tradition and in neo-liberal political thought sees society as a mere abstract category, a simple sum of individuals, each pursuing his or her own selfish gain. The canons of methodological individualism (which Schumpeter distinguishes from political individualism)[1] dictate that the explanation of any economic and social phenomenon is to be traced back to the sum of individual behaviours.

According to an older tradition, going back to Plato and Aristotle, 'man is a sociable being' (*politikon zoon*); moreover, 'the state exists by nature [and] is prior to each individual'.[2] The second statement is much stronger than the first and constitutes the core of organicism, that is, the thesis – both methodological and political –

[1] Schumpeter (1908, pp. 83–4). Political individualism corresponds to the liberal tradition's thesis of the existence of natural and inalienable rights of the person: a tradition that can be traced back to Locke (1690).

[2] Aristotle (1977, pp. 6–7), *Politics*, I(A), 2, 1253a.

whereby the collective social entity (the state, the Church) takes priority over the individual.

Organicism and methodological individualism can be considered as two extremes. The middle ground between the two is wide. One may accept political individualism as an ethical principle, that is, respect for the inalienable rights of the human person, without this implying any adhesion to methodological individualism. At the same time, one may reject organicism, both politically and as a principle of method,[3] while attributing interpretative utility to collective names, that is, terms that do not designate individual entities.[4]

Something similar applies to the contrast between the egoistic motivation attributed to *homo oeconomicus* and the social nature recognized in human beings. Methodological individualism, which calls for independence in the motivations of agents – a true assumption of solipsism – requires that analytical constructions be based on agents moved by pure egoism. With a much more subtle and balanced conception, Adam Smith speaks not of selfishness but of self-interest, a motivation tempered not so much by benevolence towards others as by the morality of sympathy (in the etymological sense of the term, feeling together) which, based on the social nature of human beings, requires us not to harm others and to respect rules of social coexistence. Moreover, the judgement that others make of us does not leave us indifferent: we wish to win 'the race for wealth, and honours, and preferments', says Smith (1759, p. 83), but if we resort

[3] For a radical critique of organicism see Popper (1945).

[4] In the mediaeval discussion on the so-called problem of universals (collective names, such as horse or rose), the opposition between nominalists (or terminalists) and realists seems parallel to that between methodological individualism and organicism (as in Popper, 1944–5, pp. 33–43): the former claim that universals have no real existence, they are mere *flatus vocis*; the latter consider the existence of a property common to the set of objects designated by the term universal to be a real essence. One of the greatest mediaeval logicians, Peter Abelard, adopts an intermediate position, defending the analytical validity of universal terms. See Roncaglia (2001, pp. 39–40) for a concise illustration. (In the close of *The Name of the Rose* [Eco, 1980, p. 473] the elderly Adso, by now rambling, combines the two positions: 'I leave this writing, I do not know for whom, I do not know about what: stat rosa pristina nomine, nomina nuda tenemus'.)

to deception 'the indulgence of the spectators is entirely at an end', and instead of admiration we get contempt.

In other words, even if we admit that we are motivated primarily by our individual self-interest, we must at the same time take into account our belonging to a community, in whose preservation and prosperity (and therefore the well-being of others) we are also interested, just as we are interested in the esteem of others. For this reason, in the difficult balance between the pursuit of our self-interest and the safeguarding of the prosperity of the community we belong to, the degree of adherence to the ethics that guide the individual's behaviour in society is crucial.

In the complex set of one's motivations, self-interest and a spirit of social solidarity can have different weights and vary over time. The spirit of solidarity can be strong within networks of limited size, such as religious communities. Here we refer to the more general social solidarity, the spirit of *fraternité* advocated by the French Revolution. Without this, it is also difficult to pursue equality and freedom. This is why it must be supported in the cultural debate, fighting the one-dimensional concept of the selfish *homo oeconomicus* on an analytical as well as ethical level, and emphasizing the links between social solidarity, the pursuit of greater equality, and the defence of freedom in all its meanings.

9.2 THE CONCEPT OF THE COMMON GOOD

The existence of a set of shared basic values is essential in order to configure another notion, that of the common good. These two notions are linked, but are not the same thing. As we have said, values concern the guiding motivations for action; the common good is the objective of 'well-meant' action, that is, guided by shared values of solidarity.

The notion of the common good is difficult, if not impossible, to define unambiguously. We can also consider it a social construct, like the value system, but the situation is even more complex. Indeed, there is hardly a unanimous consensus around it: in every society there are conflicts, distributive or otherwise, which lead to different assessments of every possible situation. This does not mean that the very notion of the common good is to be abandoned.

There are two extreme positions on this issue. The first is the organicist position, which insists on the existence of an objective common good for each social system, in the face of which individual interests must bow, possibly with sanctions for those who behave differently from this principle; this is the famous thesis of Menenius Agrippa, with his apologue of the human body in which each of the limbs needs the others. The second position is the Marxist one, which sees society as the theatre of irremediable conflicts between social classes. Paradoxically, the first position can be associated with that of the supporters of the invisible hand of the market, according to whom the optimal result for society can be obtained by allowing each individual to pursue his or her own interest: the mechanisms of a competitive market would guarantee the optimal composition of conflicts of interest between individuals, making their pursuit by other means (e.g. strikes) harmful.

An intermediate position, which seems more reasonable, admits both the existence of conflicts and the possibility of their partial resolution (and, at the same time, the possibility that an outcome achieved through conflict is worse for all protagonists than an agreed outcome). Conflict resolution, however, can only be partial, because the unequal distribution of power conditions possible compromises, thus leaving unresolved tensions open. This same logic – the convenience of a cooperative solution, which takes into account the pre-existing power structure – is present in the neo-corporative conceptions of industrial relations,[5] and even earlier, at the dawn of political and economic thought, in the *Dialogue on the common weal*, written in 1549 but published only in 1581.[6]

[5] See Tarantelli (1986).

[6] The *Dialogue* is anonymous. For more details on it, and for a broader discussion of the notion of the common good, see Roncaglia (2015).

The *Dialogue* deals with one of the hottest issues of the time – enclosures, that is, the practice of the lord fencing off within his fief land traditionally used for agriculture, and therefore directly or indirectly necessary for the sustenance of the serfs, in order to dedicate it to cattle breeding. Given the lower costs of production compared to traditional farming, this change led to a considerable increase in net income for the lord, while the serfs were driven off the land they had traditionally farmed. The conflict of interests between the lords and the serfs is obvious; at the same time, the transition entailed a sharp increase in the product per worker. If all the serfs driven off the land had found other employment, the income per capita would have increased and everyone would have been better off; but before this could happen, a lot of time could pass, and in the meantime the serfs would starve or be reduced to begging. As later in the phase of mechanization, the problem is that the progress of the economic system can lead to enormous human suffering.

In the *Dialogue,* the participants (a doctor, a knight, a merchant, a craftsman and a farmer) represent the interests and points of view of the main social classes. Faced with the problem of the economic advantages and human suffering of enclosures, the doctor (who plays the role that today should be attributed to the economist-sociologist) tries to guide the discussion in such a way as to bring out the different implications, both positive and negative, and then seek a solution which, if not the best for each, is nevertheless acceptable to all. The economic advantage of animal over plant farming, not only for the individual but also for the economic system as a whole, is such that it is difficult to give it up; but the transition must be guided in such a way as to ensure the survival of the farmers who would be driven off the land they have been cultivating for generations: a gradual transition that keeps pace with the formation of new jobs.

The doctor reacts critically to the knight's assertion that what is good for one part of society is also good for society as a whole: this might be true, but not necessarily. If it is not, reasons of ethics – but also of the sustainability of social coexistence – require that the problem of compensation of those disadvantaged by the change be addressed.

This logic requires respect for certain principles. Firstly, mutual recognition of the different interests at stake. Without this, no confrontation can begin. Secondly, an open discussion of possible ways of settling conflicting interests, which would ensure that when improvements for some groups are accompanied by the worsening of other groups, adequate forms of compensation for the damaged groups are undertaken.[7] Thirdly, sufficient confidence that discussion can be followed by action appropriate to the pursuit of the common good, without cheating to make the situation even worse. Each of these principles requires an individual morality that, while pursuing self-interest, can understand the views of others, is open to discussion, and feels bound to respect the solution once it has been identified.

Economic growth is part of this common good. In general, there is good correlation between per capita income and certain fundamental indicators of well-being, such as average life expectancy at birth, infant mortality, morbidity and average educational level. But it must be growth that respects the environment and is thus sustainable in the long term, and growth that does not give rise to strong internal differentiations in income, wealth and power, so as to avoid disruptive social tensions. It must therefore be guided growth, for example using adequate support for education systems (public, free and universal: a good level and wide distribution of education is one of the most important elements for sustainable social coexistence over time)[8]

[7] In the traditional economic theory of welfare, it was considered acceptable that compensation be virtual; but this thesis is only valid under very restrictive assumptions, necessary to disregard redistributive effects. For example, an increase in income of €1 billion euros for the richest person in a country, accompanied by a loss of income of €900 each for the poorest one million people in the country, passes the test of virtual compensation, but cannot be said to correspond to an increase in collective welfare.

[8] Gutmann (1982, p. 325) emphasizes the difficulty 'of providing an education that is neutral between substantive conceptions of the good life' and criticizes 'the conservative claim that education must perpetuate the particular values of a society and

and scientific research, with a tax system that reduces inequalities and directs consumption in an environmentally friendly direction, with an industrial policy that directs choices towards production technologies that pollute as little as possible. In many cases this means favouring public (or collective) consumption over private (or individual) consumption and, overall, significant public intervention in the economy.[9]

The possibility of finding sufficient consensus around a definition of the common good within the community and pursuing it has varied over time and space, in response to a set of elements that determine the diffusion, within society, of a 'common feeling' (Hume's tacit consent): the prevalence of the pursuit of self-interest (which includes a certain degree of altruism) over selfishness, widespread adherence to ethical principles of social coexistence and a reduced prevalence of malpractice (network favouritism, corruption, organized crime). Education and the social media can play a key role in this respect. A second group of elements concerns the political sphere: a widespread ethic of the profession/vocation of the politician, and adequate mechanisms for selecting the political class, the importance of which was mentioned above.

9.3 IDEAS ABOUT JUSTICE

Discussions on the concept of the common good intersect with those on the concept of justice. Here, too, different positions will be confronted. To begin with, there is a contrast between deontological and consequentialist conceptions of justice. According to the former, the

prepare children for necessary social functions'. Thus, 'freedom provides a better criterion than happiness for determining what, and how, to teach children'. In this text we have used the term 'education' to refer to what Gutmann calls 'nurture'.

[9] The thesis of the need for guided growth implies rejecting the thesis of the spontaneous emergence of an optimal institutional order, mentioned above (Section 6.4). Growth-guiding measures can use a variety of instruments: regulation, fiscal incentives and disincentives, and even recourse to forms of social moral suasion (such as the doctrine of social corporate responsibility, which attributes to companies, in a rather utopian way, the responsibility to take account of the external effects of their activities, for example on the environment or on employment levels).

rules of justice are derived from an authority: sacred texts, religious or political authorities, tradition. For the latter, each action (or type of action) needs to be assessed according to its consequences, taking into account its effects on general happiness.

The prevalence (never absolute) of consequentialist views over deontological ones, which arose mainly during the Enlightenment, marks a civil progress as it abandons an authoritarian approach, in which the notion of justice is imposed from above, in favour of an approach that opens the way to constructing consciously shared norms via open debate. However, deontological elements also inevitably enter into consequentialist conceptions, in establishing an order of preferences between outcomes different in nature, difficult to compare (greater growth or better protection of the environment, material enrichment or cultural enrichment, and so on) or that may have positive effects on some and negative effects on other individuals or groups of individuals (social classes, professional categories, gender or age, etc.).

A deontological view, open to a utilitarian specification of the ends to be pursued, is that proposed by Kant in his famous 'categorical imperative': 'act only according to that maxim which, at the same time, you can wish to make a universal law'.[10] In other words, the rule of behaviour is that everyone should do what they would want others to do if they were in their place. This implies that each individual should pursue some notion of the common good, thus looking at the consequences of their actions for society as a whole. Hence the consequentialist implication of a maxim with a deontological flavour, which ends up resembling the 'rule utilitarianism' advocated by John Stuart Mill (1861), in which the evaluation of consequences applies to general rules and not to individual actions.

Another possible implication of this maxim is that distributive justice is one of the main goals to be pursued. If I do not want others to behave in such a way as to take a share of what is 'due' to me (whatever

[10] Kant (1785, p. 79; BA 52).

that means), I must behave in the same way. Thus, we come back to the problem, already discussed, of the distributive rule and its evaluation, which depends upon the conception of the way a market economy works. If I accept the myth of the invisible hand of the market guiding the economic system in the best possible way, as traditional economic theory does, the distributive rule will consist in relying on the market, indeed on an ideal perfectly competitive market: everyone should receive an income proportional to their contribution to the social product.[11] If, on the other hand, I do not accept the myth of the invisible hand of the market, the pre-existing income distribution can be questioned. In any case, the pre-existing distribution of productive resources, including labour capacity, can be questioned if we consider that the chance of birth plays an important role in determining it. We must then compensate for this factor through a redistribution of wealth, primarily through tax measures such as death duties.[12]

As an extreme development of Kant's categorical imperative, Rawls (1971) proposes as a criterion of justice an increase of the lowest incomes. Before we concern ourselves with making the incomes of the middle and upper classes less unequal, we must concern ourselves with increasing the incomes of those lower down the scale. As Sen (2009, pp. 52–74) points out, if taken to its extreme, this criterion would imply that even a minimal increase in the lowest of all incomes would be considered a step in the right direction, even if accompanied by a massive shift of income from the middle classes to the richest.

[11] More precisely, we should receive an income equal to the marginal productivity of our labour and that of the productive factors – land, capital – in our possession.

[12] Nozick (1974) defends the inequalities of wealth due to birth, that is, obtained by inheritance, stressing that the rights of individual liberty, which include the preservation of private property, entail the right to dispose of it by bequeathing it to one's relatives (or anyone else one wishes). Note that the right to private property is considered an absolute right, implicit in the fundamental right to individual liberty. However, as soon as it is accepted that 'my freedom ends where the freedom of others begins' – a maxim that has been repeated with small variations countless times, from Kant to John Stuart Mill to Martin Luther King – the right to dispose of one's possessions as one pleases finds various limits, for example in the requirements of environmental protection or in the quest for distributive equity.

In short, we are faced with a long series of difficulties concerning what seems to be a shared principle, the ideal of equality. First, it must be recognized that perfect equality is not attainable. Secondly, as we shall see more clearly in the next section, the pursuit of equality has to be balanced with other elements, such as the recognition of individual freedoms. Thirdly, there is a need to clarify what the pursuit of equality means: must we apply Rawls' criterion, or the reduction of inequality in income distribution as measured by some statistical indicator such as Gini? And there is also a need to define equality: of opportunity or of outcome? With respect to income and wealth, or power, or quality of life?

In each case, other specific aspects need to be considered. In the case of equal starting points, if we recognize that being born into a wealthy and educated family is an undeniable starting advantage, how can this be remedied? With 100 per cent taxation of inheritances? By compulsory attendance at state schools, to prevent the rich from having the advantages[13] of attending prestigious public schools (such as Eton)? These questions raise a problem. In trying to reduce inequality, the importance of different dimensions needs to be weighed: should a reduction in income inequality achieved at the cost of increasing gender inequality be considered a step forward, or a step backward? How can a reduction in inequalities in career opportunities be judged against an increase in inequalities in cultural capacities? Of course, a simple answer is that we can pursue a reduction of inequalities simultaneously on all fronts. What we want to emphasize here is the multi-dimensional character of the notions of equality and inequality, which makes it difficult to define the objectives of a policy aimed at reducing inequalities.

These difficulties open the path to a further problem. When devising a strategy to combat inequality, the need to assess (to compare) the different aspects of a multi-dimensional reality means that the point of view from which we stand is important: the worldview,

[13] Not only in terms of better education, but also in terms of participation in a network of power relations that can be of considerable importance.

the value system to which we adhere. There are indeed different orientations on the importance of different aspects: education rather than wealth, for example. Now, the formation of these orientations in public opinion does not take place in vacuums, but is itself influenced by existing power relations, for example by controlling television and the press. There is a risk, therefore, that political strategies aimed at reducing inequality will be developed with a view to safeguarding those elements which, in the long run if not in the immediate future, are most relevant for the preservation of the status quo.

9.4 IDEAS OF FREEDOM

Traditionally, a distinction is usually made between the freedom of the ancients and that of the moderns, the freedom 'of' (or 'positive freedom') and the freedom 'from' (or negative freedom). These distinctions are not clear-cut, and have important nuances in actual choices.[14] In synthesis and with a certain approximation with respect to the definitions that have been given in the literature (e.g. by Berlin, or by Sen), freedom 'of' (freedom as autonomy) is the one supported by liberal ideologies: freedom for people to live and act as they like; freedom 'from' is the absence of material constraints: freedom from hunger, thirst, ignorance.[15] In the first case, the distributive problem is relegated to the background; in the second case, traditional

[14] Georgescu-Roegen (1988, p. 304) speaks of a 'penumbra' that in general makes the clear definition of complex concepts, such as those of positive and negative freedom, arbitrary.

[15] Benjamin Constant, in his 1819 lecture on 'The Freedom of the Ancients, Compared to that of the Moderns', proposes a conception of the freedom of the moderns that constitutes a point of reference for liberal thought: 'We can no longer enjoy the freedom of the ancients, which was made up of active and constant participation in collective power. The liberty which is ours must be the practical enjoyment of private independence' (Constant, 1819, p. 15). Isaiah Berlin took up and developed this thesis in his inaugural lecture at Oxford in 1958, extending it to consider the debate, very much alive at the time, between communists and liberals on freedom as enfranchisement from material deprivation and as freedom of individual action (the 1958 lecture is republished, with other texts by the same author, in Berlin, 2002). Berlin's basic thesis, simplified to the extreme, is that individual freedom should not be sacrificed in pursuit of freedom from material deprivation, as the communist regimes did. Berlin himself, however, admits the need for a balance between the two requirements, thus hinting (albeit with many

elements of political democracy (such as the existence of free and fair elections) are considered less important. In the first case, individual freedom is primarily defended against state authority (first in absolute monarchies, then in twentieth-century dictatorships); in the second case, the search for freedom from want requires the support of public action. As Bobbio points out (1990, p. 73): 'While the rights of liberty are born against the excessive power of the state, and therefore to limit its power, social rights require for their practical implementation … just the opposite, that is the increase of the powers of the state.'

What is of interest here is the link between freedom and power. From this point of view, we could say that the pure concept of freedom implies the negative of the pure concept of power, understood as the difference in potential for action between persons or groups of persons. Full freedom, in fact, implies that no-one enjoys a power superior to that of others; otherwise, the dominated would see their freedom of action restricted in some respect. Of course, a situation of full freedom, understood in this sense, is pure utopia. As has been repeated many times, we can assume as our objective the reduction, not the total abolition, of inequalities of power.

We have thus established a twofold link between the concept of freedom pursued in a given society and the problem of power. Firstly, it is the latter (directly as political power, indirectly all the elements, such as economic power or cultural hegemony, that influence political power) that determines which value system prevails in practice, and thus which meanings of freedom are in fact favoured (or sacrificed) in a given context. Secondly, however it is understood, the actual degree of individual freedom depends on the power structure and the way it is used: on the decisions of the political authorities as well as on the behaviour of others.

notes of caution) in the direction of the theses of liberal socialism. Sen (2007) considers negative freedoms as included in positive freedoms ('a violation of negative freedom implies a violation of positive freedom, whereas the opposite is not true', p. 10). This assumption favours the analysis of the interrelationship between individual freedoms and the social context, and is therefore justified in the context of Sen's analysis; but it implies a precise delimitation of the two concepts, which is very difficult in practice.

Throughout human history, the aspiration for freedom has proved to be a highly significant political objective, a motivating force to be taken into account in political action as well as in ideological battles and even in the military field. This is why the interpretation of this concept is so important in the hegemonic culture of a given historical moment and society.

Of course, freedom in its concrete manifestation also concerns the political form taken by the state. In this respect, there is a close link between freedom and democracy. Choices relating to the management of the common good concern everyone, and can constitute a constraint for those who had expressed themselves in favour of different choices. It is therefore necessary for everyone to have the opportunity to participate in shaping these choices (even if indirectly, in a system of representative democracy) and for minorities not to be unnecessarily harassed.

At a practical level, political democracy inevitably coexists with the presence of elites. Some political theorists (Mosca, Pareto) recognize an imbalance of power in favour of these elites that makes the mass of the population passive with respect to political choices. However, in an effective democracy the elites, although having more or less wide margins of hegemony, do not dominate. Thus, we have theories such as Schumpeter's 'political market', in which the different elites compete with each other for the popular vote (the so-called procedural conception of democracy). Electoral competition between parties is the most widespread form of competition between elites; only when full democracy is ensured within parties (and trade unions) can we speak of a democratic regime (which requires, however, that other conditions are also fulfilled, such as the absence of what Bobbio calls 'invisible power' and a good level of cultural education of the citizens).[16]

[16] Sartori (1987) distinguishes two types of electoral competition: the issue voting model and the model of identification with a party. Pasquino (2019, p. 136) adds a third, the

9.5 JUSTICE AND FREEDOM

The binomial 'justice and freedom', adopted as a motto by the Italian resistance movement Giustizia e Libertà and then by the Partito d'Azione, where the term 'justice' is to be understood as referring to social justice, indicates a political line that rejects both the dictatorship of the proletariat and fascist dictatorships, but also economic liberalism (the ideology of laissez-faire, or the invisible hand of the market) with its disregard for inequalities in income distribution and for the conditions of the weaker social groups.[17] In essence, it is a mediation between the abstract concept of active freedom (which alongside freedom of opinion or speech includes freedom of initiative in the economic field) and the utopian conception of absolute material equality. The freedoms 'of' – those corresponding to a democratic political system, in which there is not only freedom of thought but also freedom to openly support one's own ideas – are considered indispensable; they are accompanied by recognition of the substantial importance of at least some of the freedoms 'from' (from hunger and misery, but also from ignorance): in other words, a universal right of human beings to a dignified existence. The motto of justice and freedom thus implies, from the point of view adopted here, the objective of reducing inequalities of power, in all its various meanings, within society.

An important reference to illustrate the theses just mentioned is Carlo Rosselli's book, *Socialismo liberale* (*Liberal Socialism*).

personalization model. In such a complex framework, attempts to measure quantitatively the degree of democracy of the various countries, or to order them on a hierarchical scale, are necessarily approximate; see, however, the Freedom House website (http://freedomhouse.org). The results of empirical analyses correlating rankings or indices of this type with other synthetic indicators, such as the Human Development Index developed by Ul Haq at the UNDP, should be greeted with even greater caution.

17 The most frequent justification for this lack of interest is the trickle-down thesis, according to which economic growth stimulated by laissez-faire spreads from the rich to the poor, improving the situation of all. This thesis is flawed in its very assumption: an unequal distribution of income is a brake on growth (because of the social tensions it generates, and because the propensity of the rich to consume is lower than that of the poor, thus dampening demand); moreover, it ignores the cumulative mechanisms of increasing inequality that unbalanced growth of income can generate.

Written between 1928 and 1929, when Rosselli was on political confinement on the island of Lipari, the text was published in Paris, in French, in 1930. The book was the object of scornful judgments by Togliatti and Croce. The first thought he could dismiss it by stating, without fear of ridicule, that it was directly linked to fascist literature, probably reacting to Rosselli's harsh criticisms of Marxism and Stalin's dictatorship. The second criticized Rosselli's alleged syncretism, speaking of the notion of liberal socialism as a hircocervus, an attempt to bring together two contradictory concepts, irreconcilable with each other.[18] Despite the time that has passed and the conditions in which it was written, however, the book still deserves attention.

The first part of *Liberal Socialism* is dedicated to a critique of Marxism and the various forms of Marxist revisionism; the second part, the one we are interested in here, outlines the theses of liberal socialism. In its pre-Marxist tradition, socialism was essentially an aspiration to improve the lot of the poorer classes in society.[19] This is also Rosselli's basic view: once he had criticized Marxism, a return to the views of the origins leads him to see socialism as the step that follows 'the conquest of political freedom', insofar as the latter represents 'the beginning of the struggle for emancipation, including economic emancipation' (Rosselli, 1930, p. 93). 'Socialism, taken in its essential aspect, is the progressive implementation of the idea of freedom and justice among men' (1930, p. 82). The dimensions of freedom – individual, political and material – are inseparable from each other; the first is the premise of the second, the second is the crowning of the first. 'Freedom, unaccompanied and supported by a minimum of economic autonomy, by emancipation from the grip of essential needs, does not exist for the individual, it is a mere phantom. The socialist

[18] The hircocervus is a legendary creature, half goat and half stag. To be precise, Croce's criticism (1942) is immediately addressed to Guido Calogero's *Manifesto of Liberal Socialism* (1940), but is in fact directed at the whole strand of liberal socialist thought of which Rosselli can be considered the originator.

[19] See Spini (1992).

movement [liberal socialism] is therefore the convinced heir of liberalism.' Liberal socialism is not only gradualist (like Bernstein's, 1899), but also a process arising from below ('inductive, liberal, experimental'), not 'a plan of social organisation' (Rosselli, 2020, p. 535).

Croce's criticism arrived when Rosselli, assassinated by the fascists, could no longer reply.[20] In the climate of the time in which they were proposed, dominated by idealistic culture, such criticisms – like those of Togliatti (the head of the Italian communist party) – had a hold that they no longer have today.[21] They seem to concern, in the terms adopted in these pages, a contradiction between the pure content of a one-dimensional concept of freedom and the equally pure content of a concept of socialism as social justice, unilaterally limited to the economic dimension. As mentioned in the previous section, if we consider concepts as theoretical constructions useful to help us understand and represent the real world, and not as constitutive elements of a pure world of ideas, we cannot see theoretical contradictions where there are, more simply, practical conflicts between the different aspects of a multidimensional notion.[22]

Indeed, as Bobbio (1994, p. 57) observes, liberal socialism can be considered 'a typical expression of third-inclusive thinking', that is, 'not as a form of compromise between two extremes, but as a simultaneous overcoming of one and the other'. In fact, 'the recognition of certain fundamental social rights [is] the presupposition or precondition for the effective exercise of the rights of liberty' (Bobbio, 2010, p. 245), where the fundamental social rights are those to work, education and health. Bobbio (2010, p. 242) also recalls the 'four freedoms' –

[20] For Calogero's reply, see Calogero (1942).

[21] Einaudi's own criticism of Croce's position, which basically goes in the direction indicated by Rosselli and others – i.e. the importance of freedom from material needs as a component of a practical notion of freedom – is formulated without criticizing the method of idealist philosophy, as a position of 'practical reason' that does not deny the correctness of Croce's position on the level of 'theoretical reason'. Cf. Croce-Einaudi (1957).

[22] For the distinction between 'real opposition' and 'dialectical contradiction', see Colletti (1974, pp. 63–113).

'freedom of speech, freedom of religion, freedom from fear, freedom from want' – proclaimed by President Roosevelt on 6 January 1941, before the United States entered the war.

Criticism of liberal socialism thus appears to express cultural and political opposition to the thesis that the conquest of political freedom is not to be considered as a final destination, but as an achievement which, however fundamental, marks only one step on the interminable path towards an ideal of complete freedom and justice: 'socialism is not a static and abstract ideal, which may one day be fully realised. It is an unattainable limit ideal that is realised to the extent that it manages to permeate our lives' (Rosselli, 1930, p. 86).

9.6 THE UTOPIAS OF RAINBOW POWER

The many utopias of perfect societies[23] point to cases of societies in which coexistence between human beings is 'perfect' from some point of view – from the point of view of the absence of constraints, of equal responsibility for decisions or equality in living conditions, of rationality of behaviour that allows the maximum to be obtained with the minimum sacrifice of labour, and so on. One of these utopias, communism in Marx's version, prefigures a society in which the slavery of coercive labour, that is, the obligation to work in order to obtain what is necessary for survival and what is desired in terms of material goods and additional services, has been totally eliminated. In this case, the power of the human being over nature would be total, as would be the freedom of the individual within society.

Modern utopias look towards a fully automated/robotized society. However, as in the Solaria imagined by Asimov (1957), there remain a number of tasks that humans cannot delegate (although they can be made far less unpleasant and far less time-consuming than those we are used to in contemporary society). Technical progress allows for productivity growth, which over sufficiently long

[23] Those of St Thomas More (1516) and Tommaso Campanella (1602) are only the best known.

intervals of time makes enormous strides in living standards and, at the same time, significant reductions in the annual workload of each of us. As a result, coercive labour can be progressively reduced: our power over nature grows over time, to an extent which in the long run may appear staggering, though without ever becoming total domination. Coercive labour still remains and, with the division of labour, so does social differentiation.

Power in its various meanings is considered here not in its absolute dimension, that is, as the power of human beings over nature, but in its relative dimension, as the differential of the power of each of us over each other. The distribution of power hardly ever remains stable over time: it changes continuously, sometimes in leaps and bounds, better for some and worse for others. The problem then arises of assessing, case by case, whether or not changes in power structures linked to technological change, or more generally to historical events, go in the direction of greater equality (with the possibility of obtaining different results depending on the dimension of equality that we consider); it is then necessary to assess what interventions are possible to ensure that the change generates less and not more inequality in the distribution of power, and not simply of wealth or income.

'The decisive question to distinguish "reasonable" from "fanciful" utopias is the question of power. On what forces, concretely present in contemporary society, could a political strategy be based to realise a reasonable utopia, based on sustainable development, on the reduction of inequalities, on the enlargement of civil rights and freedom and on the creation of new channels of democratic participation?' In other words: is it possible in the society in question to coagulate an alliance of social forces around a specific objective of change, which is able to overcome the obstacle of the social forces that oppose that change?[24]

Fanciful utopias are unrealizable. It is therefore a grave error to regard them as ends for the attainment of which it is legitimate

[24] Here we take the concepts of reasonable and imaginative utopias from Roncaglia and Villetti, 2007; the sentence quoted (from p. 282) is by Villetti.

to impose sacrifices on human beings: the sacrifice of freedom, as in the 'dictatorship of the proletariat' in communist countries; or the sacrifice of the immediate standard of living, even to the point of starvation, as in the 'great leap forward' in China.

There are utopias that can be considered fanciful if designed for society as a whole, and reasonable if meant as an ethical project that can be pursued, albeit within certain limits, by individuals, families and communities. One example is the utopia of 'happy degrowth', which implies a reduction in both overall income and per capita income. While a reduction of the average per capita product can hardly be considered acceptable by the majority, a reduction of the opulent consumption discussed by Veblen (1899) and recalled in Section 3.1, accompanied by a reduction of working hours, is already pursued by many (and would be even more so, if there were more flexibility in working hours and retirement age); a reduction of the world population is also within the realm of possibility, if supported by an adequate diffusion of birth control education.[25]

Examples of reasonable utopias are: an extension of workers' co-participation in the ownership (and management) of companies;[26] a progressive reduction in working hours (such as to absorb all or a

[25] Cf. Latouche (2006), which at times tends towards a fanciful utopia but with flashes of reasonable utopia: 'Degrowth is a watchword that means radically abandoning the objective of growth for growth's sake, an objective whose driving force is none other than the pursuit of profit by the holders of capital and whose consequences are disastrous for the environment. ... more than 'degrowth' we should speak of 'a-growth''. Latouche recognizes the contribution that technical and scientific progress can make to environmental protection, but warns that 'we must not underestimate the danger that technical-scientific delirium will take definitive precedence over wisdom' (Latouche, 2006, pp. 11 and 35). On the positive side, Latouche (2006, pp. 70–1; see also p. 169) proposes 'the drastic reduction of working time, the internalisation of external effects, the incitement to the use of more convivial techniques, the penalisation of expenditure on harmful products'. Instead of a tax system with sharply increasing tax rates as income rises, Latouche (2006, p. 123) proposes to introduce a ceiling: 'the maximum allowable income'. Above all, he argues (p. 121) that 'degrowth is necessarily against capitalism, not so much because it denounces its contradictions and its ecological and social limits, but first and foremost because it questions its "spirit"'.

[26] According to the Rehn-Meidner model developed in Sweden in 1951, a share of the taxes on company profits should go into an investment fund managed by the trade

high proportion of productivity gains); a progressive extension of the welfare state (e.g. with the progressive extension not only of the years of study before starting work, but also with a strong expansion of alternating study-work experiences or recourse to part-time work for both); a policy of full employment guaranteed by the state (such as that proposed by Minsky, 2013), up to Ernesto Rossi's proposals already illustrated above (in Section 3.8) of a labour army, for a limited period of time devoted to unpleasant but necessary work, which would then entitle the person to a guaranteed minimum income for life.

If a utopia is reasonable, cultural support must be built up to make it feasible. A sufficient degree of consensus achieved by the reform project can then form the nucleus around which an alliance of social groups and strata can be constructed. Each project of change produces effects in several dimensions (changes in income, wealth, redistribution of power, development of networks of relations, and so on), which may be negative in some respects for one or other of the social groups involved; the cultural vision of support for the project is then necessary to make the sacrifice perceived as more than compensated for by the benefits. If this perception is not shared by a sufficiently large part of society, the original consensus is likely to collapse; hence a reform strategy cannot be based on an original plan that remains unchanged throughout the implementation process. Adjustments in the course of implementation will generally be necessary, and should be possible, in order to maintain a sufficient degree of consensus around the reform project to preserve cultural hegemony. In the next two chapters we shall try to consider these aspects in a more concrete way, through the concept – and some examples – of structural reforms.

unions: an experience only in some respects similar to that of sovereign investment funds, such as the Norwegian one, financed in some countries with oilfield royalties, which aim to set aside public budget surpluses to be used when the country's oilfields run out.

10 The Strategy of Structural Reforms

10.1 LEFT AND RIGHT

According to the myth of the invisible hand of the market, conflicts of interest have an optimal solution, to which a perfectly competitive market automatically leads; departing from this condition leads to sub-optimal solutions. Hayek's thesis on institutions tends in the same direction; the most suitable institutions tend to emerge spontaneously, through a process of selection.[1] In both cases, these theses lack solid theoretical foundations, but their strength lies in the fact that they constitute a useful support for conservative ideologies, and can therefore enjoy strong financial and media support that – as we shall see more fully in Section 11.3 – heavily distorts the theoretical debate.

In the preceding chapters (and more extensively in Roncaglia, 2005, 2019) we have tried to show the weakness of these theses: the optimal situation cannot be defined unambiguously, with the precision required to avoid any kind of conflict; above all, we cannot postulate an automatic tendency towards an optimal situation, however defined, or towards any situation considered desirable.

In the presence of conflicts and in the absence of a tendency towards their automatic resolution, the outcomes of social dynamics appear to be determined by power relations. With respect to these, following Bobbio we can distinguish, within a range of different positions, a right-wing orientation from a left-wing orientation. For the 'right', power differentials are (a) inevitable; (b) due not only and not so much to fate as to individuals' (or their ancestors') skills and

[1] Hayek (1973); for a discussion of this thesis, see Roncaglia (2019, pp. 79–82).

commitment.[2] For the 'left', power differentials are generally unjustified, and are often achieved by ethically condemnable methods; if they cannot be fully overcome (as the utopian or maximalist left pretends), they however call for interventions aimed at reducing them as much as possible.[3]

Of course, 'the extremism-moderatism dyad does not coincide with the right-left dyad'.[4] Also, some issues, such as support for gender equality or the defence of individual rights in sexual preferences, even if pursued independently of traditional distributive conflicts, can be considered left-wing insofar as they tend to affirm greater equality.

In the strictly economic domain, the reduction of power differentials is primarily a matter of income redistribution policies.[5]

2 Speaking of the importance of fate in human affairs, Machiavelli (1513, ch. 25, p. 99) observes: 'fate ... displays its power where there is no virtue preordained to resist it, so that it impacts where there are no barriers to contain it'. Machiavelli's observation is all the more important when one observes that the events of life (such as disease or natural disasters) had a far greater impact at the time than they do today, precisely because of the progress in the construction of barriers.

3 The total magnitude of relative power differentials can be expressed, assuming a single dimension and measurable power, as $\Sigma(i = 1, n; j = 1, n)\ |pi - pj|$, where pi and pj denote the power of individuals i and j, n the number of individuals in a population, and the differential for each pair is taken as an absolute value. The sum is divided by two to account for counting of each pair of individuals twice. The total can then be divided by $\Sigma(i = 1, n)\ pi$ to obtain an index that can range from zero to one, to be used for comparisons between moments in time or different populations. Of course, the assumption is too strong and the calculation too complicated to use in practice. The purpose of the above expression is to help distinguish the problem of variations in relative power differentials from variations in absolute power, which concern the relationship between human beings and nature (such as technical progress, which allows a generalized improvement in the standard of living, or medical progress, which allows a lengthening of life). This distinction is similar to the one made by classical economists (such as David Ricardo, 1817, ch. 20) between value and riches, i.e. between exchange values and wealth.

4 Bobbio (1994, p. 71). The right-left dichotomy has been criticized by the supporters of the Third Way (Giddens, 1998), but by reducing it to the opposition between 'old style social democracy', statist, and neo-liberalism (1998, p. 39), while Bobbio's distinctive criterion is perhaps more complex to apply in practice, but certainly much more general. The opposition in principle between state and market is not useful to evaluate what is right-wing and what is left-wing: antitrust policies are left-wing, insofar as they fight concentrations of private economic power; Soviet-style central planning, insofar as it concentrates power in the hands of the *nomenklatura*, is right-wing.

5 Traditional income redistribution policies are based on taxes and subsidies. They can be complemented by 'pre-distribution' policies, a neologism used in the last two

However, as we have tried to show in the previous chapters, it is wrong to limit ourselves to them: even if we limit ourselves to economics, policies of wealth redistribution (e.g. through inheritance rules) or those related to firms' market power margins (among other things, anti-monopoly policies), or measures regulating access to certain professions, and many other elements, also count. In this field, as in others, any public intervention has some impact on the relative structure of power differentials. In the political field, the constitutional norms that determine the configuration of political institutions, the laws that regulate electoral procedures, the form taken by political parties and their internal dynamics, and many other aspects are relevant. In the cultural arena, aspects such as copyright law, plagiarism and defamation law, the control of publishing houses, the press, radio and television, new social media, public incentive policies, the organization of the school system, and so on, play a role in determining the power structure. Finally, the interrelationships between the three aspects – economic, political and cultural – must be taken into account.

The multi-dimensionality of power implies that one person or political group may take a right-wing position on some issues, and a left-wing position on others. For instance, individual freedom rights are often recalled by right-wing politicians to oppose 'communists', but rarely include references to gender equality or freedom of sexual orientation, or to the rights of ethnic minorities or migrants; more often they concern the defence of privacy in opposition to the collection of information for fiscal or legal reasons (and more recently, during the Covid-19 pandemic, populist support for no-vax and no-mask choices). As in the case of the rejection of restrictions on the

decades by British Labour to designate policies aimed at intervening on market forces that generate inequalities. See Thomas (2017) and the literature cited therein. The line of action proposed in this paper is more radical: distributional inequalities are only one, albeit very important, component of power inequalities; given the interrelationships between the different components of power, the objective of reducing income inequalities should be pursued as part of a more general strategy of policies aimed at reducing power inequalities.

purchase of arms in the United States, these are cases of defence of individual choices that conflict with the well-being of the community: violations of the principle whereby the freedom of each person is limited by the equal right to freedom of others.

Indeed, the left/right dyad has a long history, which can be traced back to the time of the French Revolution, and has taken on a considerable variety of meanings over time: a fascinating story, accurately recounted by Gauchet (2020). Useful in representing the position of political forces by choosing where to sit in parliament, the dyad becomes a continuum (right, centre, left and intermediate positions). The appearance of the watchword 'Neither right nor left' around 1927 was the work of the fascist movements.[6]

Characterizing left or right-wing political positions is, however, difficult, not least because of the profound changes in the social structure that have occurred over time. From Italy to the United States, the right appears as a hybrid alliance of very different ideologies: nationalism, religious fundamentalism, traditional values ('God, country and family') together with neo-liberalism and extreme individualism. On the other hand, since the fall of the Berlin Wall, great confusion has reigned on the left: the traditional Marxist reference to state ownership of the means of production and centralized planning has been replaced by a fairly generalized acceptance of the market economy, albeit accompanied by redistributive policies and a welfare state, antitrust controls and regulatory policies, especially environmental protection policies; the left today seems rather to characterize itself by defending individual rights, in particular in two very different fields such as sexual preference choices and the quest for gender equality.[7]

[6] Gauchet (2020), p. 83, who adds: 'it is largely posterior ... to the simultaneous communist rejection of the two "bourgeois blocs", with which it presents an obvious symmetry'.

[7] For this latter aspect, the left overlaps with the neo-liberal right, which is traditionally individualist. Giddens's (1998) Third Way presents itself as intermediate between the traditionalist right and socialism interpreted as 'a body of thought that opposes individualism' (1998, p. 20) (thus identifying socialism and communism and disregarding

In the face of this complex historical path of the right/left dyad, the criterion of distinction proposed by Bobbio and adopted in this work is meant not as an interpretative tool of a centuries-old political debate, but as a normative reference for the elaboration of a progressive political strategy.

10.2 CRITIQUE OF THE OBJECTIVE OF ABSOLUTE EQUALITY

The objective that characterizes the left is therefore the reduction of power differentials. In this regard, two elements should be underlined: (a) just as power is multidimensional, so necessarily is the objective of reducing power differentials; (b) the ultimate objective of reducing power differentials to zero is unattainable.

Let us start with the first aspect. Let us recall Sen's (1992) question: equality with respect to what? The question is essential, precisely because of the multidimensionality of human nature. Economists who focus their attention on the economic dimension alone forget that, even if perfect equality were achieved on this dimension (with regard to both the individual distribution of income and that of wealth), there could still remain major differences in life potential between individuals. Healthy people have more freedom than people with a disability; interventions such as disability benefits tend to compensate for this difference with extra income. It is clear, however, that compensation, necessarily introduced as a general rule, no matter how hard we try to refine the rules will never be an exact compensation of the disadvantages faced by each individual.

The multidimensionality of the objective confirms that a full overcoming of power differentials is impossible. When we try to achieve equality on one dimension, it may happen that we increase inequalities on other dimensions. On the other hand, the very attempt

a liberal socialist tradition dating back to John Stuart Mill); it favours individual rights and the market economy and shares with neo-liberalism the criticism of the welfare state (considered undemocratic, bureaucratic and with perverse outcomes: 1998, p. 122), but leaves some room to redistributive policies.

to achieve full equality even if limited to the economic dimension – that is, focusing only on the standard of living – can entail very high costs for society, as the experiences of the Khmer Rouge in Cambodia and the Cultural Revolution in China remind us. The objective of equality must therefore be considered with flexibility. Simon (1972, p. 267) proposes the idea of 'satisficing' behaviour, that is, aiming to obtain a result that is considered good, even if not optimal: it is better to give up the search for perfection, which is too difficult to achieve, and to focus attention on a single aspect, and instead aim to obtain a result that is considered acceptable as a whole.

A right-wing policy consists, quite simply, in not intervening in the face of inequalities. This means letting the cumulative mechanisms inherent in the normal dynamics of social life reinforce existing inequalities. A left-wing policy, on the other hand, is about reducing inequalities, assessing goals and outcomes sensibly, and adopting the method of open discussion to agree on a definition of satisfactory behaviour as widely shared as possible.

To give a few examples, which we shall return to later, taken from the concrete experience of the first centre-left government in Italy (early 1960s), the introduction of the unified middle school was a left-wing policy because it aimed to reduce the cultural differences between the children of the rich and the children of the poorer classes; the Statute of Workers was a left-wing policy because it reduced the imbalance of bargaining power between workers and employers; the nationalization of electricity was a left-wing policy because it broke down a monopolistic concentration of economic power with a strong influence on political life, that favoured the unequal electrification of the country.[8] On the other hand, a tax (counter)reform from progressive to proportional taxation, or a law that reduces penalties for tax evasion or makes it more difficult to prosecute, as well as a reduction

[8] Consider for comparison what has happened in recent years with the fibre optic network. Companies have invested in areas with a high concentration of population; the state has had to intervene with public funding to hopefully ensure connectivity to the whole population.

of taxes on large cars, or a policy of generalized tax cuts accompanied by cuts in the welfare state, health care or public education expenditure are right-wing policies. Other examples will be discussed in the next chapter. There will inevitably be circumstances in which the distinction between right-wing and left-wing policies will be more difficult or even questionable, but on the whole we can expect the distinction to be sufficiently operational for practical purposes.

In the debate on the dimensions of public intervention in the economy, a particularly important issue concerns natural monopolies (and a similar argument applies to network services, with very high fixed and overhead costs compared to variable costs). The traditional solution involves the public management of these activities. In recent decades, under the impetus of neo-liberal economic theories, there has been increasing recourse to the creation of competition through auction mechanisms for the granting of licences to manage these activities. The relative efficiency of these two solutions deserves to be studied in depth: recent events, including dramatic ones such as the collapse of the Morandi bridge in Genoa, show that it is necessary to take into account the possibilities (and costs) of constructing a well-functioning apparatus to control the activities granted in concession.

10.3 EQUALITY AND CAPABILITIES

One of the most complex aspects of power differentials concerns the distinction proposed by Sen between different types of capabilities. The concept concerns the field of action open to the individual or, in the negative, the constraints limiting his or her freedom of action.[9] First among these constraints is undoubtedly income or, in the terms of traditional theory, the budgetary constraint on spending capacity. However, along with this we find a varied series of elements that prevent individuals from acting freely to satisfy their

[9] In this section we take up the illustration of Sen's theory presented in Roncaglia (2019, pp. 435–9).

needs and desires: belonging to a gender, or to an ethnic or caste group or to a religious minority, a disadvantaged social position, lack of education, the presence of physical handicaps. The notion of capabilities affects the notion of equity in income and wealth distribution: disadvantaged persons need more economic resources to compensate for, or at least reduce, their disadvantage in terms of freedom of action compared to others.

In all these respects we are faced with differences between individuals and hence their needs. Any attempt to move towards equality, even to define it, must come to terms with this fact. In this regard, Sen (1992, p. 45) makes a distinction between capabilities and functions, that is, between the set of all the things we are able to do and the actions we actually decide to perform. The utilitarian tradition measures the well-being achieved by looking only at the latter, but the former are also important. For example, knowing that you are in the physical condition to walk in the mountains is a good thing in itself, even more important than actually going for a walk. Sen (1992, p. 58) also emphasizes the importance of active participation in decision-making, alongside the achievement of a result (perhaps by chance, or by the decision of others).

Skills acquired through education and training are of considerable importance. However, in this respect the notion of capability concerns an upstream aspect: the capacity to acquire and develop competences, which should be distinguished from competences per se. It is partly innate, but to a greater extent acquired within the family, at school, through friendships and acquaintances; the original social location of each individual is very important in this respect.

The notion of capabilities has several important implications. For example, a Human Development Index was developed from it (by Ul Haq, at UNDP), which combines economic, health and cultural indicators. These indicators have been very successful and are used to study the condition of the least developed countries and the nature of development processes in a more articulated way than can traditionally be done on the basis of economic indicators of per capita income alone. The multi-dimensionality of human development indicators has influenced the economic theory of development.

For some issues, such as gender, the notion of capabilities should be complemented with the distinction between 'heterogeneity' and 'diversity':[10] exogenous the former, endogenous the latter, with respect to the variables considered in economic and social analyses. In the context of an analysis intended as a premise for outlining strategies for reducing power differentials, the innate aspects of gender differences (such as having to, or not having to, go through a period of pregnancy in order to have children), should be considered as differences in capabilities to be compensated for with appropriate measures. Differences deriving from legal norms, social customs, culture and prejudices should instead be combated in their premises, and only if this is not possible should their consequences be compensated for. It is precisely here, in the contrast between innate differences (heterogeneity) and differences created by the institutions and culture of societies (diversity), that the different approach of the marginalist and the classical-Smithian analyses of gender problems lies.[11]

In order to overcome gender differences, several interrelated levels of action must be considered. At the legal and institutional level, the prohibition of gender discrimination needs to be enshrined and, if necessary, active rebalancing policies, such as gender quotas, need to be introduced to counterbalance the pull of a long tradition of imbalance. In the economic field, legal-institutional interventions of this kind can play an important role (e.g. in reducing and even eliminating gender pay differentials), but they should be accompanied by specific incentive policies (e.g. for female small entrepreneurs, as already happens in some developing countries in the field of microcredit). The cultural level is probably the most important one; feminist movements

[10] See D'Ippoliti (2011).

[11] See Roncaglia (2005, ch. 4). The importance of innate differences is underlined by some of the more radical exponents of feminism, such as Luce Irigaway, who however focus their attention on the psychoanalytical aspects of gender problems, neglecting the economic and social ones. Nussbaum (1999) proposes a reading of gender problems from the perspective of Sen's capability approach.

play a fundamental role in this field and could be actively supported (e.g. with favourable legislation, similar to that in force in countries such as Italy, for candidates standing for election).[12]

In fields such as gender, ethnicity or class, the notion of capabilities opens the way to the consideration of what we may call intersectional inequalities, that is, the relationship between the various areas of inequality (income, wealth, power, health, education, social relations, etc.). These interrelationships can easily lead to cumulative processes of increasing inequalities. This is why the use of active policies is important, from fiscal policies related to income and wealth redistribution to those setting minimum quotas for disadvantaged groups, such as for university admissions.

More generally, the recognition of the presence of a plurality of goals (or values) for each individual, and of differences between the life orientations and capabilities of the various individuals, entails the need for a rational and open debate on the choices to be made. Moreover, rather than finding a perfectly just world and then trying to pursue it (both of which are impossible), the goal is to 'prevent the injustice manifest in the world'.[13] In a similar direction goes the conception of the progressive extension of rights proposed by Bobbio, referred to in the next section.

10.4 PROGRESS IS ONLY POSSIBLE

Like the notion of power, that of progress is multidimensional.[14] The indicators of human development, mentioned above, capture the

[12] Many suggestions for specific measures are available in a vast literature on the subject; see for example (both for analysis and proposals) the essays by Bina Agarwal (2016) or sites such as www.ingenere.it and MinervaLab (www.roma1.it/labminerva).

[13] Sen (2002, p. 106); for a full argumentation of this thesis see Sen (2009). See also Sen (1999).

[14] The idea of constant human progress characterizes Enlightenment thinkers, in particular Kant. Subsequently, starting with Nietzsche and Spengler, the 'myth of progress' in the most general sense of the term was criticized and, if not abandoned, at least downgraded. On the fall of the myth of progress, see Sasso (1984). Here we speak of progress in a more limited but equally broad sense, of improvement in the quality of life in all its material aspects.

main components of this notion: economics, corresponding to the average income per capita but also including its sufficiently egalitarian distribution and its environmental sustainability; health (average life expectancy at birth, morbidity, infant mortality), culture (literacy, average level of education, and the like). The development of technology affects all these aspects, especially the first two. From this point of view, on the basis of the fact that scientific acquisitions cumulate over time, it would seem safe to say that humanity is following a path of continuous progress towards higher levels of knowledge and quality of life, in its various aspects. However, things are not so simple.

Notwithstanding the multidimensional nature of the concept, it is worth distinguishing between the potential for progress and the progress achieved. The growth of scientific knowledge relates to the first aspect, but it can be used partially or imperfectly or take harmful directions – for example, building ever more deadly weapons, from those of mass destruction to chemical weapons, to drones for targeted assassinations or attacks. The availability of new technology is one thing, its use is another. In economics, this is referred to as X-inefficiency (Leibenstein, 1966): it is calculated that companies operate on average with a productivity that is about half of the maximum possible.[15] The same is true of education or health care, provided that it be possible to measure performance efficiency in these cases.[16] It is even more difficult to assess the degree of democracy

[15] Only in part does this depend on the inevitable gradual replacement of machinery with that incorporating the latest technology; to a considerable extent the productivity gap depends on organizational aspects, including those relating to the use of the workforce, and hence to human relations within the workplace. Econometric estimates (Sylos Labini, 1984, pp. 121–3) have shown that after the introduction in a factory of machinery incorporating new technology, productivity decreases at first, and then increases as organizational problems are overcome.

[16] In these fields, the gap with the optimum levels stems above all from the inadequate qualifications of those working in the sector, secondly from their inadequate motivation, and thirdly from instrumental deficiencies. The overlapping of a public and a private sector, with legislation often biased in favour of the private sector, is also a source of inefficiency (to give just one example, think of professors paid by state universities who simultaneously teach at private universities for a modest salary supplement: a situation quite common in Italy).

or civilization in a country, but even in these respects we can safely assume that the average is far from optimal. Progress, therefore, can be conceived in two ways: as a forward shift in the frontier of the possible, or as a move towards the frontier itself, starting from the situation in which one finds oneself.

These considerations apply whatever the field considered: economic, health, cultural, civil. From this last point of view, an important point of reference is the notion of progress as an extension of rights, proposed by Bobbio (1994, pp. 152–3). The idea, which goes back to the Enlightenment and in particular to Adam Smith, is that economic development (linked to the division of labour, and therefore to an increasingly complex society) allows – although not automatically determining it – a refinement of customs and a development of culture, letters and the arts.[17] All this in turn allows, again not automatically but potentially, the adaptation of legal and political institutions to the civil progress of culture in the broad sense, with the recognition of greater space for individual freedom, both in the sense of active freedom and in the sense of liberation from material constraints.

Smith (1759, pp. 283–5) gives as an example the custom – considered by him to be outdated barbarism – of exposing newborn babies in ancient Athens. The right of infants not to be put down if they were born deformed was not recognized also in ancient Sparta: when the material conditions of life left insufficient resources to keep those who could not make a productive contribution alive, handicapped infants were abandoned on mount Taygetus. Two centuries after Smith, Bobbio (1994, pp. 152–3) gives the example of the extension

[17] 'Opulence and Commerce commonly precede the improvement of arts, and refinement of every Sort. I do not mean that the improvement of arts, and refinement of manners are the necessary consequence of commerce … but only that it is a necessary requisite' (Smith, 1983, p. 137). Hirschman (1982) recalls how the so-called *doux commerce* thesis was supported by, among others, Montesquieu, Condorcet and Paine. Various authors underline other aspects of the secular process of civilization: the transition from widespread violence to respect for the power of the law (John Stuart Mill and many others), the progressive control of passions (through, for example, the development of court etiquette and its diffusion: Elias, 1939).

to animals of the right to avoid unnecessary suffering. The enormous civil space between the two orders of rights gives an idea of the path that has already been travelled, and of the path that can potentially be travelled in the future. It also supports the Enlightenment's idea of progress: a path that moves forward in time, albeit usually in small steps and with the possibility of backward steps.

In contemporary democratic societies, progress can be made through reforms, as we shall see more clearly later: that is, changes in laws and institutional arrangements, stimulated by progressive political forces, aimed at extending citizens' freedom in life choices (divorce, abortion) or with respect to economic constraints, and generally reducing power differentials.

The main violation of the long-term trend towards progress is the failure to protect the environment. From an economic point of view, the environmental effects of production activity constitute a negative externality, for which regulation and compensatory taxes are needed because it is not convenient for each individual company to take them into account directly. However, competition between national environmental regulatory systems drives each country, in the absence of general burden-sharing agreements, to avoid constraints on its own firms and consumers. If each country adopts the motto 'my country first', anthropogenic damage to the environment will continue to increase.

The idea of civil progress encompassing these various aspects constitutes, after all, the reasonable utopia of the modern era: the objective that guides the elaboration of strategies and political action (in the broadest sense) of progressive forces.

10.5 THE STRATEGY OF STRUCTURAL REFORMS: THE THEORY

The implementation of the so-called strategy of structural reforms (such as those to be discussed in the next chapter) tends, step by step, to achieve a progressive reduction in power inequalities. In this way, each structural reform helps to create the preconditions for the implementation of a further reform.[18] Each reform, in fact, requires for its implementation sufficient support within society: a widespread consensus, sufficient to overcome the obstacles posed by the concentrations of power that are affected in each case. Attempts to carry out reforms that affect concentrations of power that are too strong are doomed to failure; each such failure reduces the strength of progressive political forces and strengthens those who defend, or seek to accentuate, pre-existing power differences. Conversely, reforms that lead to an increase, in some respect, of inequalities within a society are to be considered structural counter-reforms.

A different conception of structural reforms is that of the communist side, proposed in antithesis to the Lombardian socialist one (e.g. by Luigi Longo, 1957, in antithesis to Antonio Giolitti). Petruccioli (in Macaluso and Petruccioli, 2021, p. 148) summarizes it as follows: 'There are reforms that capitalism can easily absorb, they are the social democratic reforms; and there are reforms that capitalism cannot neutralise, they are the "structural reforms" that prelude the exit from the system'. Hence the opposition, or at best indifference, of the communist party to the structural reforms (in the sense indicated above, of reducing inequalities in the distribution of power) carried out by the early centre-left, which will be recalled later: communist maximalism actually hindered progress.

One thing to bear in mind is that progress is possible, but not necessary. When there is a concentration of interests contrary to social progress, there are often steps backwards. In Italy, the defeat of the urban reform in 1963 constituted the de facto green light for a building speculation which, although illegal, has seen abuses pardoned by repeated amnesties. Not only attempts to implement policies that are too radical and doomed to failure lead to backlashes

[18] Structural reforms are different from simple reforms because the latter change something but without inducing a reduction in inequalities in the distribution of power. The term 'structural reforms', in this sense, was originally proposed by Riccardo Lombardi, who made it the core of his political strategy. On Lombardi and the strategy of structural reforms, see Villetti (2021, pp. 107–36).

that strengthen conservative alliances; demagoguery and populism also weaken the drive for structural reforms. Conservative (or right-wing) forces, on the other hand, are not sitting on their hands, but are actively working towards structural counter-reforms. The replacement of the regulated structure of the international monetary system created at Bretton Woods with the full liberalization of the international financial markets was, in this respect, an epoch-making turning point.[19]

Looking at the effects on the distribution of power, it is possible to distinguish right-wing liberalist measures from left-wing ones. In the labour market, liberalization measures often, but not always, reduce the bargaining power of workers and have to be considered right-wing. Liberalization of beach accesses (the 'Mitterrand path' that ideally runs along the entire French coast) increases the power of ordinary citizens, especially the less well-off, over the holders of beach concessions, and has to be considered left-wing. The details are important: measures of administrative simplification (the 'de-bureaucratization') can be considered right-wing or left-wing depending on how they are formulated (in general, simplifications reduce the power of bureaucracy over citizens).

When devising a reform strategy, account must be taken of the fact that it cannot be entrusted solely to specialists in the field in which one wishes to intervene: reforms of the administration of justice to jurists and magistrates, reforms of education to teachers, urban planning to town planners, and so on. This is not only because the specialists, working in their own field of action, may come into conflict of interest, but also because the interrelationships between the various fields of action make it essential to take account of the

[19] It would be wrong to imagine the existence of a plan devised *ab initio*, or a plot by the Dark Forces of Reaction, fabled at the time of the student movements of 1968. Real changes, especially in cases of this importance, are the result of a complex of elements. What comes closest to the elaboration of a wide-ranging programme of counter-reforms (considered necessary to defend the market economy and Western culture from the communist threat) is the activity of the Mont Pélerin Society, founded on the initiative of Hayek in 1948 and still active today. See Mirowski and Plehwe (2009).

repercussions and interferences between them, and thus of a multiplicity of competences. The coordination of these competences is indeed one of the main tasks of reformist politicians.

It is precisely the interrelationships between the various fields of action that need to be taken into account in order to identify the weakest points in the perverse spirals and act on them. An example in this regard is offered by a thesis sustained – for decades – by Sylos Labini regarding the problems of southern Italy: if a vicious circle has been created between economic underdevelopment and civil underdevelopment, it is necessary to intervene at the point where the circuit is most vulnerable, namely schools and training.

Structural reforms can set in motion self-reinforcing spirals: shifts in the power structure in one field of action can facilitate structural reforms in other fields. It is crucial to remember, however, that these effects are sequential, not simultaneous. Thus, it is not advisable to implement too many reforms at the same time: the risk is that a political bloc of opposition to reforming action, made up of the sum of affected interests, will form. Similarly, the failure of a structural reform or the implementation of a structural counter-reform can set in motion perverse spirals.

10.6 A FLOW-STOCK SCHEME OF POWER RELATIONS

In order to draw up a reform strategy, power relations must therefore be analysed to see whether it is possible to coagulate sufficient support for planned changes. This analysis should not be conducted statically, looking at the existing structure, but must capture (and be able to use) both the trends in progress and the dynamics that change can set in motion, given the interrelationships between the various power nexuses that are activated in historical time, not instantaneously.

The level of detail of this analysis will vary from project to project: for some aspects it will be sufficient to remain highly general, for others a more detailed analysis will be appropriate. On the other hand, if we consider the dynamic nature of the problem, we must recognize that the analysis should not only be carried out ex ante, but should be carried out continuously during the process of implementing the reform, with possible adjustments in progress.

As seen in the previous chapters, there are three main types of power: economic, political and cultural. Each of them has multiple dimensions. Economic power depends on income and wealth, but also on the role in the production process (or absence of it), hence on the social stratification generated by the division of labour, on prevailing market forms, on the structure of financial markets, and so on. Political power in a wide meaning of the term embraces not only the eventual role of the individual in politics and the different forms of state institutions, but also participation in white, grey or black networks. Cultural power involves the distinction between hegemony and dominance, the role of religion and that of the masses, access to and control of the traditional media and the new media.

Each of these main types of power conditions, and is conditioned by, the other two. The channels through which the conditioning passes may differ from case to case, and imply a set of internal links between each of the three types.

Economic power can influence political power by various means: in particular, the direct financing of political parties and movements; personnel hirings (or the supply of goods and services) made in such a way as to favour one or other political movement; the financing of newspapers or news agencies, television networks, political and cultural movements; and the use of the 'brand' of a capable person obtained through success in the economic field for direct participation in political activity. *Mutatis mutandis*, these avenues also concern the influence of economic power on cultural power.

Political power exerts a strong influence on economic power, the greater the role of the state in the economic system and the more concentrated the political power itself. In dictatorial regimes, the oligarchs are created by the political leaders and are destroyed by them (perhaps at the very moment when they feel they have achieved sufficient strength to guarantee themselves a margin of autonomy). In a state with a large system of state-owned enterprises, whose top appointments are decided by the political authority, these enterprises are directly conditioned; indirectly, through them, all economic activity is conditioned. The state also has a direct role as an employer and as a purchaser of goods and services (think of the role, in the United States and elsewhere, of military spending in guiding research into new technologies).[20] It also has a fundamental indirect role of control: over the strategy of major companies, through antitrust authorities (and, even before that, through laws); over the banking and financial sector, through the supervisory authorities (and through the monetary policy conducted by the central bank, in a regime of independence but with top appointments entrusted to the political authority); and over the advertising sector, through regulations, in particular those on privacy. Finally, legislation plays a decisive role in determining the way a market (or rather mixed) economy operates. Very important is tax legislation, and its management. Through environmental and occupational safety regulations, the state also influences the technological choices of enterprises. Through international relations – up to and including adhesion to supranational rules and communities – it influences international economic relations: trade flows, direct investments and participation in financial support networks.

The influence of culture (in the broad sense) upon politics and economics is less direct, but no less important. Culture determines patterns of behaviour, and therefore of consumption; it favours orientations that are more or less favourable to the market economy, including greater or lesser acceptance of even appreciable differences in income and wealth; it influences ethics, in particular work ethics and respect for private property, but also respect for tax regulations and laws and regulations in general. As far as politics is concerned, voters, who contribute to the choice of the governing political class, are influenced by cultural orientations often more than by material

[20] See Mirowski (2002, pp. 153 ff.).

interests: think of elements of environmentalism, or nationalism, or confessionalism or libertarianism whose importance varies from society to society and over time. Culture influences not only the ethics of the political class, but also – and this is very important – the way in which the electorate reacts to ethical violations.

These general indications are sufficient to show us how complex the network of interrelationships linking the three types of power can be; it will be necessary to specify them as best as possible in each specific case, depending on the nature of the reform programme to be implemented.

11 Materials for a Reasonable Utopia

11.1 THE STRATEGY OF STRUCTURAL REFORMS: PRACTICE

This final chapter is dedicated, mainly with reference to Italy, to concrete reforms attempted to reduce power inequalities, to their successes and to the obstacles posed by the hegemony of neo-liberal thinking, to prospects for action in the future.

Let us begin by recalling what we mentioned in the previous chapter. The strategy of a progressive political force will consist in identifying feasible structural reforms that reduce power differentials in the various fields and allow for civil and economic growth that is environmentally sustainable while maintaining a high degree of social cohesion. From time to time, structural reforms (or reasonable utopias) will have to be specified, taking into account the situation at hand.

In focusing attention on a specific objective, it will be necessary to verify that its pursuit does not conflict with other objectives. Above all, it will be necessary to consider in all their complexity the processes of change in the power structure that are set in motion, with the potential for spirals of strengthening or weakening, which, accumulating over time, may favour further steps forward or cause reversals.

Let us take a brief look at the strategy followed when reformist forces first entered government in Italy, with the centre-left, in the 1960s. The strategy adopted was a composite one, on several fronts, gradual and open to compromise. Nevertheless, it ended up being blocked, not so much by the exhaustion of the reform drive as by a violent monetary squeeze decided by the Bank of Italy first

(1963) and by a threatened coup later (1964: General de Lorenzo's 'Piano Solo').[1]

On the economic power front, we saw in 1962 the nationalization of electricity, a private centre of monopoly power with great influence on the press.[2] A compromise had to be accepted: state compensation for the nationalization of the production plants was to be paid to electricity companies rather than their shareholders. The monopoly power in a sector so vital to manufacturing was thus transformed into a centre of financial power outside the then publicly owned banking system. The rationale for this choice, strongly supported by Guido Carli (Governor of the Bank of Italy and one of the most rational leaders of the conservative front) was that it would make funds available to finance the growth of industry. In fact, this thesis turned out to be wrong due to the inability of the managers of the former electricity companies to operate in competitive markets or at least subject to a greater degree of competition, and their preference for speculative operations that in the long run proved to be wrong, rather than investments in new industrial production capacity.[3] The opposing thesis (of Riccardo Lombardi and others), according

[1] See Salvati (1967) on the questionability of the monetary squeeze and Franzinelli (2010) on the events of the Solo plan. For an overview in the context of the history of the Italian Republic, see Colarizi (2007, pp. 85 ff.). Alongside the monetary squeeze, what Caffè (1972, p. 98) calls the 'strategy of economic alarmism' was implemented, defined as 'artificially exaggerated presentation of real facts'; Caffè recalls 'the exaggerated amplifications, deliberate omissions, and unilateral presentations that concretise economic alarmism as a means of struggle in an oligopolistic power structure' (1972, p. 103). On the strategy of tension see also Pacini (2021).

[2] The subject of nationalizing electricity was (re)proposed at a conference of the 'Amici del Mondo' movement, prepared at length, at which well-considered reports were presented on the various political, legal and economic aspects; the conference was widely reported in the press and the proceedings were published with considerable speed (Bocca, 1960): an excellent example of the cultural work that must precede a structural reform.

[3] The choice, made by Carli against Lombardi's advice, failed to save the role of the large private entrepreneurial bourgeoisie as 'those billions were wasted in the wind. Worse: they set in motion or aggravated a series of negative elements of an industrial, financial and political nature, which contributed powerfully to the degeneration of the system as we know it today' (Scalfari and Turani, 1974, p. 22; their book, an accurate reconstruction of the events following that choice, shows how the failure of the entrepreneurial class gave rise to what the two authors call the 'bosses race', capable of playing both sides, public and private, to its own exclusive advantage).

to which the shareholders of electricity companies could have created a base of small businesses or, more likely, of more widespread shareowners, with a different kind of support for the growth of the Italian economy and a greater diffusion of economic power, could not be verified. However depowered, the reform nevertheless changed the situation, removing a monopoly from the scene that would have continued to use the extra profits it enjoyed to finance conservative political movements and newspapers.

A second front is the cultural one, considered decisive for the country's civil growth. The reform leading to the unified middle school, carried out in December 1962, mainly at the instigation of Tristano Codignola, eliminated special schools (such as apprentice schools) and promoted the concrete implementation of the three-year increase in compulsory schooling. The direct effect was to raise the country's cultural level, reducing the huge differences that existed at the time between social classes and geographical areas, particularly between town and countryside. On a social level, lengthening compulsory schooling means delaying the moment when the choice between continuing studies and starting work is made, and this reduces – although it is far from cancelling – the social conditioning on that choice, favouring, albeit not resoundingly, social mobility. In the same sense, a system of widespread and sufficiently rich scholarships to encourage students from the poorer classes to continue their studies would have been very useful and has been almost totally lacking. The very implementation of the reform, which required infrastructures (adequate school buildings, libraries, a new cadre of teachers) was only partly and gradually achieved, tolerating the fact that in southern Italy compulsory schooling was evaded by a substantial proportion of young people. In essence, the funds allocated to the reform, both at the time and in subsequent years, were insufficient.[4] But it was certainly an important step forward.

[4] Compare public spending per student on primary and secondary education with that of more civilized countries, and its evolution over time. (To account for differences in economic development, the ratio of education expenditure per capita to income per capita can be considered.)

A further step forward in this direction today would be the implementation of the proposal by the neurobiologist Lamberto Maffei (2021), put forward precisely with the aim of combating inequality with the motto 'children should be given the same starting line': a 'kindergarten' that would 'begin structured teaching as early as nursery school, around the age of 3–4, when the child's learning ability is at its greatest'. We will return to this proposal in Section 11.6.

A third front was that of economic policy, entrusted to the Ministry of the Budget and Economic Planning (Law No. 48 of 27 February 1967). It should have overcome the simplistic frontal opposition between laissez-faire and centralized planning through an active public intervention or, more precisely, through a coordination of public interventions in the various fields of the economy, in order to direct it towards a path of sustainable growth, which would allow the overcoming of territorial imbalances and create conditions favourable to full employment. In this case, too, we can say that the resistance to coordination on the basis of general guidelines was exhausting, so that the results were positive but limited.[5]

A fourth front, urban reform, suffered a clear defeat towards the end of the 1960s, stopping at the introduction by law (Law No.

[5] Assessments of this kind are extremely difficult, and I shall refrain from providing any material to support my thesis. To suggest the difficulty in which planning policy moved, I can recall a personal experience: one of my first assignments as a graduate in statistics consisted in reconstructing some cyclical data (the degree of capacity utilization) that Carli's Bank of Italy refused to provide to the Minister of Budget and Planning, the socialist Giolitti, but which were necessary for a correct assessment of the economic situation and the adoption of adequate policies, as proposed by an important report prepared by a study group set up at Ispe on the instructions of the Ministry of Budget and Economic Planning (Izzo, Pedone, Spaventa and Volpi, 1969). In the same period (1970) I had the opportunity to witness the clash on the evaluation of the data relating to residential building, won by the very competent and combative Dr Almerina Ipsevich, director of ISCO, against ISTAT, which, having changed the survey sample, grossly underestimated the data, thus casting the recently approved mini-reform on town planning in a bad light. In the same period, Gino Faustini, an ISPE official, was able to demonstrate – after a laborious and painstaking reconstruction of the bureaucratic process – that council house building was practically blocked by the failure to replace a ministerial official who was ill and did not sign the necessary authorizations. The last two examples show how necessary the careful work of experts on apparently detailed issues is, in order to pursue a policy of reform.

167 of 18 April 1962) of plans for council housing: the thoughtful reform project presented by Fiorentino Sullo was rejected by the Christian Democrat party (under Aldo Moro) in April 1963, in the wake of fierce opposition by builders with the alliance of large and small landowners. Indeed, the defeat, by creating an alliance of classes differing in culture and social position against the reform project, meant a setback for the whole strategy of reforms. Indeed, the risks had even been pointed out by left-wing intellectuals such as Sylos Labini. The reform, which intended to use zoning plans and a system of land grants for building, would have allowed councils to expropriate land earmarked for urban expansion in the public interest with an expropriation payment fixed at the value it had had before being used for housing, and then to carry out urbanization works (from roads to sewers) and sell it to builders at a price higher than the expropriation price, thus covering urbanization costs. This reform would have eliminated or at least reduced the weight of land rent, which has weighed heavily on economic development in Italy. However, it would also have prevented the immediate (and limited) enrichment of many small landowners, as well as the conspicuous enrichment of large landowners and developers. A less maximalist reform, which distinguished between large speculators and small and very small landowners, would have had a better chance of success: maximalism is always a dangerous opponent of reform policy.

A fifth front, the Workers' Statute, came later (May 1970) in the wake of the strengthening of the trade unions and the 'Hot Fall' of 1968. The law (Law No. 300 of 20 May 1970), which is still in force today, albeit with various amendments and ups and downs (especially as regards dismissal rules), can be considered a democratic pillar of a republic that wants to consider itself 'founded on labour', as the Italian Constitution states in its first article. Thanks to a long period of drafting, the law managed to find an elaborate compromise between the opposing requirements of the hierarchical nature of business organization on the one hand and the dignity of work and workers enshrined in the Constitution on the other.[6]

Again, the reform was subsequently challenged, with heated debates particularly on the rules on fair dismissal. The Statute plays an important role in making the balance of power between employees and employers less unequal by preventing, for example, a worker from being sacked for any political or religious views[7] or for rejecting the courtship of a superior. At the same time, it may be difficult to dismiss a chronic slacker, thief or violent person pending a conviction for proven facts, or it may hinder the internal reorganization of labour needed to reap the benefits of technological change.[8] When trade unions use their bargaining power to defend corporate interests – for example, when they push for generalized unfair promotions in the public sector, or when they obstruct job changes, even if they are temporary, reasonable and useful for productive efficiency – they weaken development and therefore employment; in the long run this undermines their own bargaining power, making a regression of industrial democracy inevitable.

The pendulum of workers' rights thus swung forwards in the direction of progress from the 1950s to the beginning of the 1970s, only to swing back (with the decisive help of the bloody extremism of the Red Brigade terrorists, but also of the violence of so many

[6] As Bagnasco (2016, p. 121) reminds us, in a market economy the position of the worker is characterized by various elements of uncertainty relating to stability of the job and professional role, health protection, working hours, on-the-job training, income and representation. Directly or indirectly, the Workers' Statute intervenes on all these fronts, increasing – in some respects significantly – the security of the worker.

[7] On the contrary, it was forbidden to collect information on opinions: a widespread practice at the time (the Fiat files, which in the 1950s and 1960s perpetuated what had been a general practice in the fascist era, caused a stir: cf. Guidetti Serra, 1984 and, for the story of the rejection of her book by Einaudi, cf. Baranelli and Ciafaloni, 2013, pp. 55 ff.).

[8] Probably the lack of an efficient arbitration forum to deal with disputes between companies and workers, together with the inefficiencies of the ordinary justice system, constituted important obstacles to a reasonable management of the legislation. It may be added that some criticisms of cases of dismissals for just cause, at least partly justified, relate more to a maximalist application of the Statute by some labour judges than to the Statute itself.

extra-parliamentary movements) from the 1980s to today. Can we hope that in the future the hard lesson of facts will be assimilated? It is not the Statute of Workers in its principles of extension of workers' rights and guarantees that should be questioned, but some aspects that lend themselves to its improper use, in contradiction with the requirements of productive efficiency imposed by competitive markets.[9]

Other reforms modifying the structure of power within society towards greater equality are the pension reform in 1969; the 1971 tax reform (Law No. 825 of 9 October 1971) introducing, among other things, value-added tax (VAT); the introduction of compulsory unemployment insurance (1976); the creation of the universal public health system (December 1978), and in general the introduction or strengthening of all the institutions that make up the welfare state. We should also mention the law introducing divorce (Law No. 898 of 1 December 1970) and the reform of family law (Law No. 151 of 19 May 1975), together with the launch of two institutions provided for by the Constitution but left until then in the dustbin, just a few days apart: regional autonomy (Law No. 281 of 16 May 1970) and referenda (Law No. 352 of 25 May 1970).

11.2 A PHASE OF RETREAT

The political events of the last decades, taken as a whole, brought about more setbacks than progress in the field of reforms aimed at reducing inequalities of power, in its various meanings. The strongest influences came from the international arena, and are of three types. The first concerns economic culture, and is the progressive affirmation of neo-liberalism, which we will deal with briefly in the next section.

The second type of conditioning concerns international economic relations. The collapse, in August 1971, of the international

[9] Giugni (2007, p. 83) pointed out that any modification of the Statute would have to be coordinated 'with a well-considered reform of social safety nets': an essential reform, which after so many debates we are still waiting for. For a reconsideration of the Workers' Statute and its evolution, fifty years after its approval, see the proceedings of the conference organized by the Accademia Nazionale dei Lincei published in *Moneta e Credito*, March 2021.

monetary system built at Bretton Woods in 1944 was followed by the oil crisis of 1973–4, with its grave effects of simultaneous rises in inflation and unemployment. Financial globalization, which exploded after the collapse of the Bretton Woods system, and measures to liberalize the main national financial systems and international trade promote systemic competition between tax and regulatory regimes. Enhanced by neo-liberalism, this competition is a heavy constraint on the adoption of national measures to protect the environment or effective rules on job security, but also on the adoption of counter-cyclical policies and on the space available for public health, pension and education systems, which are tending to shrink. This situation gives increasing room for manoeuvre to countries with a strong authoritarian component (Brazil, China, India; the so-called 'illiberal democracies' within the European Union: Poland, Hungary) and above all to 'rogue countries' that offer themselves as safe havens for tax evasion and/or the criminal economy. Moreover, it constitutes a strong constraint on the possibilities of new reforms and affects the viability of previously adopted ones.

A third element is hypothetical, in the absence of sufficient information; but it might have been important enough to make it worth mentioning. It concerns the influence exerted on politics, and through it on economic power relations, on the information sector, and more indirectly on culture, by the deviant forms taken by the 'cold war', especially after the student protests starting in the United States against the Vietnam War in 1967, and the 'Hot Fall' of 1969. In Italy, deviated secret services and Gladio, manoeuvres by the P2 masonic lodges, the Piazza Fontana and Italicus train massacres, the kidnapping and assassination of Aldo Moro and many other events are still awaiting clarification, but certainly constituted a very heavy brake on the spaces available for a reformist policy.[10]

[10] This is certainly not my field. I have followed these events as a simple citizen, trying to follow the work of investigative journalism (such as the excellent writings of the late Peppino De Lutiis).

The ambivalent results of structural reform policies in the economic field are generalized at international level, with an increase in inequalities of income and wealth within almost all countries, while in various countries – but not in all – the development of personal rights and gender equality has continued. Here we shall limit ourselves to a few comments on Italy.

The constraints of international systemic competition are directly felt in the tax field. After the 1971 reform, it is in this field that the greatest setbacks have been recorded, precisely in the decades of large tax increases (while the growth of national income was slowing down). As Scalfari observes, 'The tax has hit categories that are union strong but politically weak and has protected categories that are politically very strong .... These categories, aware of enjoying a privilege, have tolerated a corrupt ruling class.' Hence the moral question: if everyone has to pay 'taxes with the same thoroughness as employees ... the political class will not be able to continue for much longer to traffic in public wealth for private ends'.[11] Half a century later, Scalfari's words are validated: the pressure of international systemic competition has been compounded by domestic demagogy. Inheritance taxes are minimal, far lower than those (33 per cent rate) that a conservative liberal like Einaudi (1949, p. 213) considers correct; wealth taxation is substantially limited to residential property (smuggled in, moreover, as a tax on income, namely figurative rent), facilitated by the fact that international mobility is by definition impossible; income tax is concentrated on employees, given the high margins of evasion for other categories of income and the growing level of avoidance for corporation tax, linked to the increasing use of tax havens.

The use of public expenditure for patronage purposes, present in all countries but particularly high in Italy, further reduces the

[11] Scalfari (1984), quoted by Crainz (2012, p. 140). Scalfari's words are still valid today, even more so than forty years ago, and point to a field – taxation – in which a structural reform, although very difficult to achieve, appears increasingly urgent in the face of the growth of public debt and the progressive deterioration of social services, starting with schools and – as the Covid-19 pandemic has highlighted – health.

resources that can be used for constructive reforms. To give just one example, early pensions introduced in 1973 by a centre-right government (Andreotti-Malagodi: less than twenty years of work were sufficient) have since then, for decades, been a burden on public spending; they have thus absorbed funds needed for a serious reform of the welfare state, in the direction of a flexsecurity on the Danish model that could have ensured greater flexibility in the labour market compensated by a serious unemployment benefit programme and efficient worker retraining policies; flexibility would have favoured adaptation to new technologies.[12] The creation of more and more new types of temporary employment contracts, benefiting from lower contribution rates compared to permanent employment (when the opposite should have been the case), has weakened the bargaining power of workers as a whole, already compromised by globalization and competition from countries with lower labour costs.

Again for electoral reasons, given the importance of the Catholic electorate in Italy, the constitutional ban on funding public schools has been systematically circumvented, diverting resources that should have been destined to state schools. The extension of compulsory schooling has led to a sharp increase in the number of teachers; spending restraint has therefore led over the years to a reduction in their salary relative to that of other jobs, with a gradual loss of prestige, commitment and preparation. Similar cost containment has affected school management, from building maintenance (including, scandalously, protection against earthquakes) to computer equipment, laboratories and libraries. Recognition of the legal value of qualifications from private universities of a highly dubious standard has reduced the substantive value of university degrees, hindering the role of a serious university education as a 'social lift'.

[12] The Danish model consists of balancing flexibility (relative ease of dismissal by employers) with the security of income support, which is why it has a significant cost. Achieving flexibility alone, as some would like to do even though they refer to the Danish model, would lead to a sharp deterioration in the bargaining power of workers, without any compensation.

In the field of health, in recent decades the private sector has tended to expand to the detriment of the public sector (leading to recurrent episodes of the use of the public by the private sector, which can be qualified as ethical theft even though they are all too often permitted by laws and regulations). In some regions, such as Lombardy, the backwardness of the balance between public and private healthcare has shown its serious negative effects in the face of the Covid-19 epidemic.

Finally, the policy of privatization, adopted to reduce the extent of the public domain and the amount of public debt, has also affected companies operating in conditions far removed from competition (such as telephones and motorways) without organizing adequate control mechanisms, leaving a legacy of conflicts for the appropriation of positions of profit that have contributed to polluting political life.[13]

11.3 NEOLIBERALISM AND THE SHORTCOMINGS OF ECONOMIC DEBATE

Neoliberalism is a collection of different economic currents of thought, all of which tend to reaffirm the myth of the invisible hand of the market. Mistakenly attributed to Adam Smith,[14] the thesis of the invisible hand of the market is supposed to explain the market's ability to regulate itself optimally, and the consequent desirability of minimizing the presence of the state in the economy, which is considered both inefficient and a violation of individual freedoms.

Here, we shall limit ourselves to a very basic summary of four aspects: the weakness of the theoretical foundations of neo-liberalism;

[13] See Oddo and Pons (2002) on telecom and Ragazzi (2008) on motorway concessions, two different texts: the first is a good example of investigative journalism, the second is an accurate reconstruction of the mechanisms of public concessions, the work of a university professor of finance. But they converge, from the two different perspectives, in their criticism of Italian privatization. In the case of telephones, gas and electricity, companies spend enormous amounts of money on advertising (including a bombardment of telephone calls at all hours, often with misleading content), only to save on the quality of services.

[14] See Roncaglia (2001, ch. 5) and Roncaglia (2005).

the possible explanations, nevertheless, of its rise; its economic policy proposals; and its influence.

However different they may be, the various strands of neoliberalism (such as Austrian theory, monetarism, ordoliberalism) share a basic reference to the traditional marginalist conception of the functioning of the economy: the interplay of supply and demand, if free to express itself through price flexibility, tends to lead to an optimal equilibrium, which guarantees the full use of resources while respecting the preferences of consumers, the ultimate sovereigns of the system. In particular, a competitive labour market should guarantee full employment through wage flexibility. These theses have very weak theoretical foundations: they do not take into account externalities, that is, effects that do not fall upon those who make production or consumption decisions, but on third parties, for instance on the environment; criticisms of the traditional theory of capital have shown that in the presence of multiple goods, the general validity of an inverse relationship between wages and employment, which is necessary for the thesis of an automatic adjustment of market economies towards full employment, cannot be upheld; the Keynesian criticism, which starts with the presence of uncertainty affecting the decision-making processes of different sectors in different ways, leads to affirm the destabilizing role of finance and the plausibility of persistent situations of underemployment.[15]

The initial affirmation of neoliberalism, in the early 1970s, occurred at the same time as the crisis of a hybrid version of the marginalist theory, the so-called neoclassical synthesis (of Hicks, Samuelson, Solow and many others), which preserves the basic thesis of a self-regulating capacity of market economies but admits 'Keynesian' interventions to deal with possible short-term departures from equilibrium. According to the neoclassical synthesis (which uses the so-called 'Phillips curve', an inverse relationship between

[15] For an illustration of these different strands, see Roncaglia (2019, ch. 8). The critiques, and various other aspects hinted at in this section, are also illustrated less summarily in that work and in the bibliography cited there.

the rate of unemployment and the rate of growth of monetary wages, hence prices), fiscal and monetary policy interventions could have combated unemployment but at the cost of an increase in inflation, or inflation but at the cost of a slowdown in productive activity and employment. The simultaneous explosion of inflation and unemployment following the collapse of the Bretton Woods system in 1971 and, above all, the oil crisis of 1973–4, led to a rejection of this approach and a revival of monetarism, that is, the thesis that inflation depends on excessive monetary expansion while unemployment cannot be combated by resorting to Keynesian policies of public spending.[16]

A more powerful version of the thesis of the invisible hand of the market, rational expectations theory, emerged in the late 1970s and early 1980s. According to this theory, since rational economic agents take into account what they foresee will happen in the future, only unexpected economic policy interventions have an influence on income and employment trends; instead, systematic Keynesian-type interventions (fiscal and monetary policies) to combat cyclical fluctuations in the economy are inevitably useless, since they are expected, and even counterproductive because they lead to an extension of the public sphere of the economy. Rational expectations theory was considered the pinnacle of pure economic theory for a ridiculously long time; when it fell into oblivion (although it is still taught in many macroeconomics courses), the reasons for its practical failure were not investigated. Indeed, on an abstract theoretical level, given the absurd starting assumptions (a world in which there is no uncertainty, in which there is only one commodity – an

[16] In support of this thesis, the correlation between prices and the amount of money in circulation has often been cited; however, when – as is usually the case – money in circulation includes bank money, and not only legal money, the causal link goes from the rise in prices to the demand for money, and thus to the increase in the supply of bank money, and not vice versa. The cause of the inflationary explosion in the 1970s was the explosion in oil prices: if the race between wages and prices can be considered a cause of the increase in inflation after the 1969 hot autumn, with the oil crisis another contender – crude oil producers – entered the dispute for the distribution of the national product, accelerating the price-wage inflationary spiral.

essential condition for the validity of the inverse relation between wages and employment – and in which economic agents behave with perfect rationality), the theses follow logically from the premises. Abandonment of those premises undermines not only the rational expectations strand, but the whole neoliberal approach.

How could neo-liberalism establish itself, given the weakness of its theoretical foundations? Three circumstances contributed to this outcome. First, on a strictly theoretical level, criticisms were ignored. The criticisms that have emerged in the debate on the theory of capital, it has been argued, concern only the aggregate notion of capital, but not the theory of general economic equilibrium; for the latter, however, the uniqueness and stability of equilibrium, which are essential conditions for the thesis of the invisible hand of the market, are unprovable. The field of microeconomics was then distinguished from that of macroeconomics, where the simplistic assumption of a one-commodity world was quietly preserved. The assumption of rational behaviour was reinforced by the assumption of selfishness, which is much more restrictive than Adam Smith's original assumption of self-interest moderated by a sense of belonging to a community.[17] Criticism of the role of uncertainty has also been dismissed by resorting to the simplistic dichotomy between probabilistic risk, which the theory of rational behaviour of economic agents manages to deal with, and uncertainty, which is considered theoretically untreatable and therefore dismissed.[18] As the famous drunkard's joke goes, if you lose a key, look for it under the lamp post, not where it fell if you can't see well there. We shall return to the problem of externalities later.

Secondly, outside the field of economists, neo-liberalism has had an easy time presenting itself as a bulwark against statism,

[17] On the distinction between selfishness and self-interest see Roncaglia (2001, ch. 5).

[18] The subjective theory of probability allows (albeit with various problems) an axiomatic treatment within the general economic equilibrium theory, but it presents the usual problems of multiplicity and instability of equilibria and cannot be used in macroeconomics.

considered 'the road to serfdom', as the title of a famous book by Hayek (1944) puts it: not only the statism of centrally planned economies, but also that considered implicit in any form of public intervention in the economy, from the various forms of regulation to anti-cyclical policies, and above all in relation to the welfare state. The question of the merits of a theoretical approach has thus become a political question, with the conservative front's ideological adherence to neoliberalism, regardless of the validity of its theoretical foundations. Neoliberal theses have also made inroads, to some extent, into the progressive front, especially in ex-communist circles that wanted to show a total conversion to the dogmas of market economies.

Thirdly, debates on economic theory have been distorted by interventions of conservative foundations, especially in the United States,[19] by biased policies on university careers in economics, and by media control. It has gone so far as to brand those who do not accept the revealed truths of the only admissible economic theory as 'economic denialism',[20] likening them to Holocaust deniers.[21]

11.4 CONSEQUENCES AND (HOPEFULLY) CRISIS OF NEOLIBERALISM

The negative effects of neo-liberalism are such that an unfortunately belated reaction is now perceptible. Let us look at some of its various aspects.

The financial liberalization measures adopted in all major countries have favoured the financialization of the economy and financial globalization (discussed in Sections 3.7 and 4.6). Underpinned by neoliberalism, they have had negative effects on: (a) economic stability (see the financial crisis of 2007–8 and the subsequent euro crises);

[19] On the role of foundations see for instance D'Eramo (2020); MacLean (2017); Mirowski and Plehwe (2009).

[20] *Le négationnisme économique* is the title of a book by Cahuc and Zylberberg (2016), translated into Italian by Università Bocconi Editore with a preface by former Dean Guido Tabellini.

[21] We have avoided expanding on these aspects. Some bibliographic indications are available in Roncaglia (2019).

(b) the sustainability of national taxation systems, due to tax elusion, and distorting the progressivity of taxation (large estates avoid inheritance tax or personal tax more easily than small and medium-sized estates); (c) environmental, health[22] or job security regulations; and (d) the space available for the welfare state. The liberalization of international financial flows has fostered the development not only of tax havens, but also of crime, which can clean up the proceeds of its activities and even pollute large financial institutions to a greater or lesser extent.[23]

In environmental policies, the non-interventionist tendencies of neoliberalism (and nimby nationalism: Not In My Back Yard) are among the main contributors to the current disaster. When considering the problem of externalities, neoliberal theories propose compensating for them not through regulation or taxation, but through the creation of special markets – for example, carbon certificate markets. These markets have proven to be prone to speculative instability; above all, the claim that they would allow doing away with controls and regulations has distorted their functioning. In fact, companies would still have to be checked to see whether they had really reduced pollution to the extent necessary to be able to sell certificates, or whether they had increased pollution only to the extent compensated by the certificates purchased; these checks would require continuous measurements, and are therefore much more difficult than those based on simple pollution ceilings. Furthermore, the functioning

22 To give just one example, consider the intensive use of hormones and antibiotics in livestock farming, which is permitted in several countries but not in the European Union.

23 Think of events such as those of the 'Sindona system' or Calvi's Banco Ambrosiano in Italy. We do not mention the most recent cases because of the lack of reliable information (this is not my field of work), but there are many more than we think. An important contribution of information on tax havens comes from the activity of an association such as the Tax Justice Network (www.taxjustice.net), which aims at fighting tax evasion and tax elusion, therefore tax havens and opacity of financial transactions, also through the construction of a Financial Secrecy Index (www.fsi.taxjustice.net/en/) and of a tax haven indicator (Corporate Tax Haven Index). Unfortunately, the news collected by this site is not disseminated by the press (sometimes owned by the companies that use these havens…).

of these markets is not a free good: financial institutions add their mark-ups to the price of the certificates. These shortcomings, like all problems of practical implementation, hardly attract the attention of politicians, theoretical economists or the public.[24]

As already mentioned, neoliberal theses have influenced EU Treaties and the ECB Statute. The constraints upon public budget deficits impose a systematic bias towards austerity policies. The ECB Statute limits its scope of activity to controlling inflation. In the field of market unification policies, the strand of ordoliberalism has prevailed, which requires detailed microeconomic measures to ensure their orderly functioning, in particular for the qualitative standardization of products. However, the unification of markets has not been extended to the field of taxation, allowing the survival and emergence of different tax regimes within the Union (in substantial contradiction, inter alia, with the prohibition of industrial policies subsidizing companies located within the national territory).

Since the 1970s, in parallel with the rise of neoliberalism, Western economies have experienced a marked slow-down compared to the first twenty-five years after the Second World War. The global financial crisis of 2007–8, the offspring of financialization and financial globalization, led to a sharp slowdown in production and income. In Europe, the successive crises of the euro have risked setting in

[24] Discussions on environmental interventions based on cost-benefit analysis are made difficult by the uncertain quantification of the benefits of environmental measures and the length of the time period to be considered. The discount rate used is very important: if it is high, the environmental benefits achievable in the distant future lose much importance compared to the costs of interventions in the present. This explains the harshness of a debate such as the one between Nordhaus (2008) and Stern (2008, 2009, ch. 5) concerning precisely the social discount rate to be used, higher for the former and lower for the latter. In fact, it is not clear why the social discount rate should refer to an average of what happens in the financial markets, or why on an issue like the environment the present should be considered more important than the future; one can therefore assume a discount rate nil in real terms and assess future advantages and disadvantages while holding the present values of income constant (which greatly simplifies estimation procedures). Under these conditions it can be shown (Roncaglia, 1989) that even a very low probability of high environmental costs in the future, with an indefinite duration, makes it worthwhile to take action to avoid them, even if very expensive.

motion cumulative mechanisms (the importance of spreads, i.e. interest rate differentials between countries, hits both on the public finances of the various countries and on their productive apparatus in different ways) that cast doubt on the very survival of the euro and led, first in Greece and then in Italy, to a severe slowdown in these economies.[25]

The explosion of the Covid-19 health crisis led to a severe slowdown in the world economy, and required immediate interventions to support the economy. The severity of the crisis and the weight of the interventions needed in a socially dramatic situation meant that some of the main legacies of neoliberalism were violated, one after another. Within the EU, the constraints on public deficits in the Stability Pact have been suspended, albeit temporarily (and there is now open talk of their revision); the ECB has intervened, officially in support of excessively low inflation, in fact practising a decisive expansionary monetary policy; the ban on state aid to companies was suspended (Germany in particular took advantage of this); multiannual spending programmes (such as the Next Generation) were adopted, financed by issuing European public debt, accompanied by the provision of the Union's own tax sources. The new US President Biden has adopted a strongly expansive fiscal policy, probably also with a view to increasing competition with China and Russia; many other countries have done the same. International bodies such as the International Monetary Fund or the traditionally conservative OECD have taken a stand in favour of expansive Keynesian policies. The Ukrainian crisis now adds strength to these considerations.

All this, however, has never affected the consolidated power of big business. When there was talk of suspending patents on vaccines in order to encourage vaccination in poor countries (which would have slowed down the development of variants of the virus and

[25] It is not possible to dwell on these topics here. However, there are many works on the subject. Let me refer in particular to Roncaglia (2010); D'Ippoliti and Roncaglia (2011); D'Ippoliti, Malaguti and Roncaglia (2020) and to the economic papers of the Covid-19 Commission of the Accademia Nazionale dei Lincei, available at www.lincei.it.

would also have benefited rich countries), the defence of the interests of the major pharmaceutical companies ('big pharma') succeeded in blocking any initiative in that direction.

However, the need to ensure adequate public revenues to help reduce public debt, at least in a long-term perspective, has brought the issue of tax havens back into focus. President Biden's proposal for a minimum tax on multinationals that can currently make their tax burden derisory has met with agreement in principle. To this should be added, within the European Union, the issue of internal tax havens, to be considered as illegal state aid to companies registered in their territory.

Increasing attention is also being paid to environmental problems. Faced with the dramatic effects of global warming, the evidence of a situation that is almost out of control should help to overcome any nationalistic logic, whereby each country tends to avoid bearing the costs of energy transition policies, even though no one seems to want to trace the cultural responsibility for the delays in tackling what has become a dramatic problem.

Overcoming the errors of neoliberalism requires explicit recognition of its erroneous theoretical foundations: an open debate, no longer misled by political conditioning and economic interests, is essential. And it is essential that such a debate is considered of fundamental importance not only by the experts, the economists, but also by the broader public of citizens.

11.5 THE STRATEGY OF STRUCTURAL REFORMS: INTERNATIONAL RELATIONS

In this situation, the most urgent structural reform is that of the system of international relations, to avoid downward competition between states in the environmental, fiscal and generally regulatory fields, that is, the adoption of favourable treatment to attract companies and private funds: derisory taxation or confidentiality rules that encourage evasion; lack of controls on the adoption of polluting technologies, on the risks of accidents at work, child labour or product quality. It is not, of course, a question of seeking unanimous agreement between all countries in the world, but of reaching sufficiently broad agreements involving at least the largest countries, while at the same time introducing rules to prevent free riding, that is, some countries gaining an advantage in international competition by exploiting the non-compliance with the rules adopted by others.[26]

The environment is the most urgent field, but also the one in which awareness of what is at stake is most widespread and the progress made is already significant, albeit still insufficient, given the delay in taking action. The United States' re-entry into the Paris Agreement is a significant step forward, but after the lost four years of the Trump presidency, the pace needs to be stepped up. Like the European Union with its Next Generation programme, using a significant part of the resources earmarked for stimulating the economy after the Covid-19 pandemic for environmental conversion can help. It is then up to individual countries to ensure that these resources are used effectively and efficiently. Even more important than economic incentives for energy conversion are regulatory constraints, the introduction and implementation of which requires combating downward competition between the regulatory systems of different countries. Instead, the system of markets for permits to pollute should be reconsidered, and probably replaced with a system of direct regulations, which are easier to keep under control, while these markets appear to be dominated by speculation and leave unresolved the problem of checking that permits bought and sold correspond to the actual results of companies in terms of pollution control.

Taxation is the field in which competition between national systems has produced the worst effects. During the course of the

[26] On the current set-up of international trade rules and its prospects, see Mazzoni and Malaguti (2019). Before reviewing existing treaties and institutions, Mazzoni and Malaguti (2019, p. xvii) underline that more than the formalism of the analysis of written texts what counts is the realism of the analysis of power relations: 'the consideration that *law in action* weighs more than *law in the books* is valid, that is, that the concrete power relations and therefore the real distribution of power weigh more than any institutional design, even if the obligation to implement it has been solemnly assumed'.

Covid-19 pandemic, public debt increased in all countries; this constitutes a problem to be addressed, once the emergency is over, especially in the European Union given the Maastricht rules and the austere orientation of various countries (in particular tax havens, again in the name of the precepts of neoliberalism). It is no coincidence that the Draghi government in Italy has made tax reform one of its priorities. Reducing tax evasion, but also and perhaps above all tax avoidance, with a less unequal redistribution of the tax burden, is essential. However, it will be difficult to reduce elusion without sterilizing tax havens. As the debt burden has increased everywhere with the pandemic, it can be hoped that the problem will finally be tackled cooperatively at international level. Clear signs in this direction can be seen, for example, in the stance – admittedly very cautious – of the new US president on taxing multinationals at a rate of 15 per cent, which has been approved by over 100 countries. To declare victory – and it will in any case be a victory that can be considered both epochal and modest – we will have to wait for the decision to be translated from theory into practice: as we know, the devil is in the detail. Without hoping for a unanimous agreement, significant results can then be achieved with other measures, for example by establishing strict constraints on the transfer prices of oil companies or the national tax base for IT service companies (which must be the country of the purchaser of the service and not that of the registered office) and possibly for multinationals in other sectors, perhaps by shifting the tax base from net corporate income to turnover. One might also think, for example, of not recognizing the tax deductibility of expenses incurred in (direct or indirect) purchases in tax or regulatory havens, or of imposing countervailing duties (permitted, in the face of unfair systemic competition, even by WTO agreements).

In the field of health, too, the Covid-19 pandemic has shown how useful international cooperation can be, with rules to contain the transmission of contagions through international travel, to share information, and to research and produce medicines and vaccines that are affordable even for the poorest countries. Unlike former US

President Trump, the problem here is not the alleged inefficiencies of the World Health Organization, but the absence of a system of rules to support and, in major cases, enforce cooperation between different countries. A complex issue that needs to be tackled boldly is the intellectual property rights to patents by pharmaceutical companies. Despite huge public support for research, all countries have bowed to the bargaining power of these companies in the race to provide vaccines for their citizens, and in some cases some of these companies have been accused of having diverted the supplies promised in contracts signed when the vaccine trials were still in progress to more profitable markets, while proposals to share patents free of charge for faster production and worldwide distribution of vaccines have not been followed up much.[27] Big pharma (i.e. big pharmaceutical companies) is very powerful,[28] but also not very large, and apart from lobbying and economic control over information channels (largely through advertising expenditure) with no direct hold on public opinion: a determined opinion campaign can provide the ground for making reasonable proposals, without having to go as far as expropriation, which could also be justified by obvious reasons of public utility – the same, after all, that have rightly allowed the recourse to lock-downs, which also affect primary individual freedoms.

On all fiscal and regulatory fronts, decisive action is needed from the European Union, characterized by a single market and (for the core group of countries) a single currency. It must also be borne in mind that a uniform system of rules can have different effects in the various countries of the Union, when the starting conditions are different; moreover, the inevitable margins of discretion in applying the rules are often used to their advantage by the stronger countries.[29]

[27] Pharmaceutical companies holding patents could have been compensated for the costs of research – which were already largely covered by the doses of vaccine sold to the governments of the richest countries – by international development aid agencies.

[28] Le Carré's novel, *The Constant Gardener* (2001), although devoid of references to concrete events, gives a vivid idea of what we can fear the excessive power of the sector is.

[29] For example, the sanctions for excessive balance-of-payments surpluses, which should have affected Germany, were not applied.

After expansion, it is necessary to launch a robust phase of deepening the Union, which has been put off for too long, even at the cost of losing some pieces along the way (as happened with Brexit). In addition to broadening the areas of Community policy (from foreign policy to military policy, from health policy to research policy, and even migration policy), the rules of economic policy need to be revised in a cooperative sense if we are to avoid a terminal crisis of the euro: the single currency cannot hold out for long with overly rigid constraints on EU economic policy, imposed by a neo-liberal culture that has proved wrong in its premises and ruinous in its implications. It is necessary to overcome the absurdity whereby the ban on unfair competition, which prevents state aid to companies in difficulty, does not apply to tax rules (allowing the presence in the Union of three tax havens: Ireland, the Netherlands and Luxembourg) or to labour market regulations (allowing Hungary, for example, to attract investment from Germany thanks to rules that even provide for substantial payments to be made by a worker who wants to resign).

In some cases, in order to overcome possible vetoes by a minority of EU members, recourse can be made to 'enhanced cooperation', obviously envisaging (and announcing in good time) powerful disincentives for non-participants, such as the reduction of the items of the European budget that imply transfers in their favour.[30] There are in fact no substantial limits to enhanced cooperation: a possibly extreme proposal, which could in fact configure a re-foundation of the EU with a limited group of adhering states, is the one put forward by Piketty and others (www.tdem.eu, cited in Piketty, 2019, p. 1178), which foresees the constitution by the adhering countries of an Assembly composed of representatives of national parliaments and the European Parliament to which they would delegate the adoption of community taxes on corporate profits, high incomes and

[30] In fact, in the case of Hungary's 'upside-down industrial democracy', opposition to EU intervention came mainly from German industrialists, who convinced Chancellor Merkel to abandon measures on which a sufficiently broad convergence was emerging and that would not have required unanimity among the member states.

wealth, CO_2, partly to be retroceded to national budgets and partly to be used to finance energy transition projects. The EU itself can then contribute to the search for new cooperative rules at world level. In fact, it constitutes a sufficiently large and territorially compact area, and sufficiently strong economically and politically, to enable it to face up to the clash, inevitable for any structural reform, with the affected interests: the countries that are home to tax havens and the large transnational corporations.

If pursued flexibly, this reform of international and European institutional systems has a fair chance of success, in some respects if not all. It is opposed by very powerful economic interests, but limited electoral and therefore political ones. The main problem seems to be that of building a sufficiently broad consensus of public opinion around it: something that is not easy, given the distance of these issues from those of immediate interest to individuals, but not impossible, even taking into account the control exercised by the economic interests affected on the media, as we have seen in the case of the environment. The main obstacle to overcome, in this sense, seems to be the spread of neoliberal culture at all levels: in Italy, catastrophically, even in left-wing parties and movements, based on a ridiculous confusion between neoliberalism and liberalism, in the sense of respect for the rights of individual freedom. The cultural clash in the field of economic theories has, in this case, an enormous political value.

11.6 THE STRATEGY OF STRUCTURAL REFORMS: ITALY

Overcoming neoliberal culture might lead to a series of reforms in Italy as well.

In principle, large-scale reform of the state administration, which would improve its effectiveness and efficiency (thus also reducing overall costs, freeing up resources for research, education and health care), should not encounter insurmountable social and political opposition. The most difficult resistance to overcome is probably that of the bureaucracy inside those departments that would have to implement it; a precise work schedule could be useful, and could be made a condition for salary incentives for senior management. Computerization, legislative simplification (up to the creation of a single administrative code), clearly establishing the individual responsibilities of those in charge and combating cases of non-assumption of responsibility,[31] reducing the weight of ex ante controls with respect to ex post controls, which should be strengthened, could be considered as guidelines to be studied in depth by scientific commissions coordinated by the minister or, even better, by an ad hoc undersecretary devoted full time to the task.

The need for a reform of the tax system has already been mentioned. Here, too, regulatory simplification should be a priority objective. The main objective, which requires an integrated assessment of the various aspects of the reform, is to ensure that the constitutional objective of a progressive tax burden is achieved. Since any change in tax burdens might only benefit some groups and disadvantage others, there must be clear communication to the public in order to avoid demagogy in which measures that in reality only affect limited groups of taxpayers are seen as a generalized tax bill,[32] not to mention maximalist proposals such as a flat tax, the contours of which are not even clear.[33]

A reform of the justice system should also be supported by entrepreneurs, traders and the liberal professions (perhaps with the

[31] Just one example: the testing of public works postponed indefinitely. In several cases, delays are a means of inducing corruption.

[32] For instance, a rising scale of inheritance taxes, accompanied by a reduction in benefits contributions and/or a reduction in the average income tax, benefits a large number of taxpayers, while the number of those affected would be much smaller.

[33] The most common criticism, which says that a flat tax would go against the progressive taxation imposed by the Italian Constitution, is wrong: a 50 per cent flat tax accompanied by a large deduction (e.g. €20,000 per year) would ensure a tax incidence increasing with income and a revenue roughly equal to the current one. A flat tax of 15 per cent, without deductions, not only does not ensure progressive taxation, but also entails a substantial loss of tax revenue. This would have to be compensated for by cuts in public spending or increases in other taxes. Simultaneous cuts in taxation and public spending (necessarily – due to the magnitude of the cuts – on the welfare state) mainly benefit the richest and disadvantage lower and middle incomes.

sole exception of lawyers and accountants, who are interested in the additional work that unnecessarily complex procedures and excessively slow trials can entail); the wider use of telematics, which also requires investment in updating office material and skills, can contribute significantly to greater efficiency in criminal justice. This would avoid impunity for criminals through time-barring prosecution rules, such as those imposed in Italy by the recent reform, which fulfils the dreams of those who prefer to defend themselves against the trial, by lengthening its duration, rather than within the trial.[34]

All three reforms, and international cooperation on eliminating tax havens, and the transmission of information – in particular on financial deals – would facilitate the fight against crime, both organized crime and individuals or small groups of white-collar criminals, who are relatively lightly sanctioned and increasingly widespread.[35]

These reforms are not the only ones we can think about. We might well proceed on several fronts at the same time, perhaps at different speeds, at least by starting the work of in-depth reflection that must precede any such intervention. This could be the case with a reform of the school system to extend formal state schooling open to all children aged three to six. As mentioned above (Section 3.2), experts in neurobiology have established that it is in this phase of life that the brain develops most rapidly and is most ready to learn.[36] Thus, it is in this phase of life that external stimuli, from the family

[34] It is surprising how little attention is paid to the spread of organized crime (not only the mafia type), whose control of the territory and grip on politics is becoming ever stronger, in Italy as in many other countries.

[35] Sraffa rightly reminded Gramsci in 1924 that 'liberty and order' are essential for citizens and must be ensured by progressive forces (even, in the case of Sraffa and Gramsci, by revolutionary forces) before anything else. Bobbio (in Bobbio and Viroli, 2001, p. 57) points out that 'the most serious consequence of the erosion of the rule of law is the spread of a sense of insecurity'. The importance of a well-functioning justice system that systematically – not occasionally – and swiftly punishes violations of the law is a fundamental principle already recalled by Beccaria (1764, p. 62): 'When the punishment is swifter and closer to the crime committed, it will be all the more just and all the more useful'; what counts, in order to discourage crimes, is the certainty and swiftness of the punishment, not its cruelty.

[36] See, for example, Maffei (2021).

and the original social environment, can create differences in ability that hinder social mobility.

The topic of pre-school education has already been widely addressed. The United Nations included it among the Sustainable Development Goals approved in September 2015, under point 4.2 ('Equal access to quality pre-primary education'), setting targets for 2030. Among the experiences of the past, many studies on the long-term effects over a period of more than fifty years have considered the effects of the Perry Pre-School Project, which between 1962 and 1965 involved a group of 123 children of African-American origin and from low social backgrounds: according to these studies, there was a significant increase in IQ and better earnings throughout their working lives.[37] A subsequent experiment, the Abecedarian Early Intervention Project conducted by the Frank Porter Graham Child Development Institute between 1972 and 1977, found similar results.

These promising experiences, however, point to the risk that good pre-school education limited for families that can afford it will constitute a further factor in the crystallization of the social structure. Hence the proposal for universal state pre-school education.

Naturally, such a reform has considerable costs and a long lead time. It will require the construction of appropriate buildings, the training of a considerable number of teachers (bearing in mind that the qualities required of kindergarten teachers are quite different from those of teachers at later levels), and the preparation of appropriate syllabuses.[38] Most of today's kindergartens are simply places where parents drop their children off to be looked after while they go to work, and not (something much more complex to imagine and bring about) places of education. It is a common mistake to underestimate

[37] See https://youth.gov/content/perry-preschool-project and the works cited therein.

[38] Extensive discussions among child pedagogy experts (from Maria Montessori to Jean Piaget and many others) concern the role to be given to free play, guided play and formal education. From Margaret McMiller onwards (i.e. from the 1920s), pre-school education is also referred to as an important opportunity for providing free healthy food (fruit and milk) to all children and for physical exercise.

the importance of basic versus specialized education, which leads to each school being seen as inferior to the one preceding it.

11.7 HOPES AND CAUTIONS

The Covid-19 outbreak and the war in Ukraine, with their dramatic negative impact, may favour the launch of a reform strategy at both international and national level. The expansion of public deficits creates the need to catch up on tax elusion, as well as tax evasion; the increase in EU public expenditure creates the need for developing European financial instruments and a European tax system. An extensive interpretation of existing legislation against unfair competition, supported by economic logic, should make it possible to overcome tax havens within the EU; the EU and the other major OECD countries should then form a common front against external tax and regulatory havens.

Reform action does not need a master plan covering all fields of action simultaneously. The merit of each reform has to be assessed separately, and the timing of implementation is largely independent from one field to another. Unfortunately, formulating all-encompassing generic programmes has taken the place in the debate among progressive political forces once occupied by in-depth work on the elaboration of possible intervention strategies on clearly identified problems. This happened, for example, with the conferences organized by the 'Amici del Mondo' in the late 1950s and early 1960s, which had prepared the ground for the first centre-left governments, the most fruitful phase of structural reforms in Italian history.[39]

As noted in Section 10.1, the descriptive definition of the left does not necessarily correspond to the normative one. Colin Crouch's (2013) distinction between 'defensive social democracy' and 'assertive social

[39] An example to the contrary were the successive university reforms that each Italian minister tried to implement in a short time, before the government of which he or she was a member changed. The abolition of university diplomas and the simultaneous generalized imposition of three-years graduation curricula ('Berlinguer reform') has been disastrous; the current career rules hinder the movement of lecturers between universities, as well as overstretching career progression times.

democracy' is indicative in this respect; Crouch sees the latter as the only adequate response to neoliberalism, to save democratic freedoms from the risks of rupture arising from growing social tensions.[40]

Since every reform and every counter-reform creates a shift in power relations, the opportunity to create spirals of self-reinforcement and to avoid regressive spirals of retreat must be carefully assessed in practice. The political capacity to communicate the design of reforms is fundamental, and must be accompanied by the political sensitivity to grasp the greater or lesser support of the citizenship for the projects to be implemented, in the complex balance between the material interests of classes and social groups and the ideals of economic and civil progress.

The pandemic crisis and the war in Ukraine call for responses that cannot be neutral to pre-existing power structures. A renewed strategy of structural reforms can be the answer both to the ideological crisis of left-wing forces and to the economic, health and security crises that threatens to widen the sphere of poverty and exacerbate social tensions and international conflicts in every part of the world.

[40] See Bagnasco (2016, pp. 173–8), for an illustration and analysis of Crouch's argument.

References

[The year after the author's name indicates the original date of publication. The original date of writing is occasionally indicated in square brakets. Page references in the text refer to the last of the editions cited below. When this is not an English edition, the translation of the passages cited in the text is mine.]

Abbate, L. (2017). *La lista. Il ricatto alla Repubblica di Massimo Carminati*, Milano: Rizzoli.

Agarwal, B. (2016). *Gender challenges*, 3 vols., Oxford: Oxford University Press.

Almerighi, M. (2006). *Petrolio e potere*, Roma: Editori Riuniti; II ed., Roma: Castelvecchi, 2014.

Anderson, B. (1983). *Imagined communities: reflections on the origins and spread of nationalism*, London and New York: Verso; new ed., 1991; Italian transl., *Comunità immaginate*, Roma-Bari: Laterza, 2018.

Anonymous. (1549). *A discourse of the common weal of this realm of England*, new ed., by E. Lamond, Cambridge: Cambridge University Press, 1893.

Arendt, H. (1948). *The origins of totalitarianism*, New York: Harcourt Brace Jovanovich.

Aristotle [c. 350 BC]. (1977). *Politics*, Loeb Classic Library, vol. 21, Cambridge, MA: Harvard University Press.

Arlacchi, P. (1983). *La mafia imprenditrice*, Bologna: il Mulino.

Asimov, I. (1957). *The naked sun*, New York: Doubleday.

Babbage, C. (1832). *On the economy of machinery and manufactures*, London: Charles Knight; repr. of the IV ed., (1835), New York: M. Kelley, 1963.

Bachrach, P., Baratz, M. S. (1962). Two faces of power. *American Political Science Review*, 56(4), 947–52.

Bagnasco, A. (1994). Regioni, tradizione civica, modernizzazione italiana: un commento alla ricerca di Putnam. *Stato e Mercato*, 1, 93–103.

Bagnasco, A. (1996). *L'Italia in tempi di cambiamento politico*, Bologna: il Mulino.

Bagnasco, A. (2013). Economie e società nello spazio: uno sguardo in Italia. In *Antropocene: modifiche naturali ed entropiche del fragile equilibrio della terra*, Atti dei convegni lincei, n. 278, Roma: Bardi, pp. 187–94.

Bagnasco, A. (2016). *La questione del ceto medio*, Bologna: il Mulino.

Bagnasco, A. (2020). Relazione introduttiva. In *Diseguaglianze e classi sociali. La ricerca in Italia e nelle democrazie avanzate*, Atti dei convegni lincei, n. 337, Roma: Bardi, pp. 7–26.

Bain, J. S. (1956). *Barriers to new competition*, Cambridge, MA: Harvard University Press.

Banfield, E. C. (1958). *The moral basis of a backward society*, Glencoe: Free Press.

Barabási, A.-L. (2002). *Linked. The new science of networks*, New York: Perseus.

Baranelli, L., Ciafaloni, F. (2013). *Una stanza all'Einaudi*, Macerata: Quodlibet.

Bauman, Z. (2000). *Liquid modernity*, Cambridge: Polity Press.

Bauman, Z. (2003). *Intervista sull'identità*, Roma-Bari: Laterza.

Baumol, W. J. (1959). *Business behaviour, value and growth*, New York: Harcourt & C.

Baumol, W. J., Panzar, J. C., Willig, R. D. (1982). *Contestable markets and the theory of industry structure*, San Diego, CA: Harcourt Brace Jovanovich.

Beccaria, C. (1764). *Dei delitti e delle pene*, Livorno; repr. in F. Venturi, ed., *Illuministi italiani. Tomo III. Riformatori lombardi piemontesi e toscani*, Milano-Napoli: Ricciardi, 1958, pp. 27–105.

Beck, U. (1986). *Risikogesellschaft*, Frankfurt: Suhrkamp; Italian transl., *La società del rischio*, Roma: Carocci, 2000.

Bekkouche, Y., Cagé, J. (2018). *The price of a vote: evidence from France*, 1993–2014, Working Paper no. 68, INET (available at www.ineteconomics.org/workingpapers).

Bell, D. (1987). The world and the United States in 2013. *Daedalus*, 116(3), 1–31.

Bentham, J. (1791). *Panopticon or the inspection house*, London: T. Payne; Italian transl., *Panopticon ovvero la casa d'ispezione*, Foucault M., M. Pierrot eds., Venezia: Marsilio, 1983.

Berik, G., Kongar, E., eds. (2021). *The Routledge handbook of feminist economics*, Abington and New York: Routledge.

Berle A. A., Means, G. (1932). *The modern corporation and private property*, New York: The Commerce Clearing House.

Berlin, I. (1958). *Two concepts of liberty*, Oxford: Oxford University Press.

Berlin, I. (2002). *Liberty*, ed. by H. Hardy, Oxford: Oxford University Press.

Bernstein, E. (1899). *Die Vorraussetzungen des Sozialismus und die Aufgaben der Sozialdemokratie*, Stuttgard: Dietz; English transl., *Evolutionary Socialism*, New York: Huebsch, 1909; repr. New York: Schocken, 1961.

Blair, J. M. (1976). *The control of oil*, New York: Pantheon Books.

Bobbio, N. (1976). *Quale socialismo?*, Torino: Einaudi.

Bobbio, N. (1984). Dibattito sulla democrazia italiana. Il potere in maschera. *La Stampa*, 21 agosto.

Bobbio, N. (1990). *L'età dei diritti*, Torino: Einaudi.

Bobbio, N. (1994). *Destra e sinistra. Ragioni e significati di una distinzione politica*, Roma: Donzelli; IV ed., 2004.

Bobbio, N. (2010). *Elementi di politica. Antologia*, Polito P. ed., Torino: Einaudi.

Bobbio, N. (2011). *Democrazia e segreto*, Rovelli M. ed., Torino: Einaudi.

Bobbio, N., Viroli M. (2001). *Dialogo intorno alla repubblica*, Roma-Bari: Laterza.

Bocca, S., ed. (1960). *Le baronie elettriche*, Bari: Laterza.

Braverman, H. (1974). *Labor and monopoly capital. The degradation of work in the Twentieth century*, New York: Monthly Review Press.

Breglia, A. (1965). *Reddito sociale*, Sylos Labini P. ed., Roma: Edizioni dell'Ateneo.

Caffè, F. (1972). La strategia dell'allarmismo economico. *Giornale degli economisti*, 31(9–10), 692–99; repr. in Amari G. and N. Rocchi eds., *Un economista per gli uomini comuni*, Roma: Ediesse, 2007, pp. 97–103.

Cahuc, P., Zylberberg, A. (2016). *Le négationnisme économique. Et comment s'en débarasser*, Paris: Flammarion; Italian transl., *Contro il negazionismo*, Milano: Università Bocconi Editore, 2018.

Cairncross, J. (1974). *Aftyer poligamy was made a sin. The social history of Christian polygamy*, London: Routedge & Kegan Paul.

Calogero, G. (1940). *Manifesto del liberalsocialismo*, repr. in *Difesa del liberalsocialismo e altri saggi*, Milano: Marzorati, 1972.

Calogero, G. (1942). L'ircocervo ovvero le due libertà; repr. in *Difesa del liberalsocialismo e altri saggi*, Milano: Marzorati, 1972, pp. 31–41.

Campanella, T. [1602] (1964). *La città del sole*, Milano: Rizzoli.

Canetti, E. (1960). *Masse und Macht*, Hambourg: Claassen Verlag; Italian transl., *Masse e potere*, Milano: Adelphi, 1981; repr., 2015.

Canfora, L. (2004). *La democrazia. Storia di un'ideologia*, Roma-Bari: Laterza.

Cantillon, R. (1755). *Essai sur la nature du commerce en général*, London: Fletcher Gyles; repr. with English transl. Higgs H. ed., London: Macmillan, 1931; repr., New York: M. Kelley, 1964.

Carabelli, A., Parisi, D., Rosselli, A. (1999). *Che'genere' di economista?*, Bologna: il Mulino.

Castells, M. (2001). *Internet galaxy*, Oxford: Oxford University Press; Italian transl., *Galassia internet*, Milano: Feltrinelli, 2002.

Chandler, A. D. (1990). *Scale and scope. The dynamics of industrial capitalism*, Cambridge (Mass.): Harvard University Press.

Chafuen, A. A. (1986). *Christians for freedom. Late-Scholastic economics*, San Francisco: Ignatius Press.

Ciotti, F., Roncaglia, G. (2000). *Il mondo digitale*, Roma-Bari: Laterza.

Clark, J. M. (1940). Toward a concept of workable competition. *American Economic Review*, 30, 241–56.

Coase, R. H. (1937). The nature of the firm, *Economica*, 4; repr. in Coase R. H., *The firm, the market and the law*, Chicago: The University of Chicago Press, 1988, pp. 33–55.

Colarizi, S. (2007). *Storia politica della Repubblica*, 1943–2006, Roma-Bari: Laterza.

Colletti, L. (1969). *Ideologia e società*, Bari: Laterza.

Colletti, L. (1974). *Marxismo e dialettica*, appendix to *Intervista storico-filosofica*, Roma-Bari: Laterza, pp. 63–113.

Collier, P. (2013). *Exodus. How migration is changing our world*, Oxford: Oxford University Press.

Commissione parlamentare d'inchiesta sul caso Sindona (2005). *Dossier Sindona*, Milano: Kaos edizioni.

Consiglio superiore della magistratura (2015). *Il sistema giudiziario italiano. Normativa in materia di ordinamento giudiziario e di organizzazione e funzionamento del C.S.M.*, Roma.

Constant, B. (1819). *De la liberté des anciens comparée à celle des modernes*; Italian transl., *La libertà degli antichi, paragonata a quella dei moderni*, Torino: Einaudi, 2001.

Corsi, M. (1984). Il sistema di fabbrica e la divisione del lavoro: il pensiero di Charles Babbage. *Quaderni di storia dell'economia politica*, 3, 111–23.

Corsi, M., ed. (1995). *Le diseguaglianze economiche*, Torino: Giappichelli.

Corsi, M., D'Ippoliti, C., Lucidi, F. (2011). On the evaluation of economic research: the case of Italy. *Economia politica*, 3, 369–402.

Crainz, G. (2012). *Il paese reale*, Roma: Donzelli; II ed., 2013.

Croce, B. (1942). Scopritori di contraddizioni. *La critica*, 20 gennaio.

Croce, B., Einaudi, L. (1957). *Liberismo e liberalismo*, Solari P. ed., Milano-Napoli: Riccardo Ricciardi editore.

Crouch, C. (2003). *Postdemocrazia*, Roma-Bari: Laterza; English transl., *Post-Democracy*, Cambridge: Polity Press, 2004.

Crouch, C. (2013). *Making capitalism fit for society*, Cambridge: Polity Press; Italian transl, *Quanto capitalismo può sopportare la società*, Roma-Bari: Laterza, 2014.

Dahl, R. (1957). The concept of power. *Behavioral science*, 2, 201–15.

Dahrendorf, R. (1959). *Class and class conflict in industrial society*, London: Routledge & Kegan Paul; Italian transl., *Classi e conflitto di classe nella società industriale*, Bari: Laterza, 1963; V ed., 1977.

Dahrendorf, R. (1995). *Quadrare il cerchio*, Roma-Bari: Laterza.

Darvas, J., Steinmetz, K., Flowers, R. H., Gouni, L., Grieger, G., Köberlein, K., Pease, R. S., Roncaglia, A. (1991). Environmental, safety related and economic potential of fusion power. *Plasma physics and controlled nuclear fusion research*, vol. 3, IAEA, Wien, pp. 633–45.

David, P. (1985). Clio and the economics of QWERTY. *American Economic Review, Papers and Proceedings*, 75, 332–7.

D'Eramo, M. (2020). *Dominio*, Milano: Feltrinelli.

De Felice, R. (1969). *Le interpretazioni del fascismo*, Bari: Laterza; IX ed., 2007.

De Felice, R. (1975). *Intervista sul fascismo*, Roma-Bari: Laterza.

De Mauro, T. (2010). *La cultura degli italiani*, Roma-Bari: Laterza.

Dickie, J. (2011). *Blood Brotherhoods. The rise of the Italian mafias*, London: Sceptre; Italian transl. *Onorate società*, Roma-Bari: Laterza.

D'Ippoliti, C. (2011). *Economics and diversity*, Abingdon: Routledge.

D'Ippoliti, C. (2020). *Democratizing the economics debate. Pluralism and research evaluation*, Abington: Routledge.

D'Ippoliti, C., Malaguti, M. C., Roncaglia, A. (2020). L'Unione Europea e l'euro: crescere o perire. *Moneta e Credito*, 73, 183–205.

D'Ippoliti, C., Roncaglia, A. (2011). L'Italia: una crisi nella crisi. *Moneta e Credito*, 64(255), 189–227.

Dobb, M., Sweezy, P., Takahashi, K., Hulton, R., Hill, C. (1954). *The transition from feudalism to capitalism. A symposium*, New York: Science and Society.

Downs, A. (1957). *An economic theory of democracy*, New York: Harper and Row.

Eco, U. (1980). *Il nome della rosa*, Milano: Bompiani; repr., Barcellona: Bibliotex, 2002.

Ehrenreich, B., Ehrenreich, J. (1977). The professional-managerial class. *Radical America*, 11(2), 7–40 and 11(3), 7–24.

Eichner, A. S. (1976). *The megacorp and oligopoly*, Cambridge: Cambridge University Press.

Einaudi, L. (1949). *Lezioni di politica sociale*, Torino: Einaudi; repr., Milano: Vitale & Associati, 2002.

Elias, N. (1939). *Über den prozess der Zivilisation*, 2 vols., Basel: Hans zum Falken; Italian transl., *Il processo di civilizzazione*, Bologna: Il Mulino, 1988.

Elster, J. (1982). Sour grapes. Utilitarianism and the genesis of wants. In Sen A., B. Williams, pp. 219–38; Italian transl., L'uva acerba. L'utilitarismo e la genesi dei voleri. In ibid., pp. 271–95.

Esping-Andersen, G. (1999). *Social foundations of post-industrial economies*, Oxford: Oxford University Press.

Federal Trade Commission Staff Report (1952). *The international petroleum cartel*, Washington: Government Printing Office.

Ferguson, A. (1767). *An essay on the history of civil society*, Edinburgh: A. Kinkaid & J. Bell.

Ferguson, A. (1995). *Golden Rule*, Chicago: University of Chicago Press.

Ferguson, T., Jorgensen, P., Chen, J. (2019). How money drives US congressional elections:linearmodels of money and outcomes. Preprint, *Structural change and economic dynamics*.

Feyerabend, P. (1975). *Against method. Outline of an anarchist theory of knowledge*, London: New Left Books.

Fitoussi, J.-P., Sen, A., Stiglitz, J. (2009). *Report by the Commission on the measurement of economic performance and social progress.* Paris (www.stiglitz-sen-fitoussi.fr/en/index.htm).

Foley, S., Karlsen, J. R., Putniņš, T. (2019). Sex, drugs and bitcoins: how much illegal activity is financed through cryptocurrencies?. *Review of Financial Studies*, 32(5), 1798–1853.

Foucault, M. (2004). *Naissance de la biopolitique. Cours au Collège de France 1978–1979*, Paris: Seuil-Gallimard; Italian transl., *Nascita della biopolitica*, Milano: Feltrinelli, 2005; UE Feltrinelli, III ed., 2017.

Franzinelli, M. (2007). *Il delitto Rosselli*, Milano: Mondadori.

Franzinelli, M. (2010). *Il piano Solo*, Milano: Mondadori.

Fuà, G. (1993). *Crescita economica. Le insidie delle cifre*, Bologna: il Mulino.

Fukuyama, F. (1992). *The end of history and the last man*, New York: Free Press; Italian transl., *La fine della Storia e l'ultimo uomo*, Milano: Rizzoli, 1992.

Furtado, C. (1964). *Development and underdevelopment*, Berkeley: University of California Press.

Galbraith, J. K. (1952). *American capitalism*, Boston: Houghton Mifflin.

Galbraith, J. K. (1958). *The affluent society*, Boston: Houghton Mifflin.

Galbraith, J. K. (1967). *The new industrial state*, Boston: Houghton Mifflin; repr. Harmondsworth: Penguin, 1967.

Galbraith, James K. (2008). *The predator state*, New York: Free Press.

Galiani, F. (1751). *Della moneta*, Napoli: Giuseppe Raimondi; II ed., Napoli: Stamperia simoniana, 1780; repr., Milano: Feltrinelli, 1963.

Gauchet, M. (2020). *Destra/sinistra. Storia di una dicotomia*, new ed., Napoli: Diana edizioni.

Gellner, E. (1983). *Nations and nationalism*, Ithaca: Cornell University Press; II ed., 2006; repr. Oxford: Blackwell, 2008.

Georgescu-Roegen, N. (1988). The interplay between institutional and material factors: the problem and its status, in Kregel J. A., E. Matzner, A. Roncaglia, eds., *Barriers to full employment*, Houndmills-London: Macmillan, pp. 297–326.

Germani, G. (1971). *Sociologia della modernizzazione*, Bari: Laterza.

Giddens, A. (1998). *The third way*, Cambridge: Polity Press; Italian transl., *La terza via. Manifesto per la rifondazione della socialdemocrazia*, Milano: Il Saggiatore, 1999.

Giugni, G. (2007). *La memoria di un riformista*, Bologna: il Mulino.

Glattfelder, J. B. (2013). *Decoding complexity*, Berlin-Heidelberg: Springer.

Goldthorpe, J. (1992). *Revised class schema*, London: Social and community planning research.

Graeber, D., Weingrow, D. (2021). *The dawn of everything. A new history of humanity*, New York: Farrar, Straus and Giroux.

Gramsci, A. (1975). *Quaderni del carcere*, Gerratana V. ed., Torino: Einaudi.

Greenwood, R., Sharfstein, D. (2013). The growth of finance. *Journal of Economic Perspectives*, 27, 3–28.

Guidetti Serra, B. (1984). *Le schedature Fiat*, Torino: Rosenberg & Sellier.

Gutmann, A. (1982). What's the use of going to school? In Sen and Williams, 1982, pp. 261–78; Italian transl., A cosa serve andare a scuola? Il problema dell'educazione nell'utilitarismo e nella teoria dei diritti. In ibid., pp. 325–44.

Hall, P., Soskice, D., eds. (2001). *Varieties of capitalism*, Oxford: Oxford University Press.

Han, B.-C. (2005). *Was ist Macht?*, Stuttgard: Phillip Reclam; English transl., *What is power?*, Cambridge: Polity press, 2019.

Harsanyi, J. (1962). Measurement of social power, opportunity costs and the theory of two-person bargaining games. *Behavioral Science*, 7, 67–80; partial repr. in Rothschild K., 1971, pp. 77–96.

Hayek, F. von (1944). *The road to serfdom*, Chicago: Chicago University Press; repr. (with introduction by M. Friedman), 1994.

Hayek, F. von (1973). *Law, legislation and liberty, vol. 1, Rules and order*, London: Routledge and Kegan Paul.

Hayek, F. von (1999). *Good money. Part II. The standard*, Kresge S. ed., *The collected works of F.A. Hayek*, vol. 6, Chicago: The University of Chicago Press.

Heckman, J., Landersø, R. (2021). *Lessons from Denmark about inequality and social mobility*, Working Paper n. 28543, Cambridge (Mass.): National Bureau of Economic Research.

Heckman, J., Moktan, S. (2018). *Publishing and promotion in economics: the tyranny of the Top Five*, Working Paper, INET (available at www.ineteconomics.org/workingpapers).

Heimans, J., Timms, H. (2018). *New power*; Italian transl., *L'arte del potere nel XXI secolo*, Torino: Einaudi, 2020.

Herodotus, [c. 430 BC] (2015). *Historiae*, Wilson N. G. ed., Oxford: Oxford University Press.

Hilferding, R. (1910,). *Das Finanzkapital*, Wien: Wiener Volksbuchhandlung Ignaz Brand.

Hirsch, F. (1976). *Social limits to growth*, Cambridge (Mass.): Harvard University Press.

Hirschman, A. O. (1945). *National power and the structure of foreign trade*, Berkeley-Los Angeles: University of California Press; repr. 1969; new ed., 1980.

Hirschman, A. O. (1977). *The passions and the interests*, Princeton: Princeton University Press.

Hirschman, A. O. (1982). Rival interpretations of market society: civilizing, destructive, or feeble?. *Journal of Economic Literature*, 20, 1463–84.

Hirschman, A. O. (1991). *The rhetoric of reaction*, Cambridge (Mass.): Harvard University Press; Italian transl., *Retoriche dell'intransigenza*, Bologna: il Mulino, 1991.

Hobbes, T. (1651). *Leviathan*, London: Andrew Crooke; trad. it., *Leviatano*, Roma-Bari: Laterza, 1974.

Hume, D. (1752). *Political discourses*, Edinburgh: A. Kincaid and A. Donaldson; rist. in *Essays: moral, political, and literary*, Miller E. F. ed., Indianapolis: Liberty Press, 1987.

Huntington, S. P. (1996). *The clash of civilizations and the remaking of the world order*, New York: Simon & Schuster.

Huntington, S. P. (2004). *Who are we? The challenges to America's national identity*, New York: Simon & Schuster.

Innis, H. A. (1950). *Empire and communications*, Oxford: Oxford University Press.

Irti, N. (1998). *L'ordine giuridico del mercato*, Roma-Bari: Laterza.

Israel, J. I. (2006). *Enlightenment contested*, Oxford: Oxford University Press.

Iversen, T., Soskice, D. (2019). *Democracy and prosperity: reinventing capitalism through a turbulent century*, Princeton: Princeton University Press.

Izzo, L., Pedone, A., Spaventa, L., Volpi, F. (1969). *Rapporto del gruppo di studio sui problemi di analisi economica e politica economica a breve termine*, mimeo, Roma: Isco; then published as *Il controllo dell'economia nel breve termine*, II ed., Milano: Franco Angeli, 1972.

Jagose, A. (1996). *Queer theory: an introduction*, New York: New York University Press.

Jossa, B. (2010). *Esiste un'alternativa al capitalismo? L'impresa democratica e l'attualità del marxismo*, Roma: Manifestolibri.

Jouvenel, B. de (1945). *Du pouvoir. Histoire naturelle de sa croissance*, Geneva: Les editions du cheval ailé; English edn., *On power. Its nature and the history of its growth*, New York: Viking Press, 1948; paperback edn., Boston: Beacon Press, 1962.

Kahneman, D., Tversky, A. (1979). Prospect theory: an analysis of decision under risk. *Econometrica*, 47, 313–27.

Kalantzakos, S. (2018). *China and the geopolitics of rare earths*, Oxford: Oxford University Press.

Kalecki, M. (1943). Political aspects of full employment. *Political Quarterly*, 14, 322–31; repr. in Kalecki M., *Selected essays on the dynamics of the capitalist economy*, Cambridge: Cambridge University Press, pp. 138–45.

Kant, I. (1785). *Grundlegung zur Metaphysik der Sitten*, Riga: Johann Friedrich Hartknoc; Italian transl. *Fondazione della metafisica dei costumi*, in *Scritti morali*, Torino: Utet, 1995.

Keohane, R. O., Nye, J. S. (1977). *Power and interdependence*, Oxford: Little Brown.

Keohane, R. O., Nye, J. S. (1987). Power and interdependence revisited. *International Organization*, 41(4), 725–53.

Keynes, J. M. (1921). *A treatise on prabability*, London: Macmillan; repr. in J. M. Keynes, *Collected writings*, vol. 8, London: Macmillan, 1973.

Khanna, P. (2016). *Connectography*, New York: Random House; Italian transl., *Connectography*, Roma: Fazi.

Kregel, J. (2022). *La crisi finanziaria e le crisi prossime venture*, mimeo, Conference on La crisi e le crisi, April 28, Accademia Nazionale dei Lincei, Roma.

Kreps, D. M. (1990). *Game theory and economic modelling*, Oxford: Oxford University Press.

Lafargue, P. (1880). Le droit à la paresse. *L'égalité*; repr. Paris: Maspero, 1969.

Latouche, S. (2006). *Le pari de la décroissance*, Paris: Librairie Arthème Fayard.

Lazonick, W., Shin, J.-S. (2020). *Predatory value extraction*, Oxford: Oxford University Press.

Le Carré, J. (2001). *The constant gardener*, London: Hodder & Stoughton, 2001.

Leibenstein, H. (1966). Allocative efficiency vs. 'X-efficiency'. *American Economic Review*, 56, 392–415.

Lepenies, W. (1990). *Les trois cultures. Entre science et littérature, l'avènement de la sociologie*, Paris: Éditions de la Maison des sciences de l'homme.

Levi, P. (1978). *La chiave a stella*, Torino: Einaudi; repr. 1991.

Levy, D. M. (2001). *How the dismal science got its name*, Ann Arbor: University of Michigan Press.

Lindert, P. H. (2004). *Growing public*, 2 vols., Cambridge: Cambridge University Press.

Locke, J. (1690). *Two treatises of government*, London: Awnsham and John Churchill; repr. London: J. M. Dent (Everyman's Library), 1975.

Lombard (1980). *Soldi truccati. I segreti del sistema Sindona*, Milano: Feltrinelli.

Longo, L. (1957). *Revisionismo nuovo e antico*, Torino: Einaudi.

Lucarelli, S., Perone, G. (2018). La loggia P2 e il mondo finanziario italiano. Alcune evidenze empiriche basate sulla social network analysis. *Moneta e Credito*, 71(284), 369–90.

Lukes, S. (1974). *Power. A radical view*, London: Macmillan; II ed., Houndmills: Palgrave Macmillan, 2005.

Macaluso, E., Petruccioli, C. (2021). *Comunisti a modo nostro*, Venezia: Marsilio.

Machiavelli, N. [1513] (1960). *Il principe*, Milano: Feltrinelli.

MacLean, N. (2017). *Democracy in chains: the deep history of the radical right's stealth plan for America*, New York: Viking.

Maffei, L. (2021). Ai bambini bisogna dare una stessa linea di partenza. *Avvenire*, June 17, p. 3.

Mann, M. (1986–2012). *The sources of social power*, Cambridge: Cambridge University Press (1. A history of power from the beginning to AD 1760, 1986; 2. The rise of classes and nation states, 1760–1914, 1993; 3. Global empires and revolution, 1890–1945, 2012; 4. Globalizations, 1945–2011, 2012).

Marchionatti, R. (2020). Un classico di sorprendente attualità. Postfazione to the Italian transl. of Sahlins, 1972, pp. 439–52.

Marris, R. (1964). *The economic theory of 'managerial' capitalism*, London: Macmillan.

Marx, K. (1844). Zur Kritick des Hegel'schen Rechts-Philosophie. *Deutsch-Französische Jahrbücher*, Paris, 2, 71–85; Italian transl., Critica della filosofia del diritto di Hegel. Introduzione. In *Annali franco-tedeschi*, Bravo G. M. ed., Milano: Edizioni del Gallo, 1965, pp. 124–42.

Marx, K. (1859). *Zur Kritik der Politischen Ökonomie*, Berlin: Dietz; trad. it., *Per la critica dell'economia politica*, Roma: Editori riuniti, 1957; II ed., 1969.

Marx, K., [1844] (1932). Ökonomisch-philosophische Manuskripte aus dem Jahre 1844. In *Karl Marx – Friedrich Engels Historisc-kritische Gesamtausgabe*, Adoratskij V. ed., Berlin: Marx-Engels Gesamtausgabe (MEGA); Italian transl., *Manoscritti economico-filosofici del 1844*, Torino: Einaudi, 1949, II ed., 1968.

Marx, K. (1867–94). *Das Kapital*, 3 vols., Hamburg: O. Meissner; Italian transl., *Il capitale*, Roma: Editori Riuniti, 1968.

Marx, K. (1878). Kritik des Gothaer Programms. *Die Neue Zeit*, 18; Italian transl., *Critica del programma di Gotha*, Roma: Samonà e Savelli, 1968. [English transl. in Marx K., F. Engels, *Basic writings on politics and philosophy*, Feuer L. S. ed., Doubleday, 1959, pp. 153–173.]

Marx, K. (2020). *Sull'Irlanda*, Roma: Pgreco.

Mazzoni, A., Malaguti, M. C. (2019). *Diritto del commercio internazionale. Fondamenti e prospettive*, Torino: Giappichelli.

McLuhan, M., Powers, B. R. (1986). *The global village*, Oxford: Oxford University Press.

Mead, M. (1935). *Sex and temperament in three primitive societies*, New York: William Morrow; II ed., 1950; III ed., 1963; Italian transl., *Sesso e temperamento*, Milano: il Saggiatore, 2020.

Milanovic, B. (2016). *Global inequality*, Cambridge (Mass.): Harvard University Press – Belknap Press.

Milanovic, B. (2019). *Capitalism, alone*, Cambridge (Mass.): Harvard University Press – Belknap Press.

Mill, J. S. (1848). *Principles of political economy*, London: John W. Parker.

Mill, J. S. (1859). *On liberty*, London: John W. Park; repr. in *Utilitarianism, liberty, representative government*, London: Dent, 1910.

Mill, J. S. (1861). Utilitarianism. *Fraser's Magazine*, 64, 383–4; repr. in Mill J. S. and J. Bentham, *Utilitarianism and other essays*, London: Dent, 1910, pp. 272–338.

Mills, C. (1997). *The racial contract*, Ithaca: Cornell University Press.

Mills, W. (1956). *The power elite*, New York: Oxford University Press.

Minsky, H. P. (1975). *John Maynard Keynes*, New York: Columbia University Press.

Minsky, H. P. (1982). *Can 'It' happen again? Essays on instability and finance*, Armonk: Sharpe.

Minsky, H. P. (1986). *Stabilizing an unstable economy*, New Haven: Yale University Press; new ed., New York: McGraw Hill, 2008.

Minsky, H. P. (1990). Schumpeter e la finanza. In Biasco S., A. Roncaglia, M. Salvati, eds., *Istituzioni e mercato nello sviluppo economico*, Roma-Bari: Laterza, pp. 117–32.

Minsky, H. P. (2013). *Ending poverty: jobs, not welfare*, Annandale-on-Hudson: Levy Economics Institute,.

Mirowski, P. (2002). *Machine dreams. Economics becomes a cyborg science*, Cambridge: Cambridge University Press.

Mirowski, P., Plehwe, D., eds. (2009). *The road from Mont Pèlerin: the making of the neoliberal thought collective*, Cambridge (Mass): Harvard University Press.

Modigliani, F., Miller, M. (1958). The cost of capital, corporation finance and the theory of investment. *American Economic Review*, 48, 161–97.

Montanaro, E., Tonveronachi, M. (2012). Financial re-regulation at a crossroad: how the European experience strengthens the case for a radical reform built on Minsky's approach. *PSL Quarterly Review*, 65(163), 335–83.

Montesquieu, C.-L. de Secondat de (1748). *De l'esprit des lois*, 2 vols., Genève: Barillot et Fils; English transl., *The spirit of the laws*, Cohler A. M., B. C. Miller, H. S. Stone eds., Cambridge Cambridge University Press, 1989.

More, T. (1516). *Utopia*, Lovanio: T. Martens; Italian transl., *Utopia*, Torino: Utet, 1971.

Mosse, G. L. (1974). *The nationalization of the masses*, New York: Howard Ferting.

Mosse, G. L. (1977). *Intervista sul nazismo*, Roma-Bari: Laterza.

Mosse, G. L. (1980). *Masses and man. Nationalist and Fascist perceptions of reality*, New York: Howard Ferting.

Mozaffari, M. (1987). *Authority in Islam*, Armonk: Sharpe.

Neale, A. D. (1970). *The antitrust laws of the U.S.A.*, II ed., Cambridge: Cambridge University Press.

Nelson, R. (1995). Recent evolutionary theorizing about economic change. *Journal of Economic Literature*, 33, 48–90.

Noble, D. (2011). *Forces of production. Social history of industrial automation*, Abingdon: Routledge; II ed., 2017.

Nordhaus, W. D. (2008). *A question of balance*, New Haven: Yale University Press.

Nozick, R. (1974). *Anarchy, state and utopia*, Oxford: Blackwell.

Nussbaum, M. (1999). *Women and human development: the capabilities approach*, Cambridge: Cambridge University Press.

Nuzzi, G. (2009). *Vaticano S.p.A.*, Milano: chiarelettere.

Nye, J. (1990). *Bound to lead: the changing nature of American power*, New York: Basic books.

Oddo, G., Pons, G. (2002). *L'affare Telecom*, Milano: Sperling.

Onfray, M. (2019). *Théorie de la dictature*, Paris: Robert Laffont; Italian transl., *Teoria della dittatura*, Milano: Ponte alle grazie, 2020.

Ortega y Gasset, J. (1930). *La rebelión de las masas*, Madrid: Ediciones de la Revista de Occidente.

Paci, M. (2013). *Lezioni di sociologia storica*, Bologna: il Mulino.

Pacini, G. (2021). *La spia intoccabile*, Torino: Einaudi.

Pareto, V. (1896). La courbe de la répartition de la richesse. In *Recueil publié par la Faculté de Droit del'Université de Lausanne à l'occasion de l'Exposition nationale de 1896*, pp. 373–87; Italian transl., La curva di ripartizione della ricchezza. In Corsi, 1995, pp. 51–70.

Pasquino, G. (1997). *Corso di scienza politica*, Bologna: il Mulino; II ed., 2000.

Pasquino, G. (2019). *Bobbio e Sartori*, Milano: Egea.

Patel, P. (2021). *The tyranny of nations*, New York: Bifocal Press.

Pease, R. S., Darvas, J., Steinmetz, K., Flowers, R. H., Gouni, L., Grieger, G., Köberlein, K., Roncaglia, A. (1989). *Environmental, safety-related and economic potential of fusion power*, Main report by the EEF Study Group, Warrington (UK): Progressive Engineering Consultants.

Perroux, F. (1950). The domination effect and modern economic theory. *Social research*, 17, 188–206; repr. in Rothschild, 1971, pp. 56–73.

Petty, W. (1690). *Political Arithmetick*, London: Robert Clavel and Henry Mortlock; repr. in Petty W., *Economic writings*, Hull C. ed., Cambridge: Cambridge University Press, 1899, pp. 233–313.

Piketty, T. (2013). *Le capital au XXIe siècle*, Paris: Editions du Seuil; English transl., *Capital in the twenty-first century*, Cambridge (Mass.): Harvard University Press, 2014; Italian transl., *Il capitale nel XXI secolo*, Milano: Bompiani, 2014.

Piketty, T. (2019). *Capital et idéologie*, Paris: Editions du Seuil; Italian transl., *Capitale e ideologia*, Milano: La nave di Teseo, 2020.

Pinotti, F. (2021). *Potere massonico*, Milano: Chiarelettere.

Piselli, F., ed. (1995). *Reti. L'analisi di network nelle scienze sociali*, Roma: Donzelli; II ed., 2001.

Pizzorno, A. (1963). Le organizzazioni, il potere e i conflitti di classe. Introduzione. In Dahrendorf 1959, Italian transl., pp. v–xxxv,

Polanyi, K. (1968). *Primitive, archaic and modern economies. Essays of Karl Polanyi*, Dalton G. ed., New York: Doubleday; repr. Boston: Beacon Press, 1971.

Popper, K. R. (1944–45). The poverty of historicism. *Economica*, 11, 86–103 and 119–37; 12, 69–89; repr., London: Routledge and Kegan Paul, 1957.

Popper, K. R. (1945). *The open society and its enemies*, 2 vols., London: Routledge and Kegan Paul.

Pownall, T. (1776). *A letter from Governor Pownall to Adam Smith, L.L.D. F.R.S., being an examination of several points of doctrine, laid down in his 'Inquiry in to the nature and causes of the wealth of nations'*, London; repr., New York: Augustus MK. Kelley, 1967; repr. in A. Smith, Correspondence, Mossner E.C., I.S. Ross eds., Oxford: Oxford University Press, 1977, pp. 337–76.

Prebish, R. (1950). *The economic development of Latin America and its principal problems*, New York: United Nations.

Putnam, R. D. (1993). *Making democracy work. Civic traditions in modern Italy*, Princeton: Princeton University Press.

Putnam, R. D. (2000). *Bowling alone. The collapse and revival of American communities*, New York: Touchstone – Simon & Schuster; Italian transl., *Capitale sociale e individualismo*, Bologna: il Mulino, 2004.

Ragazzi, G. (2008). *I Signori delle autostrade*, Bologna: il Mulino.

Rawls, J. (1971). *A theory of justice*, Cambridge (Mass.): Harvard University Press.

Ricardo, D. (1817). *On the principles of political economy and taxation*, John Murray, London; repr. as vol. 1 in *Works and correspondence*, Sraffa P. ed., Cambridge: Cambridge University Press, 1951–55.

Roncaglia, A. (1977). *Petty: la nascita dell'economia politica.* Milano: Etas Libri; English transl., *Petty. The origins of political economy.* Armonk: M.E. Sharpe, 1985.

Roncaglia, A. (1983). *L'economia del petrolio.* Roma-Bari: Laterza. English transl., *The international oil market.* London: Macmillan 1985.

Roncaglia, A. (1989). Research in fusion as investment. *Giornale degli economisti*, 48(7–8), 293–307.

Roncaglia, A. (2001). *La ricchezza delle idee*, Roma-Bari: Laterza; IV ed., 2009; English transl, *The wealth of ideas.* Cambridge: Cambridge University Press 2005.

Roncaglia, A. (2005). *Il mito della mano invisibile*, Roma-Bari: Laterza.

Roncaglia, A. (2009). *Piero Sraffa*, Houndmills: Palgrave Macmillan.

Roncaglia, A. (2010). *Economisti che sbagliano*, Roma-Bari: Laterza; English transl., *Why the economists got it wrong. The crisis and its cultural roots*, London: Anthem press, 2010.

Roncaglia, A. (2012). L'economia della P2. In Amari G., A. Vinci, eds., *Le notti della democrazia*, Roma: Ediesse, pp. 97–101.

Roncaglia, A. (2015). Institutions, resources and the common weal. In Baranzini M., C. Rotondi, R. Scazzieri, eds., *Resources, production and structural dynamics*, Cambridge: Cambridge University Press, pp. 259–78.

Roncaglia, A. (2019). *The age of disgregation*, Cambridge: Cambridge University Press.

Roncaglia, A., Villetti, R. (2007). Divisione del lavoro: capitalismo, socialismo, utopia. In Dosi G., M. C. Marcuzzo, eds., *L'economia e la politica. Saggi in onore di Michele Salvati*, Bologna: il Mulino, pp. 265–83.

Roncaglia, G. (2018). *L'età della frammentazione*, Roma-Bari: Laterza.

Rosselli, C., [1930] (1945). *Socialismo liberale*, Garosci A. ed., Roma-Firenze-Milano: Edizioni U; new ed., Torino: Einaudi, 1973; repr., 1997.

Rosselli, C. (2020). *Scritti inediti di economia (1924–1927)*, Ghiandelli E. ed., Milano: Biblion.

Rossi, E. (1946). *Abolire la miseria*, La fiaccola; repr., Sylos Labini P. ed., Roma-Bari: Laterza, 1977.

Rossi, E. (1955). *I padroni del vapore*, Bari: Laterza.

Rossi, P. (2007). *Max Weber. Una idea di Occidente*, Roma: Donzelli.

Rothschild, E. (1994). Adam Smith and the invisible hand. *American Economic Review. Papers and Proceedings*, 84, 319–22.

Rothschild, E., (2001). *Economic sentiments*, Cambridge (Mass.): Harvard University Press.

Rothschild, K. (1971). *Power in economics*, Harmondsworth: Penguin.

Rousseau, J.-J. (1762). *Du contrat social*, Amsterdam: M. Rey.

Russell, B. (1938). *Power*, Abington: Routledge; repr., 2004.

Sahlins, M. (1972). *Stone age economics*, New York: de Gruyter; new ed., London: Routledge, 2017; Italian transl., *L'economia dell'età della pietra*, Milano: elèuthera, 2020.

Sales, I. (2021). La sfida di Falcone che tolse ai mafiosi l'antica impunità. *Repubblica*, March 23, pp. 14–5.

Salvaggiulo, G., ed. (2020). *Io sono il potere. Confessioni di un capo di gabinetto*, Milano: Feltrinelli.

Salvati, M. (1967). *Sviluppo economico e recessione nelle Relazioni della Banca d'Italia*, Roma: Edizioni dell'Ateneo.

Sampson, A. (1973). *The secret history of ITT*, London: Hodder and Stoughton.

Samuelson, P. A. (1971). Understanding the Marxian notion of exploitation; a summary of the so-called transformation problem between Marxian values and competitive prices. *Journal of Economic Literature*, 9, 399–431.

Sandel, M. (2020). *The tyranny of merit*, Harmondsworth: Penguin.

Santambrogio, M. (2021). *Il complotto contro il merito*, Roma-Bari: Laterza.

Sartori, G. (1987). *The theory of democracy revisited*, Chatam: Chatam house.

Sasso, G. (1984). *Tramonto di un mito*, Bologna: il Mulino.

Scalfari, E. (1984). I difficili destini del lodo Visentini. *Repubblica*, November 11.

Scalfari, E., Turani, G. (1974). *Razza padrona*, Milano. Feltrinelli.

Schmoller, G. (1914). On class conflict in general. *American Journal of Sociology*, 20, 504–31.

Schumpeter, J. (1908). *Das Wesen und der Hauptinhalt der theoretischen Nationalökonomie*, Munich and Leipzig: Duncker & Humblot; Italian transl., *L'essenza e i principi dell'economia teorica*, Roma-Bari: Laterza.

Schumpeter, J. (1942). *Capitalism, socialism and democracy*, New York: Harpers & Bro.; II ed., 1947; III ed., 1950.

Sciarrone, R. (1998). *Mafie vecchie, mafie nuove*, Roma: Donzelli; II ed., 2009.

Sen, A. (1992). *Inequality reexamined*, Oxford: Clarendon Press.

Sen, A. (1999). *Development as freedom*, New York; Knopf.

Sen, A. (2002). *Globalizzazione e libertà*, Milano: Mondadori.

Sen, A. (2006). *Identity and violence*, New York-London: W.W. Norton.

Sen, A. (2007). *La libertà individuale come impegno sociale*, Roma-Bari: Laterza.

Sen, A. (2009). *The Idea of Justice*, London: Allen Lane.

Sen, A., Williams, B., eds. (1982). *Utilitarianism and beyond*, Cambridge: Cambridge University Press; Italian transl., *Utilitarismo e oltre*, Milano: Mondadori, 1984, II ed., 1990.

Simon, H. A. (1972). Theories of bounded rationality. In McGuire C. B., C. Radner, eds., *Decision and organisation*, Amsterdam: North Holland,, pp. 161–76.

Simon, H. A. (1993). Altruism and economics. *American Economic Review*, 83, 156–61.

Sirianni, C. (1981). Classi, produzione e potere: un'analisi critica delle dimensioni utopistiche della teoria marxiana. *Quaderni piacentini*, 1, 57–85 and 2, 3–35.

Smith, A. (1759). *The theory of moral sentiments*, London: A. Millar; Raphael D.D., A.L. Macfie eds., Oxford: Oxford University Press, 1976.

Smith, A. (1776). *An inquiry into the nature and causes of the wealth of nations*, London: W. Strahan and T. Cadell; Campbell R. H., A. S. Skinner eds., Oxford: Oxford University Press, 1976.

Smith, A. (1795). *Essays on philosophical subjects*, London: T. Cadell and W. Davies; Wightman W.P.D., J.C. Bryce eds., Oxford: Oxford University Press, 1980.

Smith, A. (1983). *Lectures on rhetoric and belles lettres*, Bryce J. C. ed., Oxford: Oxford University Press.

Snow, C. P. (1963). *The two cultures and a second look*, Cambridge: Cambridge University Press.

Spini, G. (1992). *Le origini del socialismo*, Torino: Einaudi.

Spinelli, A., Rossi, E. (1944). *Per un'Europa libera e unita. Progetto di un manifesto*, Milano: Edizioni del Mondadori, 2006.

Sraffa, P. (1924). Problemi di oggi e di domani. *L'ordine nuovo*, 1(3–4), April 1–15, 4 (letter to A. Gramsci published anonimously).

Stajano, C. (1991). *Un eroe borghese. Il caso dell'avvocato Ambrosoli assassinato dalla mafia politica*, Torino: Einaudi.

Steindl, J. (1952). *Maturity and stagnation in American capitalism*, Oxford: Basil Blackwell; repr., New York: Monthly Review Press, 1976.

Stern, N. (2008). *The economics of climate change: the Stern review*, Cambridge: Cambridge University Press.

Stern, N. (2009). *A blueprint for a safer planet: how to manage climate change and create a new era of progress and prosperity*, London: Bodley Head.

Strange, S. (1987). The persistent myth of lost hegemony. *International Organization*, 41(4), 551–74.

Sylos Labini, P. (1956). *Oligopolio e progresso tecnico*, Milano: Giuffrè; IV ed., Torino: Einaudi, 1967.

Sylos Labini, P. (1965). *Le radici della mafia in Sicilia*, Deposizione alla Commissione parlamentare d'inchiesta sul fenomeno della mafia in Sicilia, June 21; repr. in Sylos Labini, *Problemi dello sviluppo economico*, Bari: Laterza, 1970, pp. 179–90.

Sylos Labini, P. (1974). *Saggio sulle classi sociali*, Roma-Bari: Laterza.

Sylos Labini, P. (1984). *Le forze dello sviluppo e del declino*, Roma-Bari: Laterza.

Sylos Labini, P. (1995). *La crisi italiana*, Roma-Bari: Laterza.

Sylos Labini, P. (2001). *Un paese a civiltà limitata*, Roma-Bari: Laterza.

Sylos Labini, P. (2006). *Ahi serva Italia*, Roma-Bari: Laterza.

Tabellini, G. (2018). Prefazione all'edizione italiana. In Cahuc P., Zylberberg A., 2017, Italian transl. 2018.

Tarantelli, E. (1986). *Economia politica del lavoro*, Torino: Utet.

Thaler, R., Sunstein, C. (2008). *Nudge: improving decisions about health, wealth, and happiness*, New Haven: Yale University Press.

Thomas, A. (2017). *Republic of equals. Predistribution and property-owning democracy*, Oxford: Oxford University Press.

Toporowski, J. (2000). *The end of finance. Capital market inflation, financial derivatives and pension fund capitalism*, London: Routledge.

Transparency International (2021). *Corruption perceptions index 2020*, www.transparency.org/en/cpi/2020/index/nzl

Triffin, R. (1960). *Gold and the dollar crisis*, New Haven: Yale University Press.

Trigilia, C. (1992). *Sviluppo senza autonomia*, Bologna: il Mulino.

Trigilia, C., ed. (2020). *Capitalismi e democrazie*, Bologna: il Mulino.

Trump, D. (2021). Speech to protesters, 6 January, transcript, https://apnews.com/article/election-2020-joe-biden-donald-trump-capitol-siege-media-e79eb5164613d6718e9f4502eG471f27.

U.S. Senate, Subcommittee on reports, accounting and management (1978a). *Voting rights in major corporations*, Washington: U.S. Government Printing Office.

U.S. Senate, Subcommittee on reports, accounting and management (1978b). *Interlocking directorates among the major U.S. corporations*, Washington: U.S. Government Printing Office.

Urbinati, N. (2002). *Mill on democracy. From the Athenian polis to representative government*, Chicago: University of Chicago Press.

Urbinati, N. (2020). *Pochi contro molti. Il conflitto politico nel XXI secolo*, Roma-Bari: Laterza.

Van Horn, R., Mirowski, P. (2009). The rise of the Chicago school of economics and the birth of neoliberalism. In Mirowski and Plehwe, pp. 139–78.

Veblen, T. (1899). *The theory of the leisure class*, New York: Macmillan.

Vegetti, M. (2017). *Chi comanda nella città. I Greci e il potere*, Roma: Carocci.

Vanek, J. (1970). *The general theory of labor managed market economies*, Ithaca: Cornell University Press.

Villetti, R. (1978). Lavoro diviso e lavoro costrittivo. In Villetti R., ed., *Socialismo e divisione del lavoro*, Quaderni di Mondoperaio, n. 8, Roma: Mondo Operaio-Edizioni Avanti!, pp. ix–lxxii; repr. in Villetti, 2021, pp. 31–80.

Villetti, R. (2021). *La strategia delle riforme*, Bologna: il Mulino.

Vinci, A., ed. (2011). *I diari segreti di Tina Anselmi*, Milano: chiarelettere.

Wallerstein, I. (1974, 1980, 1989). *The modern world-system*, vols. 1, 2, 3, New York: Academic Press.

Weber, M. (1904–5). Die protestantische Ethik und der Geist des Kapitalismus. *Archiv für Sozialwissenschaft und Sozialpolitik*, 20–21; II ed., in *Gesammelte Aufsätze zur Religionssoziologie*, Tübingen: Mohr, 1922; Italian transl., *L'etica protestante e lo spirito del capitalismo*, Firenze: Sansoni, 1965.

Weber, M. (1919). *Politik als Beruf, Wissenschaft als Beruf*, Berlin: Duncker & Humblot; Italian transl., *Il lavoro intellettuale come professione*, Torino: Einaudi, 1948; repr. 1976.

Weber, M. (1922a). *Gesammelte Aufsätze zur Wissenschaftslehre*, Tübingen: Mohr; Italian transl., *Il metodo delle scienze storico-sociali*, Torino: Einaudi, 1958; repr. Milano: Oscar Mondadori, 1980.

Weber, M. (1922b). *Wirtschaft und Gesellschaft*, 2 vols., Tübingen: Mohr; Italian transl., *Economia e società*, 2 vols., Milano: Edizioni di Comunità, 1962.

Weber, M. (1923). *Wirtschaftsgeschichte: Abriss der universalen Sozial- und Wirtschaftgeschichte*, Berlin: Dunker & Humblot; Italian transl. of the III ed., *Storia economica*, Roma: Donzelli, 1993.

Weil, D. (2014). *The fissured workplace*, Cambridge (Mass.): Harvard University Press.

Wood, A. (1975). *A theory of profits*, Cambridge: Cambridge University Press.

Young, M. (1958). *The rise of the meritocracy 1870–2033. An essay on education and society*, London: Thames and Hudson.

Zinn, D. L. (2001). *La raccomandazione. Clientelismo vecchio e nuovo*, Roma: Donzelli.

Index